Rising Up...
from a Long Way Down

C. C. Gross

Rising Up... from a Long Way Down by C. C. Gross

Copyright©2014 by C. C. Gross

All rights reserved

No part of this book may be reproduced, stored in, or introduced into a retrieval system, or transmitted in any form, or by any means (electronic, mechanical, photocopying, recording, or otherwise) without the prior written permission of the author.

Cover painting by Patrick James

Book and cover designed by Ellie Searl, Publishista®

ISBN-13: 978-0615950655
ISBN-10: 0615950655
LCCN: 2014930480

MOOSEJAW PUBLISHING
Milford, CT

Acknowledgments

Without the support of the following people and their motivation, inspiration, and care, this book could not have come to fruition. Many thanks to my editors, Susanne Lakin, Marian Altman and Eden Diamond; my proofreader, Barbara Smith; and my book designer, Ellie Searl, Publishista®.

To my mother, so loving and wise.
To my children, Todd and Laura, so noble, unselfish and resilient.
And to Andrew, especially, for enduring it all, and enlightening us to
Rise Up . . .
Always, I love you more.
Thank you, I love you more.

Foreword

LIKE MOST GIRLS, I DREAMED the American dream. I wanted the fairy tale—a happy marriage, handsome husband, and healthy, beautiful children. But my dream would be shattered in a moment—by a catastrophe that would throw all of us into hell. Rising from the fallout, I would be changed forever, and guts of steel would propel me to love my children as if I were an unrivaled force of nature.

I thought I was prepared to make my way in the world. At the time, I was twenty-one years old, a registered nurse, and though a bit naive, was eager to move with three friends away from Moose Jaw, Saskatchewan, Canada, to Honolulu, Hawaii. I was not prepared for a journey that would eventually transform me into a warrior in the battle of life.

I considered myself lucky. In Honolulu I met a handsome American boy who would become my husband. We moved to Connecticut, had three children, and enjoyed a comfortable lifestyle. But one day while at play, Andrew, my kind fourteen-year-old son—the popular boy who made every team, who dreamed of going to

Princeton—fell from a swing in the backyard and suffered a severe traumatic brain injury.

Everyone who knew him prayed for his survival, and he finally awoke from a six-week coma. But, like a newborn, he needed to relearn how to do everything, vividly remembering who he used to be and contrasting that with who he was now. All he wanted was to have his old friends back and life as it used to be.

RISING UP... FROM A LONG WAY DOWN portrays the story of his traumatic, painful journey and the ripple effect it had on his family and friends. Ever grateful for my nursing education, I was transformed into a lioness, constantly, relentlessly bucking the system, advocating to protect him. I would not allow this horrific trauma to paralyze me or my family. In turn, it strengthened and pushed us to limits beyond our imagination. Bad luck would not destroy us; our resilience would define who we were.

Traumatic brain injury (TBI) is called the invisible plague. There is no cure or medication available, only rehabilitation. The statistics are staggering. Every year 1.7 million people sustain a TBI, and of that number 52,000 die and 235,000 are hospitalized. A brain injury occurs every twenty-three seconds in the US, and these types of injuries are more prevalent than breast cancer, HIV/AIDS, multiple sclerosis, and spinal cord injuries. Males are more at risk for TBI, as well as children in the first four years of life and between the ages of fifteen to nineteen.

The major cause of TBI is vehicle accidents, but—of grave concern, finally—sports-related concussions are being recognized and addressed. Currently 5.3 million Americans live with TBI-related disabilities, and eighty to ninety thousand join their ranks each year. We are only now realizing the severe long-term effects of TBI. Diagnosis and treatment must be made available immediately after injury, during the golden hour, which means arriving at a hospital within sixty minutes after an injury, for a patient to have the best chance of survival and to prevent death.

Princess Diana was killed in a car accident, and she had not been wearing a seat belt. Had she survived the accident, she would have been the world's spokesperson for TBI, as she suffered a serious head injury.

Tragedy, however poignant, is as old as the story of Adam and Eve—there is always more than enough to go around. However, there is a fundamental need, which the human heart never stops seeking to fill. It is the yearning for an example of undaunted courage that heralds the triumph of faith over despair, and describes the long journey from hopelessness to happiness. My personal odyssey is not just about a life-altering and catastrophic event. It is also a story that transcends gender and even motherhood, full of insight and peace, signifying everything that is important to people everywhere. This book is a call to action—a plan to educate the nation and hopefully the world, and to develop a strong voice to serve the needs of victims and their families, who are also victims.

I have been advocating change, resources, and education while fighting the system for twenty-six years and will never give up on Andrew's plight. Hopefully this story will help you understand how complex brain injury is, and will develop in you a passion to advocate relentlessly for your loved ones, young or old.

And if you, like me, survive hell and back, you will learn you have nothing to fear.

In 1996, as a catharsis, when I knew nothing about typing, computers, or writing, I wrote a screenplay called *The Swing*. It made the first round of consideration at the Sundance International Screenwriters Lab competition, validating my story. RISING UP... FROM A LONG WAY DOWN is adapted from that screenplay.

CHAPTER ONE

IT WAS SUNDAY, JULY 22, 1986—a beautiful, warm, and sunny afternoon in Middlebury, Connecticut. I was relaxing on the patio, enjoying conversation with my mother, Elsie, who had just arrived from Moose Jaw, Saskatchewan, Canada, for a holiday. The next day would be the very worst afternoon, and also the very best afternoon. And never could I imagine the horror that lay ahead.

It had been a difficult year for me, and my family in Canada, since my brother Earl passed away. Earl was well respected in the community, with a PhD in child psychology. His life was abruptly taken from him the previous August. I had made several trips to Canada to meet with the Mounties who were working the case, and also to try to prevent my parents from learning the horrid details of his death. He had been beaten, tortured, and left to die on a prairie.

On the patio with Mom, I changed the painful conversation from Earl's death. "Let's go to the front of the house. I want to show you the flowers, especially the ones Andrew and I planted." She and I walked to the front of the house to admire my flower garden. My husband, James, was on the riding mower, in his own world. The children—Todd, aged sixteen, Andrew, fourteen, and Laura, thirteen—were at Quassapaug Amusement Park for the afternoon with their friends. My mother thought I was fortunate to live the dream and marry a handsome American and have this comfortable lifestyle with three healthy, beautiful children.

The azure sky and spunky clouds reminded me of Saskatchewan in the summer—miles and miles of sky. That's why it's called Land of Living Sky. Yes, today was a perfect day. How lucky I was.

We returned to the patio to lounge in the sun. The phone rang. Calmly, I answered, "Hello?"

The caller did not identify himself, muffling his voice. "Do you know where your children are? You shouldn't have crossed the line on Friday, scab!" *Click.*

A chill went down my spine, jolting me upright. The message was clear—I had been working at Memorial Hospital per diem, during a nurses' union strike.

My mother's eyes widened as she watched me.

I dashed from the patio to find James. "We need to get the kids right now!"

"What's wrong? They've got a ride home."

"I just got a phone call, and they threatened the kids. I'm not kidding. Someone's watching them, maybe has abducted them. They told me I shouldn't have crossed the picket line on Friday. It's my fault!"

In a few minutes we were at Lake Quassapaug, my mind in a frenzy. Were my children in danger? Were they still there? Should I call the police?

Why me? Why my children? *I'm not even part of the union! How dare they threaten me and hold health care hostage because of personal politics?*

Anger and worrying about the unknown were not going to help this situation, so I tried to calm down. I told myself everything would be fine. This wasn't really happening.

Quassapaug was a safe place for children, but it was Sunday and mobbed. How on earth would I find them? As soon as we arrived, I had them paged. No response. My heart raced. A second page. I paced, scrutinized the crowd, and squinted through the sun, trying to see some semblance of a familiar face. Time had stopped. I was hyperventilating. These things didn't happen in small affluent towns like Middlebury. Looking through the crowd I saw no sign of my children.

I was panicking, squinting my eyes with an erupting headache, trying to see through the crowd. Beads of sweat stood on my forehead. I could feel my heart thrashing. Why hadn't James come with me? Finally, in the distance, in the midst of the mob, I spotted a red shirt with a maple leaf on the front. It was Andrew, and next to him were Todd and Laura. They sauntered along, carefree, eating ice cream. The lump in my throat was mammoth.

Thank you, God.

Andrew startled when he saw me. "Ma, what's up? We told you we didn't need a ride. Jula's dad is going to take us home. And you know—we're guests and don't have to pay for anything."

"We need to go, and we need to hurry. Dad's waiting in the car. Andrew, I know Jula is a good friend, but you have to come home now."

"Oh geez, Ma. You always have to ruin everything, just when we're having a good time."

"I'm sorry. I'll explain in the car."

All three of them moaned and groaned about how I was ruining a perfectly wonderful day.

"Look, I got an anonymous phone call, and whoever they were, they followed you and knew you were here. I'm sure they're just trying to scare me because I crossed the picket line at the hospital. But your dad and I can't take any chances. Do you understand?"

They felt immortal and grumbled all the way home.

James was quiet, as if I'd made the whole thing up. And when I told him I was calling the police, he thought I was taking it too far. But when we got home I did call immediately, and the police took it seriously. They were at the house in minutes. A tall, lanky officer entered, and I told him about the threatening call. He guaranteed me they would patrol the neighborhood all night long.

And then I was on a mission. I canvassed every neighbor on the street and continued for hours, watching the shock on their faces while I tried to explain the details. "No, I didn't recognize the voice of the caller. But for some reason I'm haunted by one of the nurses who lives here in town, who is at the forefront, fighting for the strike. She's also working toward a law degree, and I wouldn't put anything past her. But threatening my children? And on Friday they called me a scab."

"You're not going to cross again, are you?" asked one of my neighbors.

"Yes, I am—tomorrow."

"But it could be dangerous for you."

My neighbors were supportive. "Don't worry we'll keep our eyes open and our lights on all week. Good luck, and be careful."

"Thanks. They vandalized property in Southbury a few days ago. It's getting dark. I've got to get home." I walked up Green Road, exhausted but unafraid. All house and yard lights were blazing.

The next morning at five thirty, a piercing alarm clock annoyed me. I pulled the sheets over my head for a few minutes, procrastinating, not getting out of bed. You'd think that after nursing for twenty-five years I'd be used to early mornings, but I wasn't. I was not about to totally give up my nursing career, so I worked per diem, though James's philosophy was that the Kane women didn't need to work outside the home. He was a successful, professional salesman with a big company—Uniron. His logic was that he made the money, and I took care of the home and children.

The alarm also activated the amorous microchip I was sure James had implanted somewhere in his body. Immediately a warm body nuzzled next to me.

"I'm getting up," I told him.

"Come on, a few minutes won't kill you."

Laughing loudly, I said, "Right, a few minutes. That's not in your repertoire, my sweet."

Begging, he replied, "I promise."

James was caressing my shoulders. His gentle touch aroused me.

"Don't start . . . I'm getting up for work."

James was amorous every morning. This was his jump start to the day and way better than the caffeine in a grande triple espresso. And now he was feeling deprived, laying the usual guilt trip. Just like a man. In the past few years, he'd developed a jealous streak. I knew it bothered his ego that I worked closely with doctors in the operating room. In his mind, I was too flirtatious, drew too much attention, and was therefore in lustful demand. Ha! I was simply a friendly Wild West gal from Moose Jaw, Saskatchewan, and a one-man woman. I was not interested in doctors, and especially not married ones.

I jumped out of bed and headed straight to the shower.

On the drive to the hospital, I stopped at the local gas station and convenience store. It was already hot out; good thing I was wearing a short skirt. I smiled at the young attendant, whose dad was the owner. He was also a school friend of Todd's.

"How are you, Mrs. Kane? Fill 'er up?"

"Yup, and I'm wonderful—I think—thank you." I winked. "Of course that might be open to debate." We laughed, I went inside, and he gassed up my wagon. A few minutes later, coffee in hand, I returned, smiling, and waved good-bye to the early-morning regulars. I was ready to start the day.

The attendant said to me, "Going to be a scorcher. Off to play tennis today?"

"Nope, I'm a working gal, heading to the hospital."

"I hear bad stuff's going on over there."

Had he heard that I called the police? In a small town of six thousand people, everyone knew everyone else's business.

I said, "You're right. But you can't threaten people and put medicine on hold. It's not right. That's why I'm going in."

I skipped to my car and turned up the radio for the local news. ". . . And the strike at Memorial Hospital enters day nine. Administration is getting nowhere with union leaders, and there are reports of alleged union vandalism to the homes of nurses who have crossed the picket line, but . . ."

That was enough news for me. I switched stations to hear Whitney Houston sing "The Greatest Love of All," and sang along. I was trying to forget yesterday and the upcoming anniversary of my brother's death.

Little did I know that today would be a day that would hurl us straight into hell.

Before I knew it, I was in the Capital Hill area of Waterbury. At one time Capital Hill had been affluent, but now was spiraling slowly downward into a slum, its buildings dilapidated and ready for demolition. At Memorial Hospital I turned into the regular parking lot, only to be immediately stopped by bold picketers blocking the entrance.

"Stop. You can't park here. There is only one entrance and exit, and that is at the front of the hospital. Go there, and they will direct you."

One by one, the picketers took their time allowing drivers to cross their line. A bus displaying New York license plates unloaded a frenzied group of supporters wearing Union 1199 shirts. Aggressive, uninformed picketers—men and women in T-shirts and shorts—had the upper hand. Something was very wrong with this picture.

The minute they donned the bold yellow signs that read, *1199 WILL PREVAIL, MEMORIAL HOSPITAL WILL NOT*, it inspired in the herd an unhealthy restlessness. And then my mouth dropped open. Standing in the midst of them was one of my coworkers, a nurse from the OR. What in God's name was she doing here? She was so unassertive and restrained by nature. This was totally out of character for Betsy.

She scowled and shouted at me. "Dirty, disgusting turncoat!"

I was stunned, shaken, and scared. The honking horns startled me, and I drove through the picket line, still staring at Betsy. The picketers were getting nasty and ugly. One of them spit at my car as I drove through.

"Scab, traitor, suck-up!"

I marched into the hospital, which looked like a ghost town. There was an ominous feeling as I entered the operating room suite. There were no patients on stretchers, no secretaries in the office, no phones ringing, no overhead pages, no individuals in constant motion—and no doctors ranting, raving, cursing, harassing, or flirting with the nurses. There was just a dark, threatening quiet.

Why am I here all alone? What propelled me to get in the middle of this fight that really isn't mine? Am I crazy?

I was edgy and hesitant to enter the changing room. I could be attacked in a matter of minutes, and no one would be the wiser. Was someone after me? Quickly, I jumped into scrubs and headed out to a vacant lounge. The sound of someone walking in the hall made me jump.

"Connie, are you here?"

"Yes, in the lounge."

It was my supervisor, Joan. She was petite and responsible and had a gentle voice, which seemed so quiet compared to the outdoor mayhem. I respected her, and that was the main reason I was there.

"Was it bad? Did you have any trouble crossing?"

"To be honest, I was scared. But I didn't have a problem—just major intimidation."

"I need to warn you. Dianne crossed on Friday, and her pool was later vandalized. The liner was cut and trashed."

"We're dealing with animals, aren't we? Yesterday we got a phone call. They threatened my children. I called the police, and they're patrolling the neighborhood."

"It's bad and getting ugly. They're busing in support."

I smirked. "Well, they don't scare me. And besides, I'm not even union. So how many cases are booked? I need to get home. I'm having a family cookout. My mom's visiting."

Joan chuckled. "From Moose Jaw, right?"

"Yes, good memory."

"We've only got a few minors. Some skin lesions and a broken penis."

"A broken penis!"

We both roared. I checked the booking slip. Flabbergasted, I said, "I know this guy."

"Don't worry, we shipped him out. He needs immediate surgery. The hospital's a skeleton. Forget anything big, especially trauma. Is he a personal friend?"

"No, but I wonder who broke it!"

At twelve fifteen, I drove into my driveway—home for another beautiful, warm, and sunny afternoon in Middlebury, Connecticut. I got out of my car to be greeted by the red roses climbing the split-rail fence and the hot-pink impatiens that Andrew and I had planted. I heard children laughing and playing. I walked around the side of the garage to see my three children standing on a bank by the swing.

Laura whined, "I wanna go first."

"No, you're the baby—you go last. I need to make sure it's safe." Andrew rolled his eyes, jesting, trying to outsmart her.

"Andrew, you're just trying to trick me, and I'm not stupid."

"And I built it, so I'm going first." Todd grabbed the swing. He swung out high above the ground, looked back, and chuckled.

Todd had engineered a thirty-foot rope swing that was the thrill of the neighborhood. Young and old alike swung on it, including James, our dentist, and the children's orthodontist. One end was tied to the top of a tree in our backyard woods; James had made sure it was tightly secured. The other end was draped over the fence and had a wooden seat on the bottom. None of the kids in the neighborhood could get their fill of the swing. Whenever there was spare time—which I thought was too often—kids were in the yard swinging on the rope. I was constantly at James to cut it down before someone got hurt. But that always made me the "mean mother," and I was overruled.

I walked into the house and to the bedroom to shower and change my clothes. The bed was unmade. It was a beautiful mahogany four-poster that we had custom-made in Jamaica by local craftsmen. James had added his unique artful taste by building a canopy and a glass mirror above it. This feature enriched the curriculum at school, when the Kane children proudly elaborated during show-and-tell about the beautiful bed their parents had. Imagine boasting about something as simple as a bed! Followed, I'm sure, by bulging eyes and probably some gossip by the teacher. Whenever we had a dinner party, everyone had to see the bed, and we'd end up sipping cocktails in the bedroom. Of course we'd leave—we weren't into swapping, and I was so naive I had no idea that anyone did such a thing.

I looked up into the mirror and adjusted my gold pendant of the Christ child. Turning up the radio, I listened to Tina Turner's "Simply the Best." I loved to dance, and after a few glasses of wine could emulate a Rockette. Fantasy was so much fun! I danced down the hallway into the kitchen and then into the family room. James was on the couch, sleeping and snoring. Beer cans were strewn on the pink carpet. Abruptly my dancing and happy mood came to a complete standstill.

I stomped over to him and said, "James, your folks will soon be here, and my mother just arrived. Please get off the couch and help me." He turned over and ignored me. Just then Andrew entered the room. I changed gears, smiled, and hugged him. "Sweetie, go out on the patio and keep Grandma company, okay?"

Andrew's eyes were downcast at the request. He tried to avoid looking at James and quietly left the room, upset.

"James, I need your help!"

He rolled over. "Nag, nag, nag."

I left the room and walked out to the patio to visit and relax with my mother, the kindest woman on earth. The children loved to have Granny visit, since she always brought several boxes of baked goods.

"Granny, the peanut butter clusters are just for me, right?" Andrew, the boy with the sweet tooth, would ask.

Granny would smile lovingly at him and pretend not to see him quickly abscond with the cookie tin and run out of sight to hide them under his bed.

"Ma, it's not fair. He's eating all the cookies," Todd would say. "We're not going to get any!" Then, somehow, more cookies would appear.

Elsie loved to holiday in the States, the land of opportunity, and was proud of me and my handsome, smart American husband. She loved James and thought I was the luckiest girl in the world. He, in turn, doted on her, and she just lapped it up, adoring the attention.

A car door slammed, and we heard James's parents: Dee, whom we called Mum-mum, and James Sr., whom we called Bumpy.

On the patio for only a matter of minutes, Dee started in. "Is everyone getting ready for Tina's big wedding at Notre Dame? Elsie, I'll fill you in."

I rolled my eyes. James and I were sick and tired of hearing Dee talk about James's sister, Trudy Lenner, and her perfect family—especially the favorite grandchild, Tina. James's father was another story and gave my mom a big wet kiss, as he did to everyone. My mother was disapproving in a quiet way.

Dee and James Sr. were too loud, always bragging, overly kissing, and just plain brassy. Dee was a striking beauty born into wealth. She had a head for business and studied the stock market, as her dad had taught her from an early age. Bumpy was from a poor Irish family, but his good looks had won Dee's heart. He married her for her legs and not her money—or so he said. He was an alcoholic and took every chance he could to sneak a drink, but he was a kind and gentle man, and I loved him. No sooner were they settled on the patio when he slyly sipped Elsie's screwdriver.

Dee pounced on him. "What do you think you're trying to pull here?"

Bumpy laughed it off. Whether he got caught or not, he really didn't care. He'd try again at an opportune moment.

I was lucky—I got along with my in-laws. They had never interfered in our business, and I respected them. But I would soon learn to eat those words. I had grown to love them as family, even though Dee didn't think I was good enough for her son. After all, he was a Kane, and I was just a simple, unsophisticated girl from Saskatchewan—and, my God, who came from Moose Jaw? I remained quiet and never confronted Dee, because that's what families were supposed to do, right? However, unbeknownst to anyone—myself included—the Americanized Connie Kane, lioness, was emerging, and soon would prevail.

"Con," Bumpy said, using the name he called me, "when are you going to become an American citizen?"

"When I can pass the test. Right now, it's way too hard for a simple girl like me."

Bumpy liked me, I liked him, and he loved teasing me. "So how is Canada? We're going to annex you soon."

Dee was quick. "Bump, shut up. You're not funny. Elsie, he thinks he's such a worldly man. Just ignore him."

Our whole family was on the patio engaged in conversation—everyone except James. Dee noticed his absence. "Where's James?"

I answered tersely, "Sleeping."

Dee detected my annoyance with James. Not skipping a beat, she turned to Todd. "So are you and Andrew ready for the big wedding?" Then she turned to Elsie. "You know that Tina, the first woman vice president of the Notre Dame student body, is getting married and—"

I was tense and interrupted, "Dee, she's heard all about the wedding."

She could be so damned annoying. Maybe it was me, and I was tired of making small talk about James's drinking and pretending nothing was going on. I needed to escape, so I politely excused myself and went inside to the kitchen. Andrew followed me and then scampered away. I tried to relax and prepared appetizers. He returned, hiding something behind his back. Knowing his impulsive theatrics, I was wary.

"So, Mr. Special Man who's taunting me with something secret— and it better not slither because you've got a birthday in a few weeks— what's your heart's desire for food for that day?"

He was momentarily pensive, and then his eyes widened, joined by a huge grin. "How about lobster?"

In return I teased and lovingly toyed with him. "Hmmm, let me ponder for a moment. Just maybe—if you behave while Grandma's here."

He kissed me on the cheek, brought his hands into view, and proudly presented me with a tiny schefflera plant I'd admired last week. I was touched. "Thank you, sweetie. Now it'll be part of our family, and it'll make me think of you, even years from now when you're away at college."

"And after Princeton, when I'm working on Wall Street, wearing a camel-hair coat and carrying a leather briefcase?"

I laughed. "Always the fashionista. And yes, I'll be prouder than ever. And, might I add—lobster for your birthday is looking good." I hugged him and he ambled out. He was the master manipulator, and I loved him to death.

I stormed back to the family room. James was still on the couch. "Dammit, James, I need your help now. Your parents, everyone, is here."

Asleep, he jolted upright, unaware of what was going on around him. Opening his eyes, he said, "Okay, okay, gimme a minute, please." Disheveled, he sauntered out of the room and into the kitchen. He opened the refrigerator door, then bent down and searched, and his pants dropped, exposing his butt. He opened a beer with that annoying *snap* that sent shivers down my spine, then procrastinated toward the bedroom.

Twenty minutes later he came out onto the patio. He was freshly showered, shaved, and looked like Mr. GQ in Nantucket reds and a pressed polo shirt. So much for an afternoon siesta. He was the center of attention—the smiling, gracious host. Mr. Personality—taking drink orders, doting on my mother, and throwing me a kiss for everyone to see.

Theatrically, he addressed me. "And what can I get my girl, my sweetie, to drink?"

I was upset with him. He was such a jerk and just didn't get it.

"Nothing." I ignored him and focused on petting our golden retriever, Maggie. Dee eyed me judgmentally and nervously twisted her three-carat diamond ring. Bumpy was just enjoying all the activity.

Andrew chimed in, "Granny, you should see our rope swing. It's like flying through the sky—awesome!"

James strutted. "I went on it yesterday, and it's great fun."

I interrupted. "And I think it should be cut down."

"Oh, for Pete's sake, let the kids have some fun."

As usual the mean mother was overruled.

"Granny, we're going on the swing. Come and watch us."

"I'll be over in a few minutes. You go ahead," she said.

Todd, Andrew, and Laura hopped from the patio and headed to the swing. Chris, their best friend, had strolled into the backyard. They slapped high fives.

Andrew picked up a patio chair and stood on it. It would make him higher on the rope and higher in the sky. He untied the swing and placed the wooden seat under his butt. Holding the rope tightly he shouted, "Watch how high I'm going! See if you can beat me. I'm Superman!"

Smiling, he swung into the woods, flying through the sky above the thirty-foot-high trees.

Abruptly, the wooden seat fell away from his butt. His support was gone.

Holding on for dear life, his knuckles blanched. The skin on his fingers and palms raw and bleeding from rope burn.

He couldn't hold on anymore—he was way too high.

Slowly his hands slipped off the rope. He screamed.

His body plunged to the ground.

A blunt *thump*.

The abandoned rope swung back to the bank.

Dead silence.

Chapter Two

Laura was frozen.

Todd gasped. "Mom, Dad—Andrew's fallen from the swing!"

James and I raced from the patio down an embankment to Andrew. He was on his back, not moving, his eyes closed and his head next to a huge rock. Oh my God, did his head hit the rock? *This isn't happening. He's playing dead. It's one of his tricks.*

We knelt on the ground. I checked his breathing and pulse. He was alive but unconscious. I waited for him to move and roll over, but he didn't, and I became more petrified by the second. James didn't speak—he was numb.

"Andrew, Andrew, can you hear me? Speak to me—it's your mom. Please say something, anything! Are you hurt, in pain? Can you hear me, open your eyes? Please tell me what's wrong—you're scaring me. Please, God, help us!"

I looked at James and started to cry. "Call 911 and get an ambulance."

James was shaking. "You call. I'll stay here."

My heart thrashed in my chest as I sprinted up the bank. I slipped on some wet leaves. *Dammit, dammit, for God's sake, help me! I think I'm losing my mind!*

I reached the top of the bank. The family had gathered around, staring mute. James Sr. clutched his chest. I flew into the house. In the kitchen I groped for the phone, fumbling, hysterical. As I dialed 911, I fought tears and my lips quivered—my voice needed to be clear. An operator answered. Before she could get out a sound, I interrupted.

"There's been an accident. My son's fallen from a swing . . . Oh my God—he's unconscious, may have broken his neck . . . It's a thirty-foot swing in the backyard. Hurry! It's Kane, Green Road, in Curtiss Farms."

I slammed the phone down and rushed back to Andrew, thinking maybe he was awake and this wasn't so bad after all. He might have some broken bones and suffered internal injuries, but we can fix all that, right God?

Andrew hadn't moved. I was petrified. "God, help me, please!" My tears fell onto his beautiful, soft cheeks. I tenderly stroked his face. "Sweetie, Mommy's here. Don't worry—I'll take care of you." Oh my God, was he dying before my eyes?

I glanced accusingly at James. "I told you to take down that damn swing. How many times did I tell you that someone would get hurt? But no, I take away all the fun. Well, how much fun is this?"

James was frozen. Suddenly I heard voices. I turned and saw three police officers and two paramedics carrying a stretcher. In shock, they glanced at Andrew, their faces drained as if afraid to speak.

I immediately took command. "I'm a nurse. He's unconscious, so you need to support his neck. It may be broken. No, forget it—I'll do it. You need to be very careful. His body needs to be very still. He can't be jarred." I scrutinized every movement. The urgency in my voice was a warning not to tangle with this lioness.

The paramedics cautiously transported him up the slippery embankment. Finally, we were on the driveway on our way to the ambulance. A group of neighbors had gathered. How quickly bad news traveled. I didn't have time to speak, but I could see the alarm in their eyes as they clutched their children. The police escorted us as Andrew was placed inside the ambulance, accompanied by one of the paramedics.

The other paramedic jumped in the front seat and swiftly turned on the ignition. I hopped in alongside the stretcher. The paramedic in the back spoke softly. "I'm sorry, Mrs. Kane. You're not allowed to ride in the ambulance — policy, you know — but you can follow behind us."

My eyes hurled lethal daggers at him. "Like hell. He's my son, and I'm not moving. I'm a nurse. Now get moving. We don't have time for this crap!"

One of the policemen nodded to the paramedic, and the door slammed shut. The siren blared as we drove down the street. I waited for Andrew to open his eyes. *Please, Andrew, I can't take much more.*

He lay too still, his breathing getting shallower.

The paramedic continually checked his blood pressure. It was dangerously low. The paramedic in the front was on the phone to a hospital. "I have an unconscious fourteen-year-old trauma victim. Fell from a thirty-foot swing in the backyard."

He listened intently. "Okay, right, the strike." He put down the radio handset and turned to me. "There's a strike at Memorial Hospital, and St. John's is full. We're taking him to Yale."

My eyes bugged out of my head, the veins in my neck engorged to explode. I was like a venomous snake on the attack. "Yale — that's thirty minutes away. He won't make it — he'll die. Call St. John's back.

Tell them they have to take him, his mother's a nurse, she worked there. And step on it—we don't have much time!"

The paramedic's brow was covered in sweat. He stammered as he picked up the radio handset again. He spoke for a few seconds and turned to me. "It's St. John's." The siren seemed louder the faster he drove.

My hands trembled. I grasped Andrew's hands. They were cold. I began to cry and prayed out loud, "My God, oh my God, please make him better!"

Finally we were at the ER of St. John's Hospital. The ambulance doors swiftly opened as the stretcher locked in an upright position. Leading the stretcher, I gripped Andrew's hands with my clammy ones. We blasted through the doors and were met by a nurse who directed us to a cubicle. In seconds the cubicle was a maze of medical personnel assessing Andrew.

Suddenly, foamy saliva oozed from his blue lips. His shorts were soaked wet with urine. His fingers and toes twitched as his body spasmed violently into a grand mal seizure. The staff allowed me to stand at the back of the cubicle. I was horrified. Things were getting worse. My face grew cold. My body trembled.

Then the overhead page blared. "Pediatric Code Three, ER, four minutes. Pediatric Code Three, ER, four minutes."

This was very bad. Andrew could die in a matter of seconds. They were summoning expert help from everywhere in the hospital to help keep him alive. His clothes were slashed from his body and discarded onto the floor. EKG leads were attached, a catheter inserted.

An ER doctor checked his eyes with a flashlight and shouted, "Get the crash cart; he needs intubating. Call anesthesia, a neurosurgeon, CAT scan, stat!"

I was frozen. A nurse handed me his yellow Swatch. I put it on my trembling wrist and stroked it, hoping to feel some hint of life, but there was none. It was cold, and I was freezing. Doctor Karney, a neurosurgeon, raced into the ER. I knew him.

He was intense, took charge, and examined Andrew. "Get him to CAT scan, stat. Call the OR to get ready. We might be bringing him up." He glanced at me but did not utter a word. I knew the situation was dreadfully ominous. An anesthesiologist I knew frantically pushed his machine into the cubicle, and within seconds Andrew was hooked up to a ventilator. I picked up his torn clothes and held them close to my body to feel his life but felt nothing. I was a zombie in a horrifying, alien zone.

I was at his side as they transported him to CAT scan.

I glimpsed at a reflection of myself in a tank top and short shorts. If Andrew woke up and saw me dressed like this, he would be embarrassed. I asked the nurse, "Can I please put on a hospital gown to cover myself? I'm so cold, I think my blood's drained out of me."

I recognized a lot of the staff, but no one spoke to me. We flew through the corridors and came upon James holding up the wall at the end of the hall. All I could see was a red face and trembling lips. All I could smell was alcohol.

He rallied to speak, and I snapped cruelly at him. "This is all your fault. Can't you see we need you? And you've been drinking." He was in shock, ready to faint. Those cruel, insensitive words would haunt and torment us both forever.

As we passed a waiting room, a TV anchorwoman was being filmed for the evening news. "A serious accident this afternoon may be the result of Union 1199 picketers who are striking against Memorial Hospital. An investigation continues in Middlebury, where fourteen-year-old Andrew Kane remains in serious condition at a local hospital, following a fall from a thirty-foot swing in his yard. The strikers at Memorial Hospital are being questioned. Repeated acts of vandalism have been reported, and the day before the accident, the

Kanes received a threatening phone call. There is concern that the swing may have been tampered with."

I squeezed my eyes shut. The reality of the situation was throwing me into a panic, clouding my mind. *This isn't happening. How could someone attack my child? What have I done wrong? How does everyone already know about the accident? Oh my God!*

We entered the CAT scan area, where I was given front-row viewing. Andrew was placed inside a coffin-like machine that made weird clicking sounds. Alone, I begged and cried, "Andrew, please wake up. Be your usual daredevil self. Pull out that damn tube." But he lay dead still.

After what seemed like an eternity, Doctor Karney trudged out. His tie was pulled loose at his neck, and he rubbed his forehead. He headed toward me, his gait labored, body stooped.

"Andrew has suffered a severe brain stem injury. His frontal bone and ethmoid sinuses are fractured, along with a subdural hematoma, and his left radius is also fractured. We don't need to do surgery, but it's very serious. Time will tell. If he makes the next twenty-four hours, we've no way of predicting how functional he will ever be."

I glanced at the clock. It was 6:21 p.m. Monday, July 21. Time had stopped. Why, why, why? My throat constricted. What had he done to deserve this—or was I to blame?

I couldn't breathe. My stomach was in a vise grip, being twisted tighter and tighter. I gagged and heaved, but nothing came up except for the taste of bile. "Oh no, God, please, please, not my Andrew. He's still my baby!"

I desperately craved James's presence, for him to hold me, reassure me, and tell me they were wrong, that we would beat this. But I was all alone, abandoned.

Little did I realize, as the clock ticked, that Andrew had passed from suffering a "mild" traumatic brain injury—experiencing less than thirty minutes of unconsciousness—to a "moderate" traumatic brain injury, wherein unconsciousness lasts from a half hour to twenty-four hours.

I stumbled over to the ICU, where they were admitting him. I sat in the waiting room and was soon joined by an old friend, Alex—a resident. How did he know? What had he been told?

"Alex, I don't know anything about brain injury."

"Let the nurses take care of him. They are excellent and know how to handle this. Just be his mother and be there for him."

Hospitals were on high alert during summer, known for no school, fun, freedom, and trauma. I couldn't imagine how terrible it was for the staff to deal with this. And now here I was, also in the middle of it. How was I going to survive? I wasn't ready to let go of Andrew. He was a fighter. He would beat this. We would beat this. I was his mother, and I knew him better than anyone.

I called home to update everyone and to say I was staying at the hospital. It was Middlebury carnival night. Todd and Laura had no idea how serious Andrew's condition was, and were driving Granny crazy wanting to get to the carnival. They thought Andrew would wake up and come home, and life would return to normal. To keep the peace, Granny let them go. This was small-town USA—nothing bad ever happened here. The kids ate cotton candy, rode the Ferris wheel, and spread the word that Andrew had been up to his usual antics but was okay and would soon be back home.

James was nowhere in sight.

For Andrew there was no cotton candy. Would he ever know the thrill and excitement of a carnival as he used to? The minutes of his coma turned into hours. He was unresponsive, paralyzed, and alive only through a ventilator machine. I shuddered, knowing he might die, but I would never admit these thoughts to anyone.

The nurse called me into the ICU. Andrew looked like a sleeping cherub posed for a portrait. The bed was neat, the white sheets pressed. It was all too perfect. I watched his chest move up and down, synchronized with the beeping of the ventilator. I moved to the top of his bed and stroked his hair, stared at his eyelashes—so thick, so long—and the cute little freckles on the bridge of his nose. His body was unbruised except for a huge shiner on his right eye. He was a beautiful child, and I began to cry. *Please, God, I know he is only a gift, but don't take him yet!*

I sat in a chair and held his hands. Without me there, he would be frightened. I vowed, calling him by his nickname, "My Gigi, I will always be with you and promise not to leave until you awaken from your coma."

One of the nurses checked in. "How are you doing? Is there anything I can get you?"

"Yes. Please find Sister Tish Shean. She's a personal friend and lives here at the convent. And could you please get me a rosary?"

Sister Tish was my best friend Maria's sister. She was a modern-day nun, dressed in street clothes. Minutes later she showed up with Sister Emirita. They brought me several rosaries and told me they would start offering daily Masses in the chapel for Andrew.

When they left I sat alone, holding my rosary in one hand and Andrew's hand in the other. I thought about Maria, who had just had the kids over to her pool a few hours before the accident. I could see them all swimming and having a wonderful fun-filled day. A tear slid down my cheek. Was that all in the past? Shame on you, Connie, for negative thoughts. This was only temporary!

The news of Andrew's accident traveled, inspiring little optimism. But I was always outwardly confident. Doctors and nurses I knew came into the ICU to visit me. They were working at St. John's because of the strike at Memorial Hospital. Their support was essential but awkward, because they were afraid to say the wrong thing. One frazzled nurse visited and proceeded to share nonstop every detail of her affair with one of the doctors. It was insensitive and I never listened, blinked, or responded. I was deaf—my focus was

Andrew. I had forgotten about the strike until one of the doctors I knew came to visit.

"I know you have a lot on your mind, but have the police checked the swing to make sure it wasn't cut by the picketers? I'll call when I leave the hospital. They need to check your yard for signs of tampering. I wouldn't put anything past this group."

Momentarily, I was stunned. This wasn't possible—we didn't know people like that. In shock and denial I dismissed it from my mind. My focus was Andrew coming out of the coma and returning home.

We passed the twenty-four-hour mark, and Andrew was alive, still in a coma. To me we had passed a major hurdle, but the doctor was cautious and not as optimistic.

"We're not out of the woods yet and need to wait another forty-eight hours," Dr. Karney told us. "His first complication has set in. He's got pneumonia."

I refused to hear bad news. "We can fix that—meds will solve that issue. We'll get over this barrier. He's young and healthy and strong."

"Another seventy-two hours will tell," Dr. Karney said.

James showed up sober and well-groomed. I was so relieved to have him there and share everything that was going on, but his negativity was still a curse. His employer, Uniron, was in the midst of a buyout. He was worried about his job and our health insurance. I was too focused on Andrew staying alive and was annoyed with him.

"We might have to send you and Andrew to Canada."

"Are you crazy?"

"I don't know what's going to happen with the buyout."

"James, you worked there for twenty years. They won't dump us. They can't."

"They can do what they damn well want."

Through pursed lips I changed the conversation. "Bring the kids up for a long stay. They need to see Andrew . . . just in case."

"Okay." He was visibly sweating.

I had made it very clear that I was not leaving the hospital until Andrew was awake. James would need to be home with Todd and Laura until I returned.

The nuns had invited me to stay at the convent for as long as I needed. I stayed for the first night in an immaculate room, relieved and forever grateful for their kindness. The convent was attached to the hospital, so if I was called and told that Andrew was out of the coma, I could be in the ICU in minutes. I was also able to attend early Mass daily.

The next morning, the worshippers at the hospital chapel and at our church prayed for Andrew. I suspected that God was getting sick and tired of all the constant chatter. Even *He* must have limits with this deluge of women with their prayers. Surely He would look down on us and answer. After Mass I went to join the nuns for breakfast and was surprised to see that James had already joined them. Things were improving.

The seventy-two hours were up. We patiently waited as Dr. Karney examined Andrew. "Andrew is going to live. However, at this point I can't tell you how functional he'll be, what his quality of life will be, or if he'll ever be able to come off of the ventilator. But he is going to survive."

I was elated. A load was lifted from my shoulders. Our sentence had been commuted. He would eventually come home, I'd take care of him, and that's all I needed to hear. *Thank you, thank you, God.*

The next step was for Andrew to wake up and start moving. I knew he could do this. I had quickly learned to live one hour at a time, often one minute at a time. Trying to look into the future, to predict what reality might be, could only sabotage the plan. I dealt with the moment and cherished each minute he was alive, ever confident about the next. I put his limbs through range-of-motion exercises, constantly touching him and talking to him so he knew I was there, even if he couldn't respond yet. The shiner on his eye was the size of a grapefruit—grotesque, purple, and yellow.

Todd and Laura arrived and surprised me. They took one look at Andrew and fear temporarily froze them. Timidly, they moved closer to the bed.

"I'm glad you're here, but where's Dad?" I asked.

They were fixated on Andrew, unable to speak. The maze of tubes, a catheter from his bladder, a stomach tube, the beeping of the ventilator, and the EKG leads monitoring his heart were too much for them.

Trembling, Todd spoke. "Ma, how is he?"

"He's getting better. Even the doctor—"

"Ma, he's always been the center of attention, foolin' around. Maybe this is just another game he's playing for attention."

I put my arm gently on his shoulder. "Todd, sweetie, he isn't playing a game this time."

Todd was now face-to-face with him. "Andrew, come on, wake up. Open your eyes. This time you've gone too far. Now open your eyes—this is no joke. Andrew, open your eyes. Wake up."

Andrew was paralyzed, trapped, and jailed, unable to respond to Todd's begging and pleading. Todd became hysterical and dashed out. He ran through the ICU, colliding with staff and visitors, and into the hallway, where he clung to a wall. I followed behind, and frantically grabbed him to hug and console, but he was inconsolable.

"The swing wasn't cut. If I hadn't built it, he wouldn't have fallen. It's all my fault."

I was flabbergasted. I looked directly at him and proclaimed emphatically, "I never, ever, want to hear you say that or for you to think that. It was a terrible accident, and it's not your fault—do you hear me? It will always be a terrible accident, but we are all going to survive this."

"Ma, all this time Laura and I have been at home laughing, thinking he deserved to fall because he's such a daredevil and so impulsive," Todd said. "That this would teach him a lesson, smarten him up, he'd come out of the coma, go back to school, and everything would be all right. What's going to happen to him?"

"Right now it's one minute, one hour, at a time. No one really knows, but he is getting better. I just keep praying for him to wake up, and praying is all we can do."

"Everyone's praying for him, and we've got tons of food from friends and neighbors. The phone rings constantly — everyone wants to help."

Tish showed up. I was relieved and knew I could count on her to take care of Todd. I motioned with my eyes, and she immediately took him away. My mom arrived a few minutes later.

I said, "I can't come home yet. I'm staying here at the hospital, but I need clean clothes. And where is James?"

Reluctantly she answered, "I'm never sure where James is. I'm sure you don't want to hear this, but yesterday when the children and I left the hospital, he was waiting for us in the car — drunk and asleep. When we woke him up, it was the ride home from hell. He showed the kids how to drive using no hands, just his knees. The car was all over the road. I sat in the backseat, praying. On the other hand, you have wonderful friends. Liz called and she's organized the Lions Club to send in dinner every night for an unlimited time."

"That drunken . . . putting you and the children through that, teaching the children to drive recklessly. How dare he abuse and threaten everyone's life?" Did I also need to protect my children from their father? Something was very wrong and getting worse by the minute. I needed to be at the hospital every day, and decided I would temporarily put up with James's drinking, but not for long.

Chapter Three

One week later the nurses tried to wean Andrew off the ventilator, but he was unable to breathe on his own. Dr. Karney took me aside and said, "I need to warn you—he may never be able to come off the ventilator."

I heard the words, but didn't believe them. I was emotionally and physically exhausted and ready to cry, but on the other hand elated. I was not ready to have Andrew die, and the fact that he was going to live was all I needed to hear. "Then I'll take him home on it."

I was running out of steam and headed to the convent to sleep. I hadn't been outside since the accident, so decided to walk around the hospital. The heat and fresh air that I loved immediately engulfed me, and for a slight moment I realized I was alive, and I smiled. It was the same overpowering reaction I had when getting off the plane in Honolulu, when I moved from Canada to Hawaii. It seemed like yesterday.

As I walked down the steps, a solemn young man was sitting, casually smoking a cigarette. Very reverently he addressed me, "Good evening, Sister."

I smiled at him. "And good evening to you, my child." I was obviously hanging with nuns so much that now I looked like one.

At the convent, now day eight, I went to my room. I looked in the mirror and saw dark circles around my eyes and a worn, distraught figure, preoccupied and unfocused. I stood for a minute disoriented, not knowing what to do or how to move. I relished the convent ambiance and slowly lay my weary body on the bed, forgetting to undress. During this time, all alone, I could deal with the shocking reality and fear that Andrew was very sick, and I questioned what kind of life lay ahead for all of us. But my strong state of denial would not allow me to think further. I clenched my rosary and bargained with God, trying not to allow the dragons that haunted me to surface, and soon I felt at peace and was comforted. I slipped a mild tranquilizer, Ativan, into my mouth and in seconds was asleep. Praise to modern medicine!

In the morning, I dressed and made sure my hair looked decent and my jewelry was in place. Even though my exterior appeared well groomed, my interior was shattered, and I felt adorned and unworthy. My gold jewelry no longer had appeal. It was materialistic and unimportant. Andrew's life was all that mattered. But when Andrew woke up, he needed to see me as I always looked, or he'd know something was wrong. The hospital surroundings would be scary enough, and he didn't need to know how grim everything was, so I decided to keep wearing the jewelry.

I arrived on the unit ecstatic. There had been slight movement on the left side of Andrew's body, and the nurses were getting him up into a recliner. He seemed to have had a growth spurt and was wearing size thirteen sneakers that resembled boats. The shiner on his eye looked horrid, but the doctors agreed—he was getting stronger.

By the end of the second week, still in a coma, he was weaned from the ventilator. I leaned close to his chest, assessed each inhalation and exhalation, and then moved closer to his face to hear the rhapsody of sweet breaths and feel the warm air flowing from his nostrils. Yes, he was breathing alone and ready to be moved out of the ICU and to a neurological floor.

In the last two weeks, I had received an extensive education. I was informed that after a brain injury—and with thorough rehabilitation—a patient can make gains for five years, the first six months being the most dramatic. Those words would be my bible for the next five years. Todd and Laura would understand that Andrew's rehabilitation would be the priority, and we'd desperately have to work as a family at his recovery. Survivors of TBI who had total family support did best, and Andrew would head that list. He would have whatever he needed to get on with his life, regardless of cost or time. We would take out loans, borrow money, whatever it took, but I would not rest until he got the best of what was available in this foreign new world. This child of mine would not be denied anything for his recovery. I was totally unaware of the trials and tribulations that lay ahead.

In my heart, I was positive that the children and I would make the transition from victims to survivors, but I was not sure about James. I needed my energy and was constantly exhausted. Since Andrew was still in coma, I wanted someone with him twenty-four hours a day. So I hired a private duty nurse to watch him during the night shift on the neurological floor. My nursing friends also took turns staying with him.

It was early morning, and I was momentarily jovial. Everything was slowly falling into place, until I exited the elevator and crashed into James. With one glance, I knew he'd been drinking, and he disgusted me, especially since he hadn't been up to see Andrew for several days. He just assumed I'd take care of everything, when in actuality I really needed his help. Instead, he was becoming more distant, and the accident was now an excuse to drink more.

I sneered, "Well, you've decided to grace us with your presence!"

"Con, please, stop."

"Like hell I will. You reek of alcohol, drive drunk with our children. What good are you?" I couldn't stand looking at him, so made a beeline for the chapel. He left the hospital.

Shaking, I entered the chapel. I blessed myself, reached inside my purse for my rosary, and popped one of my tranquilizers. I knelt in a pew and stared at the altar covered in a white corporal cloth and the crucifix. Two candles on the altar flickered, distorting my haggard reflection on the stained-glass windows as I began to pray.

God, I am numb. My brain's scattered, racing from one terrorizing extreme to another. I'm dragging, but there's no time for self-indulgence. The tears stinging my cheeks convince me I'm alive, but I wish . . . No, I'll fight this, but give me strength—don't desert me. I don't know if I can do this alone, and I doubt James . . . Please, make Andrew whole again. He doesn't deserve this. He's only fourteen years old. Take me instead.

I was momentarily transfixed and could hear Eric Clapton singing "Tears in Heaven."

I stared at the crucifix and saw Andrew hanging on the cross, unblemished, with blood trickling from the side of his head. I shook this terrible image from my mind and left the chapel.

For the first time in two weeks I was heading home. It seemed strange to drive up Green Road. So much had transpired. My mother was still here but needed to go home.

I surprised Laura. I walked into the living room and listened to her playing the piano and singing "Memories."

"Mom, you're home." She ran over and we hugged. The warmth of her body comforted me so. I had missed not being her mother.

Hopefully in the future, I could make it up to her. But neither she nor I had any idea what lay ahead for all of us. And it was best we didn't.

"And you, young lady, are going to get that scholarship to Westin. When does all the material have to be in?"

"Two weeks. How is Andrew?"

"He was just moved out of ICU to a neurological floor. He's doing well."

"Mom, what's next for him?"

"Only time will tell. He needs to wake up from the coma. But we also need to work on that scholarship for you to Westin." She had done the entire application process on her own. Attending Westin, a private girls' school here in Middlebury, had always been her dream. Little did she realize it would become a nightmare.

"Mom, the police were here. They checked the swing and said it wasn't tampered with. Then Dad cut it down."

In my heart I didn't think someone would have intentionally wanted to hurt my children. *But, God, why hadn't I made James cut the damn thing down?*

Our good friends Sue and Randy Snider came over. They were concerned with James's noticeable absence from the hospital and Andrew's progress without a father present. I welcomed any kind of intervention. James had been drinking all day.

I admired and watered the beautiful schefflera plant Andrew had given me the day of the accident. Sue and I went to another part of the house. James shouted, "Take her away and talk to her. Do something. She's in one of her moods."

Whenever I addressed his drinking, I was "in one of my moods." Randy truly cared for James and sat at the kitchen table with him. "You've got to get it together and go to the hospital. Andrew needs you now more than he's ever going to need you. His recovery is dependent on you. For God's sake, James, you're his father!"

It broke my heart to hear Randy plead for James to be a dad to his child. But James just hung his head. "I just can't do it. I can't face him. It's too painful."

They left him at the table sobbing. I had heard his answer and had no sympathy for him.

How did he think the rest of us felt? Wasn't it painful for me being there every day?

And what about Todd and Laura? James had no idea of the trauma he was causing. He was a good, kind man, but weak, addicted, and selfish. I was losing the trust and respect I'd had for him.

And I was growing stronger by the day—not by choice but by necessity. I wanted us to survive, and that goal was a permanent fixture in my brain. I wanted us to be a family, a team, and maybe my strength could make that happen. How foolish I was to think this, since we have control over only ourselves and no one else. It would take me a while to learn that.

It was four weeks after the accident. The nurses on the floor each had several patients to care for and couldn't stay with Andrew round the clock, so my friends took turns sitting with him when I wasn't there. Unknowingly, I, the lioness, upped the ante and was making nurses out of all of them. My friend Liz organized the group, and they were all given a crash course in Connie's Protocol for Taking Care of Andrew. There was a notebook at his bedside titled *Andrew 101* with these specific instructions:

1. Turn and position every two hours.
2. Rub arms, legs, and back. Don't forget bony prominences. Use special cream and finish off with a squirt of Polo!
3. Watch catheter so it doesn't pull or leak.
4. Check IV so it doesn't infiltrate.
5. Watch tube in his nose so it doesn't pull.
6. List all visitors and calls.

7. Be ready, so when he awakens from his coma, he'll see a familiar, friendly face, and you will have won the prize.

THANK YOU, THANK YOU, THANK YOU.

On the day before Andrew's fifteenth birthday, balloons and flowers were everywhere in his room, and he wore his Walkman while his favorite music played. Liz was on duty, massaging his legs. She lifted the sheets to check his catheter, and her face turned red.

"My, my, what big . . . *feet* you have! Your mother will make a nurse out of me yet!" She dusted the nightstand, his bed, under his bed. She removed his headphones, grabbed a book about golf, and held his hands. "Andrew, you must seal your lips, I don't even dust at home. Okay, here's *Ben Hogan's Fundamentals of Golf*. I'm sure your swing will be perfect after I read this to you."

Even though I had help monitoring him, I was constantly exhausted and often forgot to eat. Maybe that's why I felt so absent of feeling. My existence was now totally for my child. Would I have to program my brain and body to go through life in motion only? Unfeeling? Uncaring about the rest of the world? I speculated yes. I loved this child more than life itself, but was I to be a prisoner, in exile, devoid of happiness? Part of me had died, deep inside, and regardless of how much I yearned for freedom, death was final. I prayed, *Dear God, give me the strength to endure this, because when I think of him alive, joy so fills my heart it travels to every part of my body, and nothing can take that away. I can do this.*

Later that same day, I arrived in Andrew's room. Liz was still there. I kissed him. "Hey, handsome, how's the new nurse?"

"It's all documented in his 101 book." Liz dramatically whispered into Andrew's ear, "God forbid we don't follow the rules. And we've been gossiping. I filled him in on everything."

"Everything—even his birthday party?"

Liz rolled her eyes while addressing Andrew. "Be glad you're in a coma. I think your mother might break out in song."

Today would be special. Dr. Karney had sent a speech pathologist, Emily, to assess Andrew. I must admit I was skeptical. "Speech therapy—really? I mean, he's paralyzed, in a coma!"

Liz and I moved out of the way as Emily focused intently on Andrew. "Mrs. Kane, this is my third visit. I think he can hear me."

Shocked, I said, "Your third visit? When? Where was I? He can hear *you*?"

"At Mass." She leaned closely to Andrew.

I was impressed. A beautiful and dedicated early bird.

"Hi, Andrew, it's Emily back to visit you. I brought you some ice cream. Your mom says you love it. Maybe today you can taste it. I also want to know if you can hear me and add for me."

This was way too emotional for me, and I was unprepared to handle the fallout.

Emily continued. "I want you to add one plus two and put up as many fingers as that adds up to."

It was absolute torture as I watched Andrew's paralyzed hands lying on the bed, not moving. A few seconds passed.

"Andrew, let's try again. I know you can hear me. Add one plus two and put up as many fingers as that adds up to."

His hands still lay still. Did Emily have any idea how cruel this was for me, giving me hope when there was none? I was teary-eyed, now holding on tightly to Liz.

Emily refused to give up and said gently, "Andrew, try again—one plus two."

Very, very slowly and precisely, Andrew raised his left hand and three fingers off from the bed. I was in ecstasy and went crazy, grabbing Liz, jumping for joy. The nurses on the unit ran into the room to see what the commotion was.

As we danced around the room, Liz was crying. "Yes, yes! I knew he could hear us. His brain is working—our prayers have been answered. Thank you, thank you, God." Liz and I slapped a high five and dissolved into tears.

I leaned over to speak to Andrew. "I know I promised not to embarrass you with my theatrical and eccentric conduct, and I'm sorry. I will work on more acceptable behavior, but I can't help myself."

Meanwhile, James sat at the Twelve Ten bar, throwing back a few beers.

The word was out: Andrew could hear. Over the next two weeks visitors were constant—young, old, some I knew, others I didn't. The nuns continued to pray for him. His friends from school constantly carried on comical conversations. We knew he could hear us and that it was only a matter of time before he would wake up.

Emily believed that throughout every day he was beginning to respond. She mentioned the eight-level Rancho Los Amigos cognitive functioning test that measured coma patients. Andrew was at level two, responding to deep pain, and inconsistently and nonpurposefully to stimuli in a nonspecific manner. She also scheduled a barium swallow to check his swallowing response. And, she reiterated, rest was very important. We all witnessed the slow, dramatic, positive progression of movement, making sure it was all documented in *Andrew101*.

"He's grinding his teeth."

"Both arms went toward his head, left arm above his head."

"He's making a fist like he's ready to arm wrestle."

"He's trying to open his eyes."

"He yawned and coughed."

"He lifted his left leg."

When Andrew reached level three on the Rancho Los Amigos scale, an evaluation for Newington Children's Hospital was set. Even though I loved Emily, I thought she was dreaming. What could Newington do for him at this point? He was still in a coma, couldn't eat, was on IVs and oxygen, and could barely move. I was open to anything and anyone, but I couldn't be built up for disappointment. All I wanted was Andrew out of the coma—laughing, singing, and silly. James came with me to meet the evaluator, a mid-thirties vivacious gal from Newington. We watched in amazement and were put at ease as she spoke to Andrew, smiling, touching his fingers and arms, flicking his heels with her fingers.

"Hi, Andrew, my name is Shirley. I'm here from Newington Children's Hospital. What kind of music are you listening to?" The entire assessment took three minutes.

"Yup, he's ready for aggressive rehabilitation therapy. Let's move to the conference room so I can explain this to you."

Overwhelmed, I began to cry. I couldn't believe I felt such happiness. I reached for James and clung to him, sobbing so hard my mascara ran down my face onto his shirt. I looked up at him with raccoon eyes, and we burst out laughing.

"James, we've been given a second chance. Our little man is going to make it and come home, and we'll be a family again. It's all going to work out now, I'm sure!" I looked at James and saw the man I married. A tall, dark, handsome man presenting himself as the professional he was. There was kindness, caring, and no smell of alcohol—just tears rolling down his cheeks. This was the man I loved and wanted to grow old with, and I was still "his girl."

James was shaking. "Yes, Con, we've got our boy back."

Andrew's new program at Newington Children's Hospital would include therapies from morning till night with short rest periods throughout the day. He would wear regular clothes—sweats and T-shirts. His catheter would be removed, and he'd be put in diapers until his nervous system was healed and he was continent. His initial program would start with physical, occupational, and speech therapy, adding psychological and neuropsychological evaluations and updates. He would start schoolwork to continue his education, and also have recreational time.

And the last, but definitely the best, news was, in a few weeks, we could bring him home from Newington for a weekend visit. This was crucial in mainstreaming him back into the real world. With support, love, and acceptance from his family and friends he would be motivated to work hard. I was euphoric with everything Shirley had to say. "Is all this possible?"

"Yes, it is. He's ready to move on, and you'll be surprised by the next few months."

We shook hands with her and thanked her profusely.

James and I walked into Andrew's room. He was sleeping peacefully. I lifted his soft limp hand and kissed it. "You showed them, and I knew you would. From the very beginning I knew you'd beat this rap. Nobody knows you like your mother. I know all your special qualities, and soon you'll show the world. I love you. And by the way, Shirley said you'll walk out of Newington Children's Hospital." I watched for a nod of approval, but there was no movement. That was okay. I'd had enough joy for one day.

Chapter Four

It was August 13, 1986, and Andrew's fifteenth birthday. All day long, his room was packed—nuns, friends, family, and staff all there wishing him happy birthday and singing at the top of their lungs. I'm sure Andrew was grateful to be in a coma. For me this was the best birthday gift ever. Although he needed more rest, I was thrilled with the endless display of love and gifts.

That evening, my friend Sue helped the nurse put him back to bed. She asked him if he wanted the oxygen cannula removed, and he responded with a thumbs-up. Sue then asked him to point a finger at her if he recognized her, and he did. However, it was his middle finger.

"I will remind you of this at a later date!"

At the end of the day before the night nurse arrived, I visited once more. I held his hand to tell him that he had given us all gifts today by eating ice cream, moving, and adding. For his birthday, one of my tennis buddies, Angie, cooked up an Italian feast that filled the trunk and backseat of our station wagon. I informed him, "I stopped at the

Dairy Bar, and Mrs. Mosh said that when you are home, you can have free milkshakes every day. This I know you will not forget. Yesterday Mrs. Bruce and Trisha came to see you. Trisha visited with you, and in a few minutes she turned white, fainted, and hit the floor. You see, you're still knockin' 'em dead, even in a coma! She's okay."

I prayed constantly for James. One minute I was furious with him and the next I felt sorry for his weakness. Was I asking too much? Was I too hard and cold toward him? I shouldn't have blamed him for not cutting the swing down. Was he suffering because of me? I tried to pretend that the situation wasn't that bad and James was a good father. Sometimes we rationalize anything just to survive the typical, dysfunctional alcoholic home.

August 19, 1986, was moving day to Newington Children's Hospital. I wrote one last note in *Andrew 101*:

> 7 a.m. Dear Andrew, I've gone to Mass, and had breakfast with the nuns for the last time. They've been a tremendous source of support, and I know I couldn't have survived these past six weeks without them. You and I shall be embarking on a new journey, and I know we cannot fail. You've shown such strength and courage and probably have no idea how much you're admired. You will make a difference to the world of traumatic brain injury. There has to be a reason for all this. I'm so proud to be your mother, my Gigi.
>
> You were sleeping, so I let you sleep and then put on your headphones for music to start the day. Dr. Karney and Dr. Bizzy were in to visit. All the nurses were in to say good-bye. The administrator, Sister Rosa, came by. She was very kind to me and told me how lucky you are to have me. I look at it the other way around. She commented on how strong I am. Am I strong? I think I am just a mother. Wouldn't all mothers do the same, especially if they had a beautiful child like you?

You've had a growth spurt and are dressed in new sweatpants and a Celtics shirt. The ambulance is late, and your father's on his eighth cup of coffee. No wonder he's twitching and running to the bathroom every ten minutes. I'll need to catheterize him so he can make the trip—he's such a nerd sometimes, but we love him.

The ambulance is here. They're pushing you down the hallway. Tish and Sister Emerita are alongside. I'm teary-eyed, hugging and saying good-bye. I left candy for the staff. I hope I wasn't too much of a pain. They were all so wonderful, busy as they were, but never too busy for what you needed. Can I ever thank them enough?

We walked through the ER, where we'd entered six weeks ago. Again, a lot of hugs and thank-yous.

The sun shines brightly. The sky is very blue, a good omen. I hopped into the ambulance next to you. Your dad, Todd, and Laura will follow in the car. The ambulance is taking off for Newington Children's Hospital—no sirens.

CHAPTER FIVE

August 1986–December 1986

NEWINGTON CHILDREN'S HOSPITAL WAS SITUATED on a large parcel of land, set back on a hill, with sprawling lawns, flowers, and wooded areas. One side was flanked by an attractive children's playground, the other a large parking lot.

When the attendants moved Andrew's stretcher from the ambulance, I watched in amazement—he momentarily opened both eyes for the first time, taking in the sunlight and breathing the fresh air. I believed he'd suffered hospital psychosis from his long hospitalization and was responding to the positive aura and stimuli from nature and this beautiful temporary new home. It was an omen to me that we were finally on track.

The attendants wheeled him briskly through the entrance and stopped briefly at the reception desk long enough for the receptionist to smile and say, "Hi, we've been waiting for Andrew. He's going to Six South."

Six South, the children's rehabilitation unit, was bright and cheery, staffed by perky, smiling young women. Andrew's primary nurse, Debbie, was a tiny cute blonde. Soaking wet, she couldn't have weighed more than a hundred pounds. I was concerned how this peanut could take care of him. He was six feet tall, paralyzed, and dead weight.

Debbie explained the program and immediately put me at ease. We had entered a nursing specialty foreign to me. And then it hit me — these professionals knew much more about TBI than I did. I no longer needed to be in charge. An enormous weight was lifted from my shoulders.

The daily program ran from seven a.m. to nine p.m. with back-to-back therapies and rest periods in between. Once Andrew was settled, the focus would be on eating and drinking, so his stomach tube could be removed. I had not comprehended that he needed to relearn how to move his mouth, chew, and swallow again. This occupational therapy would require extensive work. His speech therapy would focus on the muscles in his throat and mouth and on breathing techniques using his tongue and lips. And physical therapy would get him walking again. All of these daily activities we took for granted, but now Andrew needed to relearn them. A mammoth amount of work lay ahead of him. I hoped he was up for it.

It was as if we were taking a baby the size of a man, and teaching him the basics that most babies arrive into the world knowing. But when they put diapers on him like a baby, it nearly killed me. I would bring more sweats and tops since the nurses changed him as soon as he was soiled. The staff maintained respect and dignity for all the patients at all times.

Todd and Laura had their priorities and quickly acquainted themselves with the hospital, roaming around seeking adventure.

They were proficient with who was housed on which floor, and where the gift shop, cafeteria, pool, and gym were located. The outside play area, ramps, and woods were an added bonus.

Todd was excited. "We can take Andrew on an adventure into the woods to explore once he's in a wheelchair. Laura, you can plot the course, and I'll be the driver. Andrew will love it. It'll be like we're home in our woods."

They knew this would be Andrew's home for several months and perhaps longer. But it pained me to watch them, so young with so much being forced on them, yet they never complained. This catastrophe would haunt them for the rest of their lives.

The nurse measured Andrew—he was now six feet two. All that special stomach-feeding formula had been good for him. His friends wanted to know what it was and where they could buy it to grow a few inches themselves. Not surprising to me, Andrew had discovered the fast track to growth. It was just like him to be one step ahead of everyone, even in a coma.

Finally, late in the afternoon, after the extensive admission process, James and I, followed by Todd and Laura, kissed and said good-bye to Andrew. We were again a family—exhausted, but relieved—with much to assimilate. I assured him I would return tomorrow. We stopped for dinner before starting home. It seemed like forever since we had all sat down together as a family. It was the way it should be. It all felt good. James's eyes were soft and every now and then they teared up. His face was warm and comfortable as he focused on his family during dinner conversation. I was on cloud nine.

We arrived home to the phone ringing off the wall. It was my hysterical mother-in-law, Dee. "I've been trying to get you all day. Everyone's been calling me, and I had no news for them. You'd think you would have called."

She continued to rant and rave and never once asked about Andrew or us. I could hear Bumpy shouting at her in the background, upset with her call. It was all about her. I slammed the phone down. That was a first for me—not my style, but necessary. James overheard enough and walked away, disgusted at his mother. This was progress and also a first. Their relationship was strained, and I knew deep down it bothered him that his mother was so selfish and unsupportive. But this was just the tip of the iceberg.

When I arrived next morning at Newington, Andrew had already finished a physical therapy session and another was scheduled. I marveled at how precisely and smoothly the unit ran. Every therapist was on time, to the minute. In a few days I was told I could take him outside, using a moving lounge chair. In our constant, though one-sided, conversations, I informed him of the entire goings-on, who was coming to visit and when. Now that he was no longer at St. John's, there would be fewer daily visitors, but weekends would be hectic.

He never refused to do anything the therapists asked. And I watched every move he made. Within a few days he appeared to be holding his head with more control. Even though his body looked like a propped-up Raggedy Andy doll, it was his face that tormented me, totally absent of expression, his eyes void and blank as if someone had robbed him of his feelings. Where was the boy who was so happy, spontaneous, confident, and full of life? I hoped he was still inside, somewhere.

Laura accompanied me on the next visit. She enjoyed telling Andrew all the down-and dirty scoops on his friends. She treated him as if nothing had happened, which amazed me. She bounced around the room, talking nonstop, sometimes singing and laughing, but mostly loving him desperately. It added peace to my aching heart to see this. She playfully made fun of Todd, to entertain and amuse Andrew. "He's home with a babysitter playing with his Tonka trucks."

Andrew was physically there but emotionally in lockdown.

Todd was caddying to pay for books for his senior year at Holy Redeemer, a secondary Catholic school. I had just made a trip to the school to see the principal. I asked him and the guidance department to keep an extra eye on Todd, and informed them that Andrew would not be returning for his sophomore year. Saying the words out loud tore me apart. At this point, furthering Andrew's education seemed a million miles away. I just wanted him to live and come home. I would not accept any other option.

As I was frequently uncertain about the intense rehab program at Newington, it became obvious that the only way I would survive Andrew's catastrophe was to take it one day at a time. That way I could focus on enjoying the small improvements and feel some joy. We were also told that for the next five months we would see rapid progress. After that, it would slow down, but improvements would continue for five years.

The physical therapist felt Andrew was ready for the tilt table, which to me looked like a torture chamber device. His body was strapped on, and a motor moved it upright to a standing position. The sight of him standing fortified me. He was tall for his age and so handsome. Thank goodness I didn't miss this.

I took him outside for fresh air in a reclining wheelchair, when suddenly we saw our dog, Maggie. James walked behind, sober, dressed in a suit and tie. Maggie nuzzled her wet nose on Andrew's lap and wagged her tail with glee as he tried to move his left hand to pet her. His response was encouraging, as his breathing became heavier and heavier. It was as if he were fighting to escape a locked cage. I knew it was now just a matter of time before he was totally out of the coma, and that someday he'd romp with Maggie again. I would never give up that dream.

James and I were like ships passing in the night. He informed me that his sister Trudy, her husband, their daughter Tina—the new bride—and her husband were coming to visit.

They arrived on a beautiful warm weekend while I was at the hospital and stayed an hour. It was good to see them, as I had grown to love them, and they seemed optimistic and concerned with Andrew's recovery. Tina was teary-eyed as she and I spoke. I congratulated her on her wedding. She was a kind and compassionate young lady and was sincere in wanting to come to visit again. Both she and her mother, Trudy, wrote in Andrew's notebook, inviting him out for pizza, weekends with them, and to Notre Dame football games. But these things would never come to pass.

After a few weeks, Andrew was enduring hour-long therapies, able to roll back and forth on his own. On the day we celebrated Todd's seventeenth birthday, he and Laura wanted to take Andrew on an adventure trip into the woods. Todd wheeled him in his wheelchair as I followed casually behind. I felt so serene, observing the three of them playing as if nothing had happened.

But serenity was jolted as Todd raced and popped wheelies with Andrew in his wheelchair. He presumed Andrew enjoyed the jerking starts, stops, and dangerous turns, and he probably did, but I envisioned Andrew flying out of the chair and landing on his head.

"Todd, please stop."

"Ma, he loves this and keeps giving me a thumbs-up for more."

"I'm sorry, birthday boy, but that's plenty for now. I think Andrew and I have had enough excitement for one day."

When Labor Day rolled around, James chose to spend the holiday weekend partying with old friends. He didn't have time to visit Andrew, which made even his parents furious with him.

That day the hospital was quiet. It gave Andrew and me extra time to relax outside in the sun. Andrew quietly worked on his tan, and I was content just watching him be alive. When I left, I kissed him good-bye. "Happy Labor Day. I had a wonderful time with you, sweetie. I'll see you tomorrow. I love you." I walked out of the room.

Early that evening, Andrew was alone in his room. The sun shone through the windows. Just then his nurse walked by his room. From afar she observed as he began to wake up from his "nap," and open his eyes all the way for the first time. They stayed open, and the fog was gone. He blinked several times like he was trying to see where he was. The nurse guessed he was having a terrifying nightmare, that he felt something very terrible had happened. And later we learned from him that he thought he'd been abandoned and put in a strange place. He said he felt confused, only able to barely move his left hand and not his right. He tried to speak but was unable to open his mouth. He wondered where he was and thought he was by himself and trapped. He remembered his face felt hot and his forehead was wet with perspiration. Then he felt tears roll down his cheeks.

He was out of the coma, had awoken, and his mother was not there. He was alone and petrified. My greatest fear had become reality, and I was terribly guilt ridden for not being there with him.

No one was home for me to share the news with, so I quickly rushed back to the hospital. It was around eight p.m. when I arrived at the unit. It was very quiet. I entered his room and for the first time saw him with both eyes wide open. I gave him a big hug and joked, "Hey, my Gigi, you've finally opened both of your eyes, and it's about time, young man."

But I was unprepared for his reaction. He looked right through me with a vacant stare. He still couldn't speak, but I knew this was huge and we were moving forward. Now I would be even more vigilant about spending all day with him while he worked his therapies, and would go home around four p.m. I couldn't remember when I last cooked a meal, since friends and neighbors were still delivering dinners. My schedule at home was hectic, as I tried to get Todd and Laura to and from school and their extracurricular activities. I tried to save some energy for them, but they noticed my emotional and physical absence.

Several weeks passed. I continued to arrive early at the hospital to catch Andrew's first physical therapy session. That was when I saw the greatest improvements, which fortified me. He had learned to stick out his tongue ten times and was rewarded with a grape popsicle, even though he couldn't hold it. He was able to sit up by himself for several minutes, and was starting to use his right arm and leg. The therapist would ask him to lift his arm and legs ten times and he would always do more. His right side was permanently partially paralyzed, called a hemiparesis, and would never be as strong as his left side. And he had to change dominance from his right hand to his left. I knew he could do this. For many victims, it would be easier to roll over and die, but not my Gigi. He was a fighter and the most courageous person I knew.

The nurse informed me he was entering level four on the Rancho Los Amigos Level of Cognitive Functioning scale. This level could find a patient confused and frightened and not understanding what he feels or what is happening to him. Patients have difficulty following directions and can overreact to any situation by hitting, screaming, and using abusive language, and often need to be restrained. Because of this, Andrew was placed in a crib with a net over the top so he couldn't crawl or fall out. The sight of this made me gasp, even though I knew it was for his safety. He was now aware of his environment and was frightened. My presence was vital.

During one physical therapy session, he struggled to point to some paper and a pencil. Upon being given these, he attempted to write. It took a long time for him to scratch out "prisoner in a foreign country."

His therapist and I were stunned. What was going on in his mind? Shocked and in tears, I ran out of the room to regroup. When I returned, his therapist was speaking to him. "Andrew, you're not in prison. You're in a children's hospital. You had an accident and fell from a swing, but you're getting better. Before you know it, you'll be walking and back to school with all your friends."

How I wished that might be true. I never let him or anyone else witness the fears or uncertainties I felt. Every day that he improved I was sustained. Between the tears, I was strengthened and able to smile—if not for myself, for him.

At that point I felt Andrew must never know that he had been near death or that he has a severe brain injury. And that even if he worked his therapies for five years, he might still be disabled with deficits. The words made me shudder.

A few weeks later in physical therapy, I admired him kneeling, which showed how strong his legs were getting. "Gigi, you'll be walking soon!" I was overjoyed, but his face was dead—a totally flat expression, and it worried me.

Before I left the unit, the head nurse took me aside and said, "Mrs. Kane, we've had to put him on Elavil, an antidepressant."

I could not hide my pained reaction.

"We found him in bed with the pillow over his face."

I gasped, horrified. "As if he were trying to smother himself?" Was death the only option for this boy, or was this part of the healing process? It took me a few minutes to compose myself. I tried not to cry. After all, I was his strength. He must always know that I was there for him and would never give up.

It will get better, Andrew, I promise. God, do you hear me? Please, I need your help.

"You're here every day. I think you need to take a few days off for yourself. Don't worry about Andrew—we've got our eye on him every minute."

I was skipping meals and losing weight, and obviously I looked stressed. I didn't realize the emotional and physical toll it was taking on me. I certainly could not leave him now. But by the next week I realized I needed a break. "Andrew, Aunt Leah has invited me to her spa, and I'm going there for a few days. I need a little rest. You don't mind, do you?"

He was rather quick on the uptake and slowly shook his head from side to side. Could it be that he was a bit relieved to be rid of me for a time? Was I annoyingly nurturing?

Oh no, not the girl from Moose Jaw.

James's uncle Don and his wife, Leah, had been very supportive since Andrew's accident, actually more so than James's parents were. They had just renovated a grand old home on fifty acres in the Litchfield Hills and turned it into a magnificent spa.

I was grateful for the invitation. Not only was I invited, but Leah asked me to bring eight of my friends who had impressed her with their generosity. I arrived at the spa a day early. It was a vision to behold. I joined Leah in her lavish office, admired the décor, and sank into a soft, voluptuous chair.

Leah, however, had something on her mind other than the posh surroundings. "Connie, I don't know what you're running on, but you better start taking care of yourself. This could go on for a long time. I also know you are doing most of this alone and that James is literally of no help. In fact, I don't think James is very stable, and I wouldn't be surprised if he attempted suicide."

My jaw dropped open in shock. Thanks for sharing—just one more thing to worry about.

The bottom line was that James's problems were evident to all. Uniron had been bought out, but his position remained unchanged. So did the excellent medical coverage as our bills mounted. I wasn't sure of anything with him, but I did not think he was suicidal, even though his drinking had escalated. And it wasn't fair to pile him onto my plate to fix. He was responsible for himself, and he was sinking. I was furiously swimming to stay afloat while holding up our three children.

The next day my friends joined me at the spa, and I was elated to see them. However, Leah's words kept echoing in my head. For a few days, though, we were totally pampered. Adjacent to the mansion was a contemporary addition that housed an enormous pool, sauna, Jacuzzi, and gym, with rooms for facials, makeup, and massages. The staff catered to our every whim. The price tag for a week was $3,500. My eight friends and I would be pampered free of charge. Thank you, Leah Kane.

During a massage I entered into a deep, hypnotic sleep that prohibited the trespass of the real world, but I awoke to a vision of Andrew's lifeless face. I prayed, *Please, God, make him better.* Andrew still consumed my every breath, heartbeat, and thought. There was no escape, nor did I ever consider one. After three days of pampering, we were rejuvenated and eternally grateful to Leah. She told me to come back whenever I needed a break.

We all met outside in the sunshine to bid farewells. I looked at everyone in admiration and love and said, "I am the luckiest person in the world to have you as my friends." We kissed and hugged, but noticed one of the group was missing. And then suddenly she fled the house and headed toward us. She was flustered, panting, red-faced, and glowing with a whisker burn. She had just "done" the masseuse. We all roared, shaking our heads in disbelief. Certainly, an unforgettable, dramatic ending. I'd almost forgotten how to laugh.

Two weeks later, I brought Andrew home from Newington for his first day pass. Todd and Laura met us in the driveway. Todd got the wheelchair out of the trunk, and I opened the car door. Smiling, I said to Andrew, "Remember how we practiced. Let's do it."

Andrew was focused on pushing his body into position. He twisted, lifted his legs, pushed his knees, grabbed the door with his new dominant left hand, stood up, and sat in the wheelchair. He had it down. I adjusted and hid the diaper that peeked out from under his shorts. Todd and Laura pushed him to the front doors and lifted him inside. Todd stared at Andrew. "Something's different . . . uh, the tube from your nose is gone. I was gettin' used to it."

Andrew gave a thumbs-up. He had pulled the tube out, but was eating enough so he no longer needed it. Everyone shouted, "Yay, Andrew!" For the first time since his accident, there was a faint smile on his face.

"Gigi, you're smiling." My eyes welled up as I knelt to give him a hug.

Todd squirmed. "Ma, leave the poor kid alone!"

I jested, "Be quiet or you're next."

Everyone was jovial. No one mentioned that James was absent. He told me he had errands to run, but I knew what that meant.

As soon as the word was out that Andrew was home for the day, the phone rang constantly. Everyone wanted to come over. His hairdresser was first, to give him a haircut. Friends wheeled him in and out of the house. They included him in a basketball game even though he was a passive observer. Sitting in his wheelchair he watched them running, jumping, shouting, and laughing—doing what he used to do. I wondered what he must be thinking. Was he able to totally comprehend all of this? What kind of prison might this be for him, and for how long?

He impulsively tried to get out of his wheelchair. I told him, "Soon, my sweet, soon." He was impulsive, defiant, stubborn, and even uncooperative. I realized he was still at level four on the Rancho Los Amigos scale and highly agitated at this point. I would need someone to help me drive him back to Newington, and Todd offered. Andrew constantly tried to unbuckle his car seat all the way back to the hospital.

Newington had stressed the importance of home visits and returning to normalcy as soon as possible. I would let nothing interfere with this and brought him home every weekend.

I took a personal oath to be mother, nurse, and occupational, physical, and speech therapist. I was naive and unaware of how emotionally and physically difficult it would be, and I was no replacement for a father.

My parents sent us a ten-thousand-dollar check to use however we thought best for the family, even though they didn't have the money to give. People we hardly knew sent gifts. On the other hand, Dee, who was rolling in dough, had not given Andrew a gift of any kind. James was hurt, and it seemed to give him another reason to drink.

Chapter Six

In October, months after his arrival at Newington Children's Hospital, Andrew refused to attend group and speech therapy. He liked physical therapy because he was successful. But he still hadn't uttered a sound, and group interaction was painful for him. A new patient, Brad, was assigned to his room. The staff hoped this interaction would be beneficial for both of them. They were the same age and comfortable with each other. There was one main difference: Andrew still needed a wheelchair, but Brad could walk without problems. Brad's dad was the CEO of a large insurance company and had box seats to numerous sporting events. I begged James to attend the games they invited us to, but he was too busy. So Brad, his dad, Andrew, and I went to the Hartford Coliseum and took in a few basketball games. Andrew loved the VIP attention and understood the sport much better than I did, and I was momentarily happy for him. But moments were fleeting, and reality would soon return.

Between therapies, we would often just sit and relax in a glass atrium at the hospital, letting the warm autumn sun engulf us. Andrew would smile and rest his head on my shoulder, grab my hand with his left hand, and gently squeeze it. And then I would feel a pang in my heart as I watched his right hand, barely able to move. He still could not speak but understood everything I said, and he communicated by thumbs up and down. Writing would take a little while, as he was just getting strength back in his arms and hands during occupational and physical therapy, and he had to change his dominance from his right hand to his left. We would sit quietly, not speaking, locking the world out and enjoying the peaceful energy of the moment. We would always be linked together, bone to bone, muscle to muscle, blood to blood, breath to breath. Nothing could change that, not even death. And I would focus on the unit chief's words: "He will make dramatic gains in the first six months, and he will walk out of here. And I see no reason why he cannot finish high school, attend college, and some day get married."

The next weekend during his visit home, I made my special pancakes that would challenge even Julia Child. Andrew ate nonstop and wanted more. Was he starving? Didn't the hospital feed him, or did he have a tapeworm? I could flatter myself that it was my pancakes, but they were only pancakes. I called the hospital and was informed that his brain still couldn't distinguish when he was full, and he could continue to eat until . . . They suggested we bring him back before he exploded.

Andrew was now past ten weeks post-accident and home for the entire weekend. It was demanding work, as he needed to be helped with bathing and dressing. He still didn't have the strength to stand and was irritated and embarrassed by wearing diapers. He was starting to use a urinal, but often couldn't hold himself properly in place and then spilled all over himself. It was absolutely painful to watch him, and I couldn't imagine how he felt about all this as he was now aware of everything going on around him. The hospital assured me that it was only temporary, but the interim was difficult. I slept in a sleeping bag on the floor next to his bed, fearful he might try to walk or roll out of bed.

James offered no help. I no longer even asked and was so disgusted with him that I'd moved out of our bedroom and into the den. In response, he did not communicate and was becoming a stranger to Andrew as well. That was my punishment.

One Saturday evening when he was on a weekend pass, I helped Andrew brush his teeth. I tucked him into bed, kissed him good night, and slipped into my sleeping bag. The bedroom door was ajar, and suddenly we heard footsteps coming from the master bedroom. We both lifted our heads to see James, dressed to the nines. I called out, "Where are you going?"

"I need to get out and see my friends."

I was so exhausted—I had no energy to care. But when I saw tears running down Andrew's face, I seethed. I said under my breath, "You bastard, James. I hate you, and you'll pay for this."

Andrew cried into his pillow, and I did the same. I cried mostly for Andrew but also for myself—and yes, for James. I was beginning to realize there was no way out, and I simply didn't know what to do.

A few days later I received a call from Rosemary Shean, a family friend and holistic therapist. She offered to help and asked me to come see her. She had known James since he was a youngster. She liked him and remembered him as a respectful, thoughtful kid. She knew I needed her assistance if we were to survive. She was right on, even though at that time I couldn't see it. I made an appointment, telling myself it was not because I needed a therapist but because she was an old friend and I respected her. I'd take time out of my busy day, once.

Her office was housed in her garage and full of potted flowers. I felt an aura of comfort, safety, and trust. Rosemary was a very vibrant and self-assured woman. Little did I realize then how valuable a role she would play, how I would revolve my life around our visits, how I would forever thank God for sending her to me, and that she would save my life. Her ever-generous gift was to take on me and my never-ending problems pro bono. My friends were wonderful.

Andrew was again home for the weekend. Laura tried to play games with him and would prod him. "Come on, we can write notes back and forth, like we're in school. It'll be fun!"

Twice Andrew shoved the book away. He then took the pen and very slowly wrote, "I'm hungry, want an apple."

Laura called to me in the kitchen. "Mom, Andrew is hungry and wants an apple."

Immediately I forgot about what I was doing, cut up an apple, and took it to him on a tray. Pretending I was his waiter, I placed it on his lap. "For you, kind sir."

He was semi-reclined on the couch, relaxed. I gave him a kiss and left the room, enjoying the sight of him and Laura together. Andrew began to eat the apple, shoving one piece after another into his mouth, forgetting how to chew or swallow. Suddenly he coughed, his face turned red, he drooled, and he was choking.

My pulse raced. Eyes bulging, in a full body tremor, I screamed, "Todd, where are you? Come quick! Andrew is choking. Go next door to Dr. Sean's and get your dad!"

Todd sprinted next door and barged in, where James and Dr. Sean were relaxing over a cup of coffee. He cried, "Dad, Andrew is choking!"

In panic I shouted to Laura, "Call 911!"

I tried to pull Andrew's feet to the floor and get behind him to perform the Heimlich maneuver, but he was dead weight, and I couldn't move him. His head hung, his face was red, and his mouth hung open. I swished my finger through his mouth but found nothing.

James ran into the family room. Together we pulled Andrew to his feet and performed the Heimlich. The apples flew out of his mouth. We could no longer hold him up, as he was too heavy and wobbly, so we laid him down on the carpet.

I looked at James, forgetting all the bad between us. "Thank God you were here. You saved his life." I wanted this moment to never end, but the EMTs rushed into the room.

One of the obviously inexperienced young men tried to do a verbal assessment. Frantically and rudely I snapped, "We don't have time to assess—he has a TBI."

He innocently responded, "What's a TBI?"

My mouth dropped open—this person had no idea what he was dealing with. I demanded, "Young man, I'm a nurse, and we need to get to an ER. I'm not losing my son now, not after what we've been through. Let's move before his airway obstructs. Do you understand what I am saying?" The EMTs quickly and quietly transported Andrew into the ambulance. I jumped in the back and we sped off, siren blaring, but this time Andrew remained conscious.

At St. John's Hospital, Andrew was put into a cubicle, and to my relief a doctor assessed him as a TBI. He approached him with an X-ray and a tongue depressor. Andrew had not aspirated any food into his lungs. The doctor moved with ease toward his face. "Now, I want to examine your throat to make sure you haven't injured yourself with all that choking. Open your mouth wide for me."

He prodded around. "Now say *ahhh*."

Andrew did as he was told and said, "Ahhh." His face illuminated, eyes widened, eyebrows raised at the one-syllable sound.

I yelped and moved closer. "Give me that tongue depressor." I grabbed it out of the doctor's hand. He jerked back. I pressed it down on Andrew's tongue. "Andrew, say *ahhh*."

Andrew responded again, "Ahhh." As clear as a beautiful church bell.

The doctor stared, confused.

"Do you realize what just happened? This is the first time Andrew has made a sound since his accident ten weeks ago." Andrew and I were both in tears. I hugged him, "Gigi, you spoke. I knew you would."

I called Newington Children's Hospital. They wanted him back immediately with all the details of the day. It was seven p.m. when I left the unit. I reiterated, "Remember, when he speaks again, regardless of the time, even in the middle of the night, I want to be called."

At twelve thirty a.m. the phone rang. I jumped out of bed and ran to the kitchen. It was a nurse from the unit at Newington Children's Hospital. "Mrs. Kane, you told us to call. As the night nurse was making rounds, Andrew spoke. It was very slow and slurred, but he said, 'Please close the door.' Then he asked her if she would help him get down on his knees to pray and thank God for giving him back his speech."

I was light-headed and sat down. My eyes glazed over, and then tears flowed down my cheeks. I wanted to share this news with James, but we were sleeping in separate rooms, and I wasn't sure just what shape he was in. I gingerly entered his bedroom, overwhelmed by a bouquet of beer and smoke, and a roll of snorts and snores. I expedited a quick return to the den and hopped into bed. Andrew's speech had given me a new surge of energy. We were putting the pieces back, and he *was* becoming Andrew Kane again.

The next morning when I arrived on the unit, there were several speech pathologists at the nurses' station. Andrew was all smiles, a celebrity popping wheelies in his wheelchair. Everybody seemed to be buzzing with heightened energy, or perhaps it was just my state of euphoria. Later that day I met with the head speech pathologist, who confessed, "We thought Andrew would never speak again, and we were afraid to tell you."

I was stunned. That had never entered my mind. And now a new plan was put in place, directed to intensive speech therapy. Andrew would need to relearn breathing and placement of his tongue, lips, and cheeks, in order to speak and to be understood. It was a tedious process. He worked diligently on a special Zaison Computer ESC a friend of ours had donated for his use, and got his picture in the newspaper, sitting at his terminal, modeling it for Newington Children's Hospital as new state-of-the-art equipment. He still loved to be the center of attention. Prior to the accident he prided himself on having a command of the English language. In ninth grade he had even been chosen for a Spanish poetry contest. Perhaps it was his theatrics, but all of this must have been in preparation for his future.

After a few months, however, the speech process was going slowly. He sounded guttural, garbled, throaty, hyper-nasal. I wondered if he would ever be understood. This medical condition was called dysarthria. I continued with a strong front, but deeply prayed and bargained while grinding my teeth.

He began water therapy. The buoyancy allowed him to move spontaneously, and I was thrilled to watch, imagining a beautiful dolphin. I tried not to miss a session, as this affirmed that he would walk again. Of this, I was a fanatic believer.

Life for me was being at the hospital for most of the day. A cell phone would have come in handy, but no such gadget existed in 1986, so to communicate at home I instituted a "communication book." We wrote, for example:

Wednesday:
    Todd, I'll pick you up for appointment at 1 p.m. Stick around.
    xo Ma

James, please take off screens from windows, empty your ashtray and beer cans.

The cat is hiding in the house, please find and put out. — Todd

Laura, please do load of whites, add Clorox, put outside on line.

Do I also put in Tide? — Laura

Where have I gone wrong? Yes, my dear. xo Ma

Since I was often late at the hospital, I asked Dee to help me out with some of the chauffeuring of the kids. One day I asked her to pick up Todd from track practice at Holy Redeemer. Not knowing this, Todd hitched a ride home while she was waiting for him. With nostrils flaring she then drove to our home. "Why didn't you tell me Todd wasn't going to be there? How dare you let me sit there and wait, when I should be home putting Bumpy's potatoes on?" That marked the end of Dee's services.

By November, Andrew was using a walker independently. He also started on a school program. We had to transfer him to the public school system, Regional School District #10, where they would provide academics as well as the special PT, OT, Speech, and Special Resource Learning Center services he needed. He could not return to Holy Redeemer, since it was a Catholic school and not a state school, and they were unable to provide this.

We scheduled a team meeting with Dr. Jinnie, the director for special services at the Region 10 high school, to coordinate the transfer. I had known Dr. Jinnie for many years and liked her. However, right from the beginning, we seemed to be a bit at odds, but I was sure it was me and that we would iron it out. Was I in for a surprise!

Andrew was doing well in the school program while at Newington, but needed constant reinforcement to stay on task. He also continued to use the computer program our friend had donated, which reviewed and taught basic skills like reading, math, and language arts. I was computer illiterate, couldn't figure out how to turn it on, and would never purchase one. And that was final!

Discharge from Newington was slated for early January 1987. Andrew would then start a day rehabilitation program at Daview Rehabilitation Center in Danbury, thirty minutes from our home. The looming question was whether to start him back into the Region 10 school system now or wait until the fall. He still required intense occupational, physical, and speech therapy, and Daview could also incorporate academic tutoring provided by Region 10. We ruled out the campus school environment for now. Missing a year was not the end of the world. He had other mountains to climb. He was impulsive and stubborn and needed constant limit-setting, as did any fifteen-year-old—but especially more so as one with a brain injury.

In preparation for Andrew's continued academic success and eventual return to the Region 10 high school, Dr. Javorn from Newington Children's Hospital was beginning a neuropsychological evaluation. This would be an invaluable and detailed resource to point out his strengths, weaknesses, and special needs. The process took days, but I was skeptical of the results that intricately detailed all his deficits. I thought it was much too early to test accuracy of visual perception; language manner; intellectual, conceptual, and verbal subtests; or visual problem-solving. Andrew's daily progress was invigorating, and that's what I placed more stock in.

Christmas would soon be here. I loved the holidays, decorating the house, and the smell of fresh pine from a real evergreen tree. It was at these times that families grew closer, and in my heart I hoped that would be the case for us. Andrew was pushing himself, determined to walk again without aids. And joyously, our first Christmas present was from him — a progress report from Newington, stating that during his school time he was doing well academically and behavior-wise. His study habits had improved with excellent effort, and he was a valuable contributor in group discussions and getting along with classmates. That was my Gigi!

We were hosting Christmas dinner and invited a few close friends. James loved cooking the turkey and making his special chestnut dressing. He was much better than I at preparing holiday fare, and I repeatedly praised him.

In the twenty years James and I had been married, Dee and James Sr. had always spent Christmas with their daughter Trudy. We thought perhaps this year, because of Andrew, they would stay with us, but it seemed they just didn't care. Trudy expected them to be with her, and so that's what they did. The children and I were upset, but James was devastated. It just reconfirmed to him that his place in his family was not that important. When I first met Dee, she told me James was an accident and she never wanted him. I was shocked. How could a mother be so callous as to admit that to a total stranger? Dee and Trudy were hatched from the same mold.

Our children also felt the pain. They asked, "Why don't Grandma and Grandpa Kane ever stay here and watch us open our presents?" Despite all this, on Christmas morning I was happy. I was seeing Rosemary, my therapist, on a regular basis, and the antidepressant Trazodone had kicked in after the typical six weeks to build up effectiveness. I had more energy and optimism with every day. Christmas would be festive, and we had so much to be grateful for.

It was a mild winter day, and I went to say Merry Christmas to a neighbor. After a brief, fidgety encounter, she burst out, "Are you having an affair?"

I laughed and thought she was joking, but her face told me she wasn't. I was hurt and angry. "Are you kidding me? Do I have time for an affair? Andrew's my priority!"

"You were seen having breakfast with someone, and it wasn't James."

"Really? By whom?"

"I can't say, but it's a friend who knows you well."

"Obviously she doesn't, and she's not a friend. And I can't believe you, who are like family, would ever think that of me!"

I was dumbfounded, and then a light bulb went off. One morning, weeks ago, I had had breakfast with an old friend, Wayne—the anesthetist who intubated Andrew and saved his life, and who sat with me for hours in the ICU at St. John's. After breakfast he had followed me to Newington to visit Andrew. That's when I was seen. How cruel for people to think only the worst when I was going through hell. To top matters off, I really didn't look my finest. I was downright haggard. This was only the beginning of estrangement from my so-called friends and family. I pondered, what had I done wrong to become a target for gossip and rumors? When you're down and out, do people really want to just step on you? The answer was excruciating.

Returning to Newington after Christmas was difficult for Andrew. He'd had it with the five months of hospitalization there—the average stay was three.

The final day at Newington arrived. The plan was to pick him up early in the morning and take him directly to Daview Rehabilitation Center. We went over his discharge plan. He was now independent with his personal hygiene, dressing, and transfers. He was using the wheeled walker but required constant reminders for safety as he was impulsive, stubborn, and needed constant limit-setting. Independence with supervision was still encouraged. He had to stay on Dilantin for seizures, and if there were any problems, we were to call Newington immediately. The entire staff, many with tears in their eyes, stood at the nurses' station to say good-bye and good luck.

Andrew donned a new Boston Celtics hat and jacket, a gift from a friend, and we were ready to leave. He was confident, composed, and proud. Using his walker, he walked independently to the door of Six South Rehab. For the last time he turned around and gave everyone a huge smile, tipped his hat, and exited. My face beamed, and I thrust my chest forward proudly. We were climbing that hill of recovery and would not stop until we reached its pinnacle. One day, one minute, one moment at a time. Forever my modus operandi.

Smiling, I held the door open. I tried to hold back, but my eyelids went into spasm, and tears glazed my eyes. The Newington treatment team had kept their word — he was walking!

Thank you, God.

CHAPTER SEVEN

January–December 1987

DAVIEW REHABILITATION CENTER WAS LOCATED in Brookfield, Connecticut. It was thirty minutes from home and considered a vital and essential element in Andrew's continued success. I would now have more free time since Daview did not allow family to be present on a daily basis. In fact, their "program" was well documented in a rule book that I needed to read, agree to, and sign off on. I was taken off guard with the initial rigidity of the plan. Newington had recommended Daview, and I had an unwavering high opinion of and trust in Newington's every word, but I was not prepared for the countless confrontations that lay head, or for the frustration this so-called wonderful program would impose.

At the same time, James's job was on the line. The corporation that bought Uniron kept him on, but now under close scrutiny, he needed to continue and start producing again. He had spent twenty years building a territory that almost ran by itself. I knew it was only a matter of time before James's drinking became evident to the new corporation. I should have been more understanding of his situation and his demons, but I was exhausted trying to stay afloat for Andrew, Todd, and Laura. When I had a free moment, I would go for a walk to reenergize myself rather than argue with an alcoholic. In not dealing with him, I could preserve myself for the mayhem that was building. Or so I thought.

The first day at Daview, Andrew was very tense. Maybe he sensed my discomfort, since this was the only day I could visit, aside from monthly family conferences. The atmosphere seemed negative compared to Newington. Protocol was important. I was seated in a conference room with several packets in front of me, instructed to read them carefully. Aggravation mounted with the rigidity and rules we were all to follow, and this was only the beginning. What had happened to that sweet law-abiding girl from Moose Jaw?

I read on, questioning and pondering the rules and schedules. This was so strict in comparison with Newington. Consistent tardiness would not be allowed. The case manager was always to be notified, and contacted if you intended to leave the building (and only with prior permission). Computer time was strictly scheduled, and turned off immediately after use or your case manager would be contacted. Inappropriate language was not tolerated, telephone calls were not allowed unless . . . It went on and on. Finally it read, "or you will be discharged from the program." They took their work very seriously — which I certainly approved of — but it seemed so rigid and cold. We were used to kind, nurturing nurses for the last six months. This was a stark contrast I was not prepared for.

Daview had completed a formal assessment on Andrew's progress and listed the goals they set for him. Long-term speech therapy would increase his volume, reduce breathiness, and improve intelligibility and intonation. They would address cognitive memory, reasoning, sequencing, organization, and auditory comprehension, with the hope of increasing more acceptable behavior and social skills. Physical therapy would improve range of motion, balance, posture, gait, and endurance, while occupational therapy would focus on upper extremity muscle strength and coordination to increase independence with daily living skills.

Daview concluded that he was capable of handling bed transfers, personal hygiene, and grooming, although he was unsafe for standing to shower. He could dress himself but needed help with fine motor tasks, such as working buttons, hooks, and zippers. Sitting in a chair independently and cutting his food were still difficult. His right hand was nonfunctional for writing, and attempts with the left were slow and the results barely legible.

Daview's director, Dr. Joan Musser, judgmentally stated, "Presently Andrew exhibits intrusive, impulsive, and egocentric behavior, which will interfere with therapies."

I resented her immediate negativity, but knew Andrew would prove her wrong.

He had school tutoring for ten hours a week. His reading improved, working with a dedicated tutor who used periodicals such as *National Geographic, Smithsonian, Natural History,* and *Discover.* The tutor called Dr. Jinnie at Region 10 a second time, to ask again for materials she had not received. That alone should have been a red flag for me.

In language arts he was lower than ninth-grade level, but motivation was high. Thank God for motivation. I needed a few scraps of optimism. Daview's assessments certainly did not concur with the glowing reports I used to get from Newington. Had I been deaf, stupid, or not listening?

His psychological evaluation, done by Dr. Musser, really blew me out of the water. She wrote that at first he was agitated, showed anger and hostility, and was poorly focused, which resulted in loss of therapy time. He perceived "slights" and "threats" and was suspicious of peers. Interaction in group situations was problematic—he perceived he was being treated unfairly. Time-out periods were necessary to prevent verbal outbursts. His individual sessions were nonproductive due to inflexible thinking. His expression remained both childlike and grandiose, and his frustration tolerance was low. Dr. Musser further noted, "He appears to be experiencing the full impact of his injury and relies on denial for coping. Projecting blame on others is his primary means of coping and defense."

I was overwhelmed with Dr. Musser's destructive assessment, and my blood pressure skyrocketed. There would be a team conference every three weeks, which I was *not* allowed to attend. The results would be sent to us. But I had to attend the monthly family conference, with perfect and timely participation foremost. Would I also have to salute this commander-in-chief?

Oh no, the Moose Jaw gal was getting feisty.

Meanwhile, it was Super Bowl XXI. Somehow James got some tickets to the game, and since it fell on his birthday, January 25, it was crucial for him to go away for a few days with the usual group of guys. I hoped the time away would be therapeutic and he would come back a man ready to make positive changes in his life. Super Bowl, however, proved not to be the prescribed therapy. I was a naive, eternal optimist—forever hopeful, forever disappointed.

My mother and my sister Pat came to stay with me during James's absence, temporarily lifting a weight from my shoulders. My sister returned home to Regina, Saskatchewan, to discover her husband had moved out. Somehow I felt that the lingering cloud of doom hanging over me had transferred to her.

My mother was heartbroken as she continued to support us. The life she had known for more than sixty years was slowly unraveling. The previous year she had lost my brother, and now she endured Pat's and my troubles. No matter what your age, you always feel your children's anguish and misery. I was grateful for my mother's strength, courage, and love. And I will thank God for the rest of my life for being blessed to be her daughter.

At this point I needed a break from the exhausting pace to reenergize myself if I was to continue. So when James returned from the Super Bowl, I again dipped into the money my parents had given us and flew to Puerto Vallarta for a week on a special super-saver deal. At the last minute, a girlfriend joined me. It was hard for me to relax, as I was used to an exhausting pace and now it had come to a standstill. We started each day going to Mass. That was the hardest, as all I thought about was Andrew and felt guilty being on vacation, but my mother and therapist told me I needed to do this. I didn't realize how ghastly and gaunt I looked. One morning we listened to a Mexican mariachi band practicing for a wedding. The trumpets blared and awakened our souls as we danced in the back of the church. It was refreshingly beautiful and innocent, yet solemn. For the first time in months, I was at peace. Even though I missed Andrew, I knew I could only continue this job with newfound strength. I could only imagine that James had everything under control and he would ask his parents to step in for added support. I slept twelve hours a night and by afternoon we were on the beach. As the waiter walked by, I quickly flagged him. "Another Corona, please." And I disliked beer!

I returned from Mexico tanned and refreshed to face a very drained James. My heart broke for him.

He said, "I can't believe my parents never once called or offered any kind of help."

Again, more of their apathy and aloofness. They had completely removed themselves from our lives. We were a burden to them. They pretended everything was the same, yet we had no time for anything but our family. Our priorities had changed. We were exhausted and stressed. This reality didn't fit into their lives, and we would just need to deal with it. But we'd show them. Andrew would get better, and so would we.

Meanwhile, we received the first team conference note from Dr. Musser, which was disturbing. "He's progressing in all areas but is emotionally five years old."

We were going backward with her negativity. Weren't we supposed to focus on the positive to help this boy get ahead? Dr. Musser's tactics were not my style, and I made that all too clear. Maybe I was flirting with paranoia, but I felt she just didn't like any member of my family. What was there not to like? I was such an agreeable, calm, pussycat — and from Moose Jaw! But then, maybe in my advocating for Andrew I'd grown too intense?

By March, Andrew continued to plug along, feeling no one liked him. He was struggling with denial of his injury — and who wouldn't be, especially a fifteen-year-old? I constantly reassured him that was not true and that he was a role model due to his hard work. He developed knee pain from Osgood-Schlatter disease, common in active young adolescents during a growth spurt. The easy solution was to limit activities, but one leg was now longer than the other, which required orthotics. All of this we would fix.

But we couldn't fix Dr. Musser's attitude. "Mother is cooperative, but I question her being realistic about what Andrew can do." I was livid. How dare she question my support and love for him? If I gave up, who would he have? She had no idea what it was like to walk in my shoes. However, I determined I would continue to reach for the stars, and Andrew would beat this.

There was now a constant war between Andrew and his speech therapist, Dawn, so behind Daview's back I contacted his first speech therapist, Emily, at St. John's Hospital, to evaluate him. Andrew was elated — speech was his priority, as he had always wanted a command of the English language, and a program was begun. Somehow,

Daview got wind of the extra therapy, and I was called in for a special conference.

I argued, "I feel he needs and wants more aggressive voice and dysarthric elements in his program."

The speech therapist agreed. "I will pursue a more aggressive approach to his therapy, but it will be dependent on his behavior."

Dependent on his behavior? Now I was really pissed off. He had a brain injury, and it was her job to keep him motivated and focused, and not distracted to the point of bad behavior. And then, I had to sign a new document that I agreed to all that.

There was a difference of day and night between the two speech pathologists and their philosophies. I paid no attention to the conference or the document, and Andrew continued to see Emily at St. John's Hospital. I would pick him up from Daview and then drive him to St. John's. Emily had a special gift, and I wasn't going to deprive Andrew of this opportunity.

At times I observed him practicing special speech mouth-and-lip exercises in front of the mirror, talking with a tongue depressor in his mouth or doing exercises using a pencil—moving his mouth without dropping the pencil. I knew someday this would pay off. He was beginning to like who he was and what he saw, and I might have been prejudiced, but he had grown into a drop-dead handsome young man. Emily also recommended a physical therapist at St. John's. He had outstanding skills, and Andrew looked forward to the extra sessions that erected no hurdles. I was at ease with this approach that was similar to Andrew being at a gymnasium with a trainer in a real world.

One evening I received a phone call from Father Gossler a priest from our parish, St. John of the Cross. He had visited Andrew and suggested Andrew join his confirmation class.

I had totally forgotten about his religious education program and felt he was more than prepared to receive the sacrament. Andrew was elated, but I was wary. He would be joining his classmates for the first time since his accident. It seemed things were slowly falling back into place.

In May 1987, Andrew stood in line for the celebration of the sacrament of confirmation. He was on a personal mission, and although he was supposed to use his walker, he was determined to walk alone. The tallest in his class, he was positioned last in the procession. He was so nervous he was sweating. I scrutinized the plan, with my adrenaline on high alert, and my right foot at the ready, halfway out of the pew. As everyone turned to see their children, Andrew struggled down the aisle, shuffling, weaving, wobbling, and trying to stand tall. Attempting to genuflect, he lost his balance and started to fall, but he clutched the pew just in time. His walking was better than it appeared to be, but he was petrified with the entire scene. There wasn't a dry eye in the church. I was limp, and my heart thrashed relentlessly. I anticipated this event would be difficult, but had not expected it to be excruciating. Fortunately, I had taken a tranquilizer before the service.

The ceremony was exceptionally touching. I watched Reverend John F. Whealon, archbishop of Hartford, make the sign of the cross on Andrew's forehead and anoint him with the perfumed holy oil chrism. In the Catholic faith, the oil signifies that the Catholic must always be ready to profess his faith openly and fearlessly. I shuddered as I vividly remembered the last time he'd been anointed. It had been the sacrament for the sick and dying when he was in ICU at St. John's. I closed my eyes and prayed. *Please, God, make him better. Make him whole like he used to be. Make him be just like his friends.*

After the ceremony, photos were taken, and Andrew was the center of attention. He smiled and listened. While everyone else laughed and talked nonstop, he was very nervous, knowing he couldn't speak clearly and join in the conversation. He smiled as if he was totally engaged. It tortured me to watch because I knew exactly what he was thinking. It was supposed to be a happy day, but was it? Or did it confirm how really different he was now?

I nearly begged his friends. "Please come by and visit anytime. His routine is eight to four-thirty, and he's home every weekend."

Andrew's gains in physical therapy, especially since using a recumbent bike, made him happy and independent. However, Daview's report termed his behavior poor. "He appears to listen to his mother more than anyone."

Of course he listened to his mother—we were a team. His friends were in a different school, and we rarely saw them. I had gone to Daview to take him out to lunch a few times, only to be reprimanded. "Mrs. Kane, please don't make a habit of taking him off the premises." I felt there was no flexibility or compromise with this rehab program. We had been spoiled by Newington's hospital program and their protocols.

Todd was now in his senior year at Holy Redeemer and a track star. I was trying to attend more of his meets, as I knew I had neglected him. However, he never complained. He understood how broken Andrew seemed to be. At the final sports banquet of the year, he was going to be awarded with letters and a trophy. I begged James, "Please come, this is important to Todd."

He yelled, "No, you moved out of the bedroom."

Yes, I had moved out. Sleeping with James was a nightmare. He was up and down all night long, inebriated. On one occasion in the middle of the night, he ended up in the kitchen, cooked, made a mess, and left it. The next day, when I turned on the stove, I smelled rubber burning. He had put a plastic container of cold cuts and cheese in the oven instead of the refrigerator. My neighbor also informed me that all the lights had been on, and she had seen him cooking stark naked!

After Todd's graduation from Holy Redeemer, I decided to send him for a postgraduate year to a boarding school in Cheshire. My mother was thrilled her money was helping with the children's educations. If I needed Todd, he would only be thirty minutes away. And it would give us more time to start college hunting, which had been put on hold due to Andrew's accident and which James refused to help with.

My ultimate goal was to get one of the children out of the house and save at least one of them. Those words would eventually haunt me. Laura had won a partial scholastic and music scholarship to Westin, the school she had dreamed of attending. Otherwise, we would not have been able to afford to send her there. She was ready to start in the fall.

In June, we received the latest team note that Andrew's behavior had improved, and he was constantly incorporating, using, and improving on the many therapies he had learned. Most importantly, his speech had improved, and even though it was slow, he could be understood. Finally, some positive reinforcement. Soon thereafter, on one occasion, James picked him up from Daview. It was a rarity, and I was thrilled. Andrew was starting to walk on his own but still needed to use a walker, which he gently flung into the backseat, and climbed into the front. He eyed his dad, who had a major buzz on.

"Yup, pretty soon you'll be driving, Gigi."

Andrew playfully manipulated his dad with slow, slurred, but intelligible speech. "Why not today, Dad? I can drive—really I can. Just pull over and I'll show ya. We won't tell Ma."

James looked at Andrew in a drunken stupor. "Oh, Son, I don't think you're ready."

"Come on, Dad, I am. Look how good my walking is."

"Okay, you're right. Today's the day, but never tell your mother."

"Course not, Dad, she'd major flip."

James pulled the car over to the side of the highway, staggered around to the passenger side, and got in. Andrew climbed over to the driver's side, and the car slowly snaked onto the road. Andrew drove to within a few blocks from home, where James took over so I wouldn't know. However, Andrew did tell me later.

Months earlier I had requested an educational evaluation from Daview to obtain a profile on Andrew's learning and present academic skills. I needed to be well aware of his needs in order for optimal placement at the Region 10 high school, come fall. In part the evaluation read: "His injury had resulted in a combination of denial and processing deficits that were impeding his academic retraining progress. This radical change from his pre- to post-morbid condition was unbearable for him. Every aspect of his life was complicated."

Despite this assessment, in September Andrew would be on campus, enrolled as a part-time sophomore in the Region 10 high school, starting with two classes. He would be in a small group for individual instruction, to be monitored by an educational specialist. Also, as part of the review, Dr. Musser noted, "Therapist met with family and recommended much-needed family therapy. Father seems more realistic." I was furious. The reason we weren't doing family therapy was James vehemently refused to go. I continued to see my therapist, Rosemary, and occasionally a psychiatrist, Dr. McMase, who prescribed my antidepressant. And James continually made fun of my "happy pills." His view was that I was weak. Later he would revisit this with a very different opinion.

By summer we desperately needed a family holiday. Everyone knew we were burned out, financially and emotionally—everyone except for James's family. They didn't view our situation as a priority to use the family cottage on Nantucket. James was in tears after speaking with Trudy. It was obvious they just didn't give a damn. So we dipped into the money my mother had given us and rented a house.

I had learned to love Nantucket, despite the fact that on my first visit I had just come from Hawaii, and there were no palm trees. It was a tiny, safe island—no murders, assaults, or violence. James's grandmother had bought a small cottage in Sconset for six thousand dollars in 1952, when he was twelve years old. He was familiar with the island, their neighbors, and the locals, from going there every summer with his mother and grandmother.

We also had fond memories of our small wedding at Our Lady of the Isle Church and the family reception of fourteen at the Chanticleer Inn. We hadn't planned to marry, and our wedding came as a surprise to both families. James had always told me he wasn't getting married until he was thirty and successful, and perhaps he should have waited. He'd graduated from Boston University, and then been drafted into the Army from the National Guard for not attending meetings. Now with all of that in the past he was ready to enter civilian life, get a job, and make his mark. And I was moving to San Francisco with my roommates from Hawaii, but decided to fly east to visit him before I left.

He then asked me to marry him—we were in love and decided to get married quickly, without a dime between us. His mother wasn't happy, as she had only met me briefly and felt he could do better with a wealthy young girl she had hoped he'd choose.

And on our wedding day, true to form, by the end of the day we were fogged in, unable to fly back to the mainland. Undeterred, James thought nothing of this, ready to stay with his friends and family at the family cottage. "We'll party today and start the marriage tomorrow." That decision would eventually deceive him. I remember feeling betrayed but trying to forget it. Alone, I went to visit my family at the cottage where they were staying. I wondered what my parents thought about all this. I know I felt uneasy, but then, staying with James's parents prior to the wedding had been difficult. It was my first time in the East, and everything and everybody was new and strange. James had reassured me he loved me and I had nothing to worry about. I believed him.

Two hours later James showed up to pick me up.

We couldn't afford a honeymoon, since we were heading to a one-room apartment in New Jersey, where James was starting his first job with Uniron and I was beginning work in the OR at St. Anne's Hospital. I worked for two years before Todd was born, and we saved my entire paycheck—which I wasn't happy about. Especially when payday came and the nurses I worked with headed out to get their hair and nails done, and I couldn't go because we didn't have money for such a lavish lifestyle. We used my money to make a down payment on a little house. I respected James's decisions. He was good with finances, then.

For our family Nantucket trip, Andrew was granted a two-week vacation from Daview. The usual permitted amount was one week, but I think they realized he'd worked hard, made dramatic advances, and needed time off. I was hoping it would bring all of us together again, especially James and me.

On July 1, our wedding anniversary, we arrived at Hyannis to board the ferry. James stayed in line with all the vehicles, each packed to capacity with coolers, bikes, fishing equipment, and tennis rackets. I think I even saw a grandmother strapped on top. One would do almost anything to get to Nantucket. Indeed, the start to a perfect vacation. The children dashed on board to get their favorite spots and waved to everyone. Maggie's tail swayed in unison as if she sensed the fun and frolicking that lay ahead. I observed it all and basked in momentary wonderment.

As we arrived in Sconset, we were greeted by a smiling sun and a romantic rose-covered cottage. An enchanting scent, reminiscent of fond memories and times gone by, filled the sparkling sea air. I was positive that aura would prevail. Andrew slowly climbed on his bike and started up a narrow path shouting, "Hurry up, guys. I bet I can beat you!" The hundreds of hours spent in PT and on the recumbent bike had paid off, and I no longer needed to hover over him.

"Don't be wanting to beat everyone—you're just off that walker," shouted a fretful Todd.

I was in a trance watching. So much had happened in one year. Did I ever think Andrew would ride a bike again? Of course I did. There was no doubt in my mind. But a little voice whispered, *Liar, liar, pants on fire!*

Deep inside me, a vault that I kept strictly hidden suddenly opened. In my mind I saw a perfect Andrew, dead, lying peacefully on white silk in a funeral casket. I glanced away, wiped off the tear, and helped James unpack the car.

Immediately I changed gears. "Let's walk to the ocean. Unloading the car can wait."

Quietly, hand in hand, we strolled in the soothing sand. It forced us to take pleasure in a romantic setting sun. On top of the waves, sparkling diamonds jumped and played tag, a perfect playground for the frolicking birds and singing seagulls. I heard them chant, "Welcome to Nantucket. You are going to have a magnificent experience." And I believed them.

The next morning, James and I sat outside, sipping coffee in the backyard. The beautiful azure sky and puffy white clouds engulfed us. For a moment I was relaxed and back on the prairies of Saskatchewan, where sky dominated.

"It's going to be a great beach day. This is heaven on earth. You wait and see—everything's going to be fine."

"I hope so, Con. You're always the optimist. Let's invite a few old friends over for cocktails."

Raising a mischievous eyebrow, I said, "Good idea, but do you remember that time on the beach in Hawaii? I was the shy Canadian from Moose Jaw, and you were the slick dude from the East?" I put my feet on his lap, and my toes stroked his thighs. James squirmed, and his eyes twinkled as he rubbed my legs.

We invited guests for the next evening. I couldn't remember the last social occasion we'd hosted or attended. That night we were fashionably dressed, and well groomed, the perfect couple with the perfectly beautiful children. Just like it used to be. Once again James was the host. It was tranquil and fun. I knew things were going to change for the best.

While James and I were enjoying our guests, the children were riding their bikes around town looking for tennis balls for Maggie while searching for adventure and celebrities. They came onto the patio to say hi. Andrew lingered, as everyone wanted to chat with him and hear about the catastrophic details of the past year. Our guests marveled at how great he was doing. I just watched him, so proud.

The last to leave, Andrew went into the kitchen, where an assortment of liquor sat on the counter. Scrutinizing the bottles, he peeked out the window to make sure no one was coming in. He then grabbed a bottle of vodka, took two pills from his pocket, threw them into his mouth, and chugalugged them down with vodka.

At that moment, Todd entered and grabbed the bottle from him. "Are you crazy? What are you doing? You can't touch that stuff. Mom will flip. Get your ass out of here. You're not as quick as you used to be." He strong-armed him out of the kitchen. We were none the wiser.

The next morning we awoke to another beautiful beach day. James prepared a lavish breakfast, and I started to pack a lunch. I noticed Andrew was a bit jumpy. I thought to myself that it would take a few days for him to relax—his body had been through so much. We drove to the small beach, five minutes away, and found a place everyone agreed upon. We all sat down together, close to the water. The children ran into the waves. They were accomplished swimmers—a gift from James, who was an excellent swimmer. They'd had years of lessons and had been on various swim teams. The water was cold and soon they were back sitting on the sand, building castles. James and I opened books to read, a rarity for us, but it was difficult for me to unwind. I said, "I hope you're keeping an eye on Andrew. Remember you're the strong swimmer, not me."

"You worry too much. Relax."

"Maybe I do. I just want this vacation to be a new start for all of us. But something's not right with Andrew."

"Con, you're overprotective. Let the kid breathe!"

I was quickly defensive. "Well, someone's got to be protective, and it's certainly not you." He had some nerve referring to me as overprotective, and I saw red at the implication. I jumped up from the beach blanket to go for a stroll to calm down, only to be intercepted by Laura running to me out of breath.

"Mom, it's Andrew. He's acting weird — says he's hearing voices and wants to go swimming in the big waves. He says he can't sit still. I'm scared."

I raced to where Andrew was rocking in the sand.

"Andrew, what's the matter?"

He began to speak loudly, his speech slow and slurred, difficult to understand.

"Andrew, please calm down. Slower, clearer."

"Ma, I feel real funny. My body wants to jump out of my skin, and my head's racing. I'm dizzy and confused. I can't think straight and couldn't sleep last night. I'm prickly all over. I don't know what's going on."

I took him back to where Todd, James, and Laura were sitting. "Okay, we're going to the hospital. Everyone pack up."

Todd and Laura tried to help Andrew up, but he pulled away, limping, covering his ears, becoming more agitated. Then Todd told me, "Mom, there's something you have to know. Andrew's been drinking your liquor and taking Vivarin tablets. He said he wanted to be alert and not miss any of the vacation."

My mouth dropped open. Not my Andrew. How could this be? Why?

I was not condoning his actions, but I understood how desperately he wanted to savor every moment here, wanting his life to return to some form of normalcy. And again I couldn't help but look at James accusingly, but I did not utter a word. James remained mute.

Laura joined in. "Mom, you also need to know that last month at the Westin dance, the chaperones kicked Andrew out. They thought he was drunk because of his slurred speech and wobbly walk. He swore at them, and it was a nasty scene. I don't know if he was drinking or not. He just can't win. It sucks."

"I hate that word."

"Well, Mom, it does!" said Laura.

"I know it does."

I knew how hard it was for Todd and Laura to rat Andrew out, but we had openly discussed his progress and how very important the truth was. And the truth stank, but it would only help their brother in the long run.

James walked over. "Con, don't you think you're overreacting?"

"Overreacting? What are we supposed to do—just sit and watch him go through this torture? James, where's your brain?" I had no idea how this incident might affect his already compromised brain and worried that he could escalate even more. And then what? None of his doctors were around for guidance, and I was petrified.

He backed down. "Okay, okay, you're right. I'm just sick of hospitals. You know how I feel."

"Yes, I know, but it's not your feelings I'm concerned with."

We arrived at Nantucket Hospital about four o'clock. Andrew was out of control, thrashing, often screaming out or crying. He held his ears tightly, trying to shut out the world that had invaded him. I was scared stiff and furious with James's lack of support. As the receptionist began with the usual paperwork, not relevant during a crisis, Andrew escalated. The doctor arrived, and I rambled out his history.

When the doctor asked, "What is a TBI?" I flipped out.

"Traumatic brain injury!"

Softly, the doctor responded, "Oh, yes."

I was not at ease with this Einstein, but we didn't have a lot of choices. It was a tiny hospital, and he was the only doctor, too young and obviously inexperienced. I asked myself, *Did he graduate at the head of the class, or the bottom?*

At this point, Andrew was swinging his fists, kicking at everyone, begging for relief. They had to put him into four-point leather restraints. That nearly killed me. I was impatient, waiting for the doctor to medicate him with something, anything. I assumed he needed to leaf through a PDR—*Physicians' Desk Reference*—for medication, dosage, side effects. Andrew was becoming more violent.

Finally, at five p.m., the doctor entered the room with a 5mg injection of Valium, which had little effect. At five thirty the dose was repeated. The doctor called poison control about the caffeine from the Vivarin he took. The four capsules, equal to eight cups of coffee, along with the vodka he drank, could be causing the delirium he was experiencing. At six thirty he was given 10mg of Valium, and blood was drawn for a toxicology screen to check if any other drugs were in his system. By six fifty he was calmer, his speech was clearer, and he apologized for his behavior.

I asked the nurse, "Can you please take the restraints off? He doesn't need them anymore." She checked with the doctor, and he okayed their removal. At seven thirty he was docile and wanted to go home. Andrew was then discharged and walked out of the ER. Final diagnosis: acute caffeinism and alcohol intoxication.

We drove home, grabbed a couple of pizzas, and went to bed early. Sleep did not come easily. I was exhausted, still pumping adrenaline, and turned to my rosary beads.

We had gone 180 degrees from coma to out-of-control. When would we get to the middle and coast forever? *Please, God, let it be soon.* A few months later I found out that Valium should never be prescribed for someone with a TBI. It was the worst choice of drug. I knew that doctor was inept. It should have been given to me!

For a long period of time Andrew was remorseful. I believed this was healthy, as he needed to understand how his actions and choices affected all of us. We were in this together for better or worse. He returned to Daview with a better attitude. Now, *I* was the problem. They had found out about the extra speech therapy with Emily and said it was interfering with his progress and insinuated that if I did not comply, he was out of the program. I resentfully signed the paper, acknowledging that I would cooperate fully and stop his therapy with Emily. They had won this round. But I was fed up with Dr. Musser, her attitude, and her treatment of my child. In plain English, I just didn't like her.

I adamantly requested another neuropsychological evaluation for Andrew's part-time placement with Regional School District #10 in the fall. This would be necessary and advantageous for him to make another transition, and I would not take no for an answer. At my insistence, an outside psychologist was brought in. She found him a warm, calm adolescent who was subject to mood fluctuations, with difficulty understanding the perspective of others. He was highly self-conscious and acutely aware of how his recent trauma identified and separated him from others. The psychologist stated, "These characteristics were not unusual, for adolescence." Finally, an optimistic opinion from an outside source.

I resented Dr. Musser even more now, and felt she was an obstacle in Andrew's progress. I regretted not seeing this earlier. I would need to be more direct in my advocacy. From here on in I would need to listen more to my gut feelings as a nurse and mother. Was it right or wrong for Andrew? I would make that choice. It was not about anyone but him. He had the accident, and it was his life we were trying to rebuild. That would remain foremost. On the plus side, in the eight months at Daview, Andrew had made overall gains, and his IQ had gone up seven points.

In September, Andrew would start at the Region 10 high school part-time. He would be there during the morning and then return in the afternoon to Daview for his rehab program. I met with Andrew's new school team at the high school. The guidance counselor, and the occupational, physical, and speech therapists were present. Dr. Joan Jinnie led the meeting, giving details about Andrew's condition and program. Everyone had a copy of the four-page detailed neuropsych evaluation. We all concurred that he was in for a lot of work to make continual gains toward that now-four-year recovery deadline we all knew was dangling in front of him. A partial academic load was put into place. Even this would be difficult, as he was highly self-conscious and acutely aware of how his recent trauma identified and separated him from other students. It seemed that the team genuinely cared, and I was finally at ease. That feeling would be short-lived.

Though he had little time left at Daview, he was miserable. He told me, "Ma, I hate it here."

And yet he was also ambivalent about reentry into a new school system and special remedial classes. "I don't want to be with the dumb kids. I'm not mentally retarded. Ma, I hate the new Andrew!"

My heart shattered hearing him speak this way. I felt his pain, and it temporarily crippled me, but I continually reinforced. "Sweetie, it will get better. I promise." Quietly, I had a conversation with God. *When, when, are you going to make him feel more confident with the wonderful person he still is? Please!*

Dr. Musser submitted another progress report to Region 10. She stated, "Andrew does not like the term TBI and does not want to be associated with it. His present goals are a need for more community exposure to increase his self-confidence and curb his immature behavior." She also noted he was more focused, so his educational program was being upped ten more hours per week. His scores were up: word attack from grade 5.7–8.1, word comprehension from grade 5.5–9.7. Verbal ability eighty-ninth percentile. Science and sociology were at a tenth-grade level. Math scores were low and that was okay with me. He couldn't be perfect in everything, yet.

Her psych evaluation was now more positive: "He was very cooperative and responds to positive reinforcement and compliments, but still wants to socialize with normal people. Occupational, physical, and speech therapy saw him more relaxed, less impulsive, and working hard in everything."

And I asked myself, "Why wouldn't he want to associate with normal people? He *is* normal." I looked at the report and thought, *Wasn't this always my modus operandi*? I thought, if only James spent more time with him, things would be even better. But he had no time for Andrew or any of the children, and I needed to live with that.

Andrew's friends were now few in number and rarely dropped by. They seemed afraid of him. For socialization, I took him shopping, always keeping a sharp eye on him. He would take a cart and roam around the store independently. Even though he had special orthotics, he still walked with a right leg limp. At least this got him out of the house, among normal people.

But later, when Todd took him to a local convenience store, it was another story. Andrew was caught shoplifting. He had no history of stealing, and I was shocked. The owner of the store did not make an issue over the incident, fully aware of our circumstances. However, a neighbor who witnessed the scene called me, feeling I would want to know. And, yes, I did. Andrew was the kid everyone wanted around, the altar boy everyone requested for weddings and funerals, the boy who would help the elderly with odd jobs. What was going on?

Shortly after that, another episode occurred. He confessed—he'd been drinking alcohol from our liquor cabinet. Following these incidents, for two long weeks the effect of alcohol on an already-compromised brain reared its ugly head, manifesting in paranoia, hallucinations, and delusions, creating confusion and disorientation. He had wanted to numb his pain. Only, that had backfired, terrorizing him and his friends, and pushing them even further away. I was determined to stay ahead of this problem and was ever more vigilant with everything he did.

In September, Todd left home for Cheshire. I would miss him terribly, and we were both nervous. We found his dorm and unpacked. I gave him a three-page detailed list on how to do laundry, which he glanced at quizzically. And then that painful moment came.

"Well, Spark"—his nickname—"it's time for me to go." We hugged and I kissed him, leaving with a big hole in my heart.

"Thanks for everything, Mom. I love you and worry about you. I don't know how you do it."

"I'll be all right. You just help me by taking care of yourself. Promise."

"I promise."

To further alter the family dynamics, Laura would start her freshman year at nearby Westin. I was confident this prestigious private school would open doors for her. Because she would be a day student and live at home, I felt no separation anxiety as I had with Todd. Laura wasn't one to feel any separation anxiety anyway, as she made friends easily.

And then there was Andrew. I received another disappointing report from Daview about him. "Since school reintegration to the half day spent at Region 10, he is refusing tasks, cursing, and demanding, with attention-seeking behavior, projecting and distorting situations. He views continued therapy as a reminder of his injury, yet he agrees treatment is still necessary. He feels therapists are yelling at him and has difficulty with limit-setting. He's rude and not getting the full benefit from treatment due to his secondary behavior. In therapy, he shows little insight, clings to other patients, and often makes fun of others' impairments. Continued psychotherapy is necessary. The half day he spends at Region 10, with returning to Daview and spending full afternoons on therapies, is draining and tiring to him." She recommended he be discharged totally from Daview.

And so be it. Daview was now past. Andrew had made significant improvements, but the cost had been high for him and me. We both cried and instantly felt relief as the return to normalcy was now even closer. Or so we thought. If I had thought I had options for Andrew and had support from James, I might have looked further. But Newington felt strongly about him going to Daview, and I listened to them. Brain injury survival and rehab were all new frontiers. He should have gone on to a rehab program where he would stay 24/7, but at that time the only one that existed was out of state. And I'm not sure I could have sent him that far away, but I will never know.

And then, wham-o. Dr. Musser contradicted herself and stated Andrew would *not* benefit from further psychotherapy. I was livid. How could she make such a foolish statement? Andrew was entering a new school, handicapped from a traumatic brain injury, with no friends, and she thought he didn't need psychological counseling? This was gross negligence on her part.

Because I witnessed Andrew's traumatic and excruciating social integration, I knew how imperative psychological help was. I contacted a male therapist, Dr. A. Smine, in Cheshire, CT. I felt a male therapist would relate better to Andrew, and within a few weeks they started therapy.

And then the axe fell. I pointed out the importance of counseling to Dr. Jinnie, but she informed me that because Dr. Musser had not written it on the Planning and Placement Treatment Plan, or PPT, Regional School District #10 was not required to provide or pay for Dr. Smine's services.

I was livid! Andrew desperately needed psychotherapy, and it was the responsibility of the school system to pay for it.

Counseled by a specialist, a friend of Tish's, I placed a call to Special Services of the State of Connecticut to discuss this critical situation and to advocate for Andrew. The specialist told me it was imperative to use these words in order for the school to pay for these services.

In order for Andrew to meet his educational needs, he needed psychological counseling. Those words were crucial and law in the State of Connecticut, which Dr. Jinnie arrogantly denied. If I had to take this to the highest court in the land, I would not back down. They had incensed the lioness from Moose Jaw. No one ever attacks her cubs.

Get ready for war, Dr. Jinnie.

I called my lawyer, Bill Jones. I was suing Regional School District #10.

Chapter Eight

January 1988–June 1989

It was Super Bowl time again. James informed me he was going to New York for a few days to celebrate with the guys, whether I liked it or not. There was limited communication between us, and "the guys" were obviously more important than his family. He had been let go by the company that had taken over Uniron, but had put in twenty years and was eligible for a pension plan. He landed another job with a Canadian company, and we immediately had health insurance, even though he hadn't started working yet. Bumpy called to speak to James, and when I answered the phone we talked.

"Con, he's a good kid. I also know you're a good mother and trying to do the best for everyone. But he's my son. What am I supposed to do?"

"Thanks, Bumpy, it's okay. He's a grown man and has to do what he has to do . . ."

James's guy friends all liked to drink but could stop when they wanted to. I loved a vodka tonic with a wedge of lime in the summer but that was in the evening or before dinner. For years before the accident, we'd get together with other couples and take vacations. As the years went on, I often accepted dinner invitations without him, openly telling everyone he was home in bed, only to have him show up a couple of hours late, looking great, after sleeping it off.

The year before the accident was turbulent on our social life, with my brother's unexpected death, and me flying home several times trying to help my parents cope with their sorrow. I also grieved his untimely death.

James's usual Friday night buddies who met weekly at the 1210 Restaurant also warned him about his drinking.

"Don't worry, I have everything under control," he'd tell them. It sounded so authentic, and I think he really believed it. His alcohol abuse had progressed slowly and instilled in him an untouchable, grandiose attitude. In his mind he was still Mr. Smooth. And perhaps it was my fault, but addressing his drinking only led to another fight that I didn't want to have in front of the kids. He had to do it his way.

I, on the other hand, wanted a much-needed family vacation to Disneyworld, where we had never been. It would be the last opportunity for a winter family vacation, which we had never taken with the children, since next year Todd would be in college. I begged James to go, but he refused. So I pulled the kids out of school for a week and bought a Gold Card Package, which entitled us to nonstop full access to the Disney Kingdoms and the best restaurants, while staying at a great hotel. There was nothing the children couldn't do. They were ecstatic. Again, thank you, Mom and Dad.

We arrived at Disney the first week of February to mid-seventies temperatures and the Polynesian Hotel, which made me feel like I was back in Hawaii. It brought back those wonderful carefree days when I'd lived there, and the memories brought tears to my eyes. The first day we took pictures with the Disney characters. The children ate each meal like it was their last, going back for seconds and thirds. You'd have thought I'd been starving them. No wonder they were so skinny. Good thing child services wasn't observing.

Laura shouted, "First, let's go horseback riding!"

"Okay, and then we've got to play golf," Todd added.

And Andrew wanted to zoom around in the water on the mini boats. A plan was agreed upon. I just wanted us to be a family and have fun. On the third day they chose to go horseback riding. I explained Andrew's brain injury to the staff and was guaranteed that he would be strictly monitored at the stable in the Magic Kingdom. I was told not to worry about his safety. Laura loved horses and had been riding since she was six. Her years with the Litchfield Pony Club had rubbed off on Todd and Andrew, and they also rode in town at a good friend's barn, where there were several horses. My agenda was shopping and a quiet lunch at the Contemporary Hotel.

I had just purchased a handsome Irish mohair wrap for my mother, when I heard my name coming from the overhead page.

"Connie Kane to the hospitality desk. Connie Kane to the hospitality desk." No one knew I was there. Who could be calling me? Something was very wrong, and I panicked. Unfamiliar with the hotel, I began to run blindly to find the hospitality desk.

When I got there I said, "I'm Connie Kane. You're paging me!"

"You need to call the Polynesian." The receptionist dialed the number.

I said, "This is Connie Kane."

"Mrs. Kane, your children are here and fine. However, Andrew was running and slipped and fell. We think he's broken his arm and have made arrangements for him to see an orthopedic surgeon at the Orlando Clinic. We have a car waiting to take you there."

I put the phone down in a momentary trance. I was relieved but wondered if this would ever end. Thankfully it was Andrew's right arm, the one with the hemiparesis (partial paralysis). The X-ray showed fractures of the radius and ulna bones. Since there were no misalignments or angulations, a fiberglass cast was applied. Andrew was instructed to keep his arm above his heart and exercise his fingers, of which he now had only about five percent usage. He was fully compliant, but the mini boats kept calling, and he continued riding them with blue fingers that everyone thought were going to fall off.

The hotel staff did cartwheels to help us. I think they were afraid I was going to sue, since Andrew was injured on Disney property and they were liable, but I had no such intention. Andrew's arm would heal, and that was all that mattered.

Only many years later would I learn the real story of the fall. Apparently Todd, Andrew, and Laura did go to the stables, but riding wasn't scheduled until later in the day, so there was no staff present. And since Laura loved horses and no one was there, she talked her brothers into saddling up, and they went for a short unsupervised ride on their own. Andrew's horse started to gallop, and he couldn't hold the reins with one hand. He lost control and fell off, but was okay. Realizing they might be in trouble, they quickly dismounted, ran back to the barn with the horses, and Andrew slipped in wet mud and fell again. This fall broke his arm.

The last night of our Disney visit we had dinner reservations at an elegant restaurant that required a jacket and tie. The restaurant was on a ship, and its interior matched any upscale New York restaurant. Todd and Andrew made the clean-plate club, loving every minute of it. Laura had come down with a stomach bug and was too sick to join us. The management of the Polynesian Hotel went out of their way and provided us with a babysitter for her. I think they were cautious, awaiting our departure—the sooner the better, especially after Andrew's broken arm.

We returned home again to "rehab reality" for Andrew. Since leaving Daview, Andrew was now enrolled in a rehab program at

Easter Seals. I knew we had made a good move, as he no longer complained about attending the sessions. The PT and OT goals remained consistent: improve speed and dexterity of his right arm, improve motor control of his now dominant left arm, and continue strengthening his legs for various walking activities.

In speech they worked on improving language comprehension, parameters of speech, and cognitive functioning, with emphasis on carrying over and using what had been learned. The therapist's comments were positive. "Very cooperative, but quiet, polite, and eager to improve." Once again I was relieved.

We were moving forward again.

Along with Andrew's daily school commitments and his Easter Seals program, he also went for extra speech therapy with Emily, extra PT at St. John's Hospital, and saw his psychologist, Dr. Smine. It was a full plate. James still hadn't begun his new job, and I was able to go back to work part time in the OR at Memorial Hospital. One could never have too much health insurance, especially for the unknown . . .

I was energized and happy to be back at work. Everyone was supportive. I could, however, feel residual tension from the strike. I continued to see my therapist, Rosemary, and it seemed she and I made all our family decisions. I had no relatives to talk to, and the less my family in Canada knew, the better. I didn't want to worry them when they were so far away, or try to make them understand the ramifications of my messed-up life.

Laura spent many overnights at Westin. Administration thought it easier for her, given her home situation. In actuality, they knew very little about it.

Meanwhile, my attorney, Bill Jones, called to update me on the lawsuit against Region 10. I was furious at them for refusing to pay for Andrew's psychotherapy but more importantly because they just didn't seem to care about my child. The reason we had transferred

Andrew to the public school in our district was because, by law, they had to provide for the special needs of handicapped children, and Andrew needed all these services in order to be successful. All services required for a child must be written in the PPT, which Dr. Musser had not done, which was in fact downright immoral and illegal and the reason I was suing the public school system.

All this made me advocate all the more furiously. I contacted the National Center for Handicapped Children and Youth for information on pertinent Connecticut state resources, as well as the State Board of Education in Hartford, and the Connecticut Parent Advocacy Center. My lawyer had given Region 10 notice of legal action, and in turn, they started due process. I knew I would be triumphant, not only for Andrew but for every other child who required special services, and also for the parents who were too drained to fight the system and accepted what they were advised as the gospel truth. This would be my chosen path.

In preparation, I obtained letters from ten of Andrew's doctors and therapists, all of whom supported without question his need for psychotherapy. Dr. Smine, Andrew's new therapist, wrote a profound letter. It read:

> Dear Dr. Jinnie,
>
> Pursuant to our telephone conversation of 12 February 1988, I am sending this letter outlining some of Andrew Kane's emotional needs, their impact on his academic functioning, and relevant goals of psychological intervention. As you know, Andrew sustained a traumatic brain injury. Resulting from his fall, however, was more than a compromised central nervous system. Because of his dramatically altered cognitive, sensory, and motor functioning, Andrew's very sense of self has been traumatized. The self-concept, which Andrew had been working on, was in an instant shattered. The previous

physically agile, articulate, and academically gifted young man was transformed into a person struggling to adjust to a new way of being in the world. In a real sense, Andrew sustained a traumatic self-injury in addition to adjusting to a new self-concept, diminished skills, and lost abilities.

Andrew finds himself coping with the loss of friends who could not adjust to his complex transformation. There is no good time to have a brain injury. When such injuries occur in adolescence, there is cause for both concern and hope. Concern for the obvious and hope because with adequate assistance an individual may be helped to resume growth in the cognitive academic spheres. Development in these areas, however, intersects with and depends in great measure on continued emotional growth.

To help Andrew achieve his academic potential is one of the objectives of my psychological intervention. This will be accomplished directly through my support, guidance, and suggestions, whenever appropriate. Also, helping Andrew to work on the ongoing social and emotional trauma of his injury, which interferes with his ability to attend, concentrate, remember, and sustain other challenging academic efforts, constitutes a major goal of psychotherapy.

Dr. Jinnie, I hope you and your team find this information helpful.

With ten letters in hand from the medical community, adamantly articulating the profound importance of continued psychological counseling for Andrew, I marched to Region 10 and presented them to Dr. Jinnie. "These letters are for you." Standing tall, I promptly exited. The mediation was now set in motion for the following week.

That morning before I got ready, I checked and watered the schefflera plant Andrew had given me that was now almost three feet tall. Then I donned a suit and heels. I was dressed for success, as they say. In my advocacy pursuit, it would later be known as the "power suit." People do pay attention to you when you make a presentation in proper attire. Never would I wear jeans.

Dr. Jinnie and Region 10's three attorneys sat on one side of the conference table. Bill Jones and I sat across from them. I leaned over to Bill. "They don't have a chance. I've done my homework. If they dare deny services, I'll take it to court and make as much noise as I can—newspapers, television, whatever it takes." I was fired up, but let Bill do the talking. He spoke professionally and eloquently, and we were successful.

As a result of the mediation, Andrew would receive a neuropsychological evaluation at Newington Children's Hospital, scheduled as soon as possible, and Region 10 would assume financial responsibility for the evaluation. If the recommendation from Newington Children's Hospital stated that psychotherapy was necessary for Andrew's continued educational program, then Region 10 would pay the cost for such psychotherapy, retroactive to February 1988.

Two of my letters in support of psychotherapy came from Newington—from the head of the rehab program and from the neuropsychologist, Dr. Javorn. I knew it was a done deal.

I walked out of the meeting gloating, but kept it to myself. Then I gave Bill a big hug. "Thanks so much," I told him. "We showed them, didn't we?" One should never underestimate a girl from Moose Jaw.

The neuropsych evaluation came back. Continued psychotherapeutic support was strongly recommended to facilitate a greater acceptance of cognitive limitations as well as social difficulties that might arise. Andrew should be followed neuropsychologically with a subsequent evaluation performed in one year to monitor changes in neuropsychological functioning. The testing revealed that

Andrew's IQ had moved up a few more points. Thus, he was functioning in an overall average range of intelligence. I was ecstatic.

Dr. Javorn, the neuropsychologist, also suggested a sleeping EEG, or electroencephalogram, to determine if Andrew had a seizure disorder. He had had one grand mal seizure at the time of the accident and had been on Dilantin for seizure control since then. The results showed he did not have a seizure disorder and no longer needed Dilantin. I was so grateful to Newington, I swore that if I ever made any money, I would leave it to that facility.

Sometime later, the local newspaper made it known that the Region 10 high school had spent sixty thousand dollars to send a very emotionally challenged child to a special school because they felt that if it helped the child, they were obliged to do so. I seethed at the article. Dr. Jinnie had made it seem that what I wanted for Andrew was something out of the norm, and that I was a bitchy, demanding mother. I was prepared for a long battle over any minor infraction during his three remaining years in high school, but remained resilient. I would spare nothing, would not negotiate easily, and would never compromise on what I felt Andrew needed.

A few weeks later I arrived at Region 10 high school to pick him up for an appointment. As I sat in the car waiting, I envisioned how difficult school must be for him. I had no idea how horribly traumatic it truly was. His day consisted of attending a school he was not familiar with, with kids he didn't know, adjusting to a system of periods set up for academics in regular classrooms, then to the OT room for therapy, the PT room for therapy, and finally Speech in the special room designed for speech therapy. It was a lot of quick moving around from one area to another, especially when he was still concentrating on perfect walking, posture, balance, and follow through. He didn't want to stand out even more by having the teachers and aides help him.

He strolled out of the school, wobbling more than usual, his book bag slung over his drooping weaker right shoulder. In the car he flung the bag in the back, reclined his seat, and closed his eyes to the world. I sensed something was not right, patted him on the leg, and cautiously asked, "How was your day, sweetie?"

It was obvious he wanted to block out his gruesome, difficult world — a world he now must survive in.

"Terrible! I worked so hard in PT that I was dripping with sweat. It takes me so long to change my clothes, and I didn't want to be late for history class, so I went all stinky. As I rushed in the hallway, I lost my balance, bumped into a bunch of girls, tripped, and another girl fell on me. Everyone stared at me, and I got so nervous I couldn't speak. They looked at me like I was a freak. I am a freak. Ma, this is so hard. I don't know if I can do it or take much more." He put his head in his hands and sobbed uncontrollably.

Tears flowed down my cheeks, and my voice cracked. "Andrew, you are the strongest and most courageous person I will ever know. It will take time, but it will get better, I promise." Inside my aching heart I truly believed this.

I had a session later with Rosemary. I arrived early, took off my shoes, lay down on the white wicker sofa, and covered myself with a soft Irish mohair throw. I was already beginning to feel at peace. This was my healing time. I could say anything and everything I feared to say to anyone else. I could open the vault deep inside me and share my innermost feelings. I could laugh or cry without judgment. I was safe here, and it was all about *me*. Mainly it was about learning, surviving, and someday experiencing true happiness. This was my only option.

Rosemary entered, wearing one of her festive Mexican caftans. Her blond hair mixed with the bright colors gave her a lighthearted look. I needed and yearned for that. She greeted me with her usual smile — not too much, yet just enough. I'd probably want to kill her if she was too happy when I was so miserable.

"So how are things this week?"

"Rosemary, I don't know any more. My heart is breaking for Andrew." I relayed the incident from earlier in the day. "It's a daily struggle. It takes him forever to get dressed in the morning. I'm still tying his shoelaces. I don't mind, but he does. And can you blame him? He's sixteen and still needs his mother to lend a hand. Seeing him like this is so painful. I remember him before the accident. He was the master of ceremonies, singing, dancing on stage. The chosen one for the Spanish contest, the boy who always made the team, who wanted to go to Princeton and someday conquer the world."

I buried my face in my hands and cried openly. I took my time, and when I was finished, I regrouped. Now there was work to do. We ran through his program to make sure everything was in place and working optimally. We discussed Todd and Laura and where they were emotionally, and then we spent a lot of time on James. Rosemary had known James since high school, and she was optimistic he would turn things around and stop drinking. She suggested I up my antidepressant. She was right—I needed more help and energy.

It was time to start college hunting for Todd. This should be fun quality time for James and him, but James had no time. He'd need to be sober and not drink all day, and at this point he couldn't do that. So he made the excuse, "Con, you're better at this than I am."

I hadn't gone to college in this country, so it would all be new to me, but I relished the time spent with Todd. He was my rock and foundation, but I kept that a secret so as not to put too much pressure on him—or I thought I did. We combed Connecticut, Massachusetts, and New Hampshire, and he settled on Northeastern University in Boston, MA.

At the time that Todd was graduating from Cheshire, James and I had been going for days without speaking to each other. We drove separate cars to the graduation. Laura and Andrew came with me. When James arrived, he reeked of liquor. His drinking stressed everyone, putting a damper on the festivities. I was furious with him and embarrassed for Todd.

Rosemary suggested I try Al-Anon—a support group of relatives and friends of alcoholics who share their experience, strength, and hope in order to solve their common problems. They believe alcoholism is a family disease and that changed attitudes can aid recovery. Al-Anon has one purpose—to help families of alcoholics understand the alcoholic through using a twelve-step program. I tried one meeting and sobbed uncontrollably the entire time, unable to speak or share my pain. It took too much time and hurt way too much. I never returned.

Summer finally arrived. Laura was babysitting. Todd was working at a factory during the week and caddying at a country club on weekends. Andrew had a job as an aide with disabled children at a municipal recreation department. On weekends he washed dishes at The Country Inn Restaurant in Middlebury. The staff loved him. All was well. The only problem was picking him up after work, usually around one a.m. Often one of the staff would drive him home, but if they didn't, I had to do it. I had stopped working to drive him to his summer therapy programs, which were more important than my job. James also viewed this as my responsibility since he was now working.

Andrew continued summer rehab at Easter Seals, hassle free, since school was not in session. I drove him every day and was in constant communication with the therapists. The setting was much less rigid than Daview, but I was concerned. He looked very thin and gaunt, so they involved a nutritionist in his program. I worried why he wanted to look this way and what it all meant. Perhaps it was his only form of control. In the fall, Andrew would return to Region 10 and continue his rehab program there and wouldn't need any more shuffling, except for psychotherapy in Cheshire with Dr. Smine. I tried to make the psychotherapy a fun excursion, throwing in some shopping and going for ice cream. It worked for a while.

The final discharge summary from Easter Seals was positive with gains in all areas. They had discharged him home, with a program he worked daily. I admired his drive and motivation. He was beating this rap.

Finally, in September he started full time at Region 10 school. All his therapists and teachers had been well prepared and were openly compassionate about his needs. They realized how important this was to his total well-being. And, just maybe, they'd heard of his mother, who'd taken Dr. Jinnie and the system to mediation and won. What they would soon find out was that I was just a mother taking care of her child and loving him more than I loved myself, and that I would give up my personal dreams and put everything on hold until he was completely healed. I never realized or was realistic about how long the healing would take, or what the future would hold. I was blind with love for this child.

Before school started I requested a reevaluation at Newington Children's Hospital to help establish recommendations for his school program. There could be no confusion or error. I didn't know if a child with a traumatic brain injury had ever been enrolled in the school, and I needed his program to be precise in order for him to meet his educational goals. It's not that I didn't trust the school, there was just no room for error. As usual I could always count on Newington. They suggested these interventions:

1. Divide larger assignments into smaller components and provide feedback.
2. Provide instruction in a systematic, step-by-step fashion, with opportunities to apply strategies to various situations.
3. Provide written outlines of task expectations.

4. Deliver directions in brief segments with repetition of key elements.
5. Request verbal feedback from Andrew to make sure he understands.
6. Allow flexible time constraints.
7. Provide written notes of lengthy verbal information (lecture format).
8. Provide opportunities for Andrew to review lectures with a peer or the instructor.
9. Allow utilization of a tape recorder during lectures.
10. Provide assistance in developing study plans.

Meanwhile, my friend Tish Shean, nun and principal of Sacred Family High School, a coed Catholic school in Waterbury, asked me to accept a position there as the health educator / coordinator for the upcoming year. The school system complemented Andrew's schedule, and I'd be able to transport him to his many therapies and doctors without missing a beat. Hopefully the list of ten would soon start to dwindle.

I told her, "I'd be honored to join Sacred Family. I've always wanted to teach, and this will be an excellent opportunity." The pay was not commensurate with the work, but the health benefits were great, and the program would last one hundred and eighty days. Little did I comprehend that this move would be my salvation and make Andrew and me near celebrities.

I now joined the ranks of the teachers. Tish gave me the health book that was used probably twenty years prior, which focused on bubonic plague and other such vital issues. Totally not the focus for teenagers. I looked her straight in the eye and said, "Tish, I can't teach this. These kids need to learn about drinking, drugs, smoking, sex, AIDS, and self-esteem. They need to understand the consequences of risky behavior in order to survive today."

"Okay, you've got carte blanche with the curriculum."

I tossed the book in the garbage and put together a program that I felt would benefit students. I had a great deal to share with them, and if I touched only a few of the students, I would have done my job. They needed to know about the importance of their own health. And they needed to know how quickly it could be taken away. I would share Andrew's world and enlighten them about their misperception of immortality. This was going to be a challenge, but I was looking forward to it. I was beginning to feel that my life had purpose and I was somewhat in control.

Todd started college, Laura was in her sophomore year at Westin, and Andrew was a sophomore at Region 10. Region 10 had also set up after-school tutors to work with Andrew at home. Things were looking up. I hoped Andrew would make some new friends, now that he would be at the high school all day. I was thrilled to once again watch him playing, in effect, one-handed basketball in the driveway, even though it tortured me to see him always playing alone. I made sure he couldn't see my tears.

James seemed excited about my new job. The excellent additional health coverage made him comfortable and took a weight from his shoulders.

On my first day of school, at an informal breakfast to greet old and new staff, I was overdressed for the occasion. Subconsciously, I was anxious to get out of OR scrubs. As I was introduced, I felt it necessary to give a speech and hand out copies of *Fifty Known Stress Relievers*. I genuinely hoped the staff would read the material and have a less stressful year. No one else felt it necessary to stand up and speak, so I was sure they were all rolling their eyes, wondering and whispering, "Where did Sister find this beaut?"

I was a great believer in prophylactic medicine, trying to ensure that all necessary precautions were taken to prevent unhealthy or negative events from impacting the body. But then, why hadn't *I* cut down that damn swing and practiced my own prophylaxis? Would I always be haunted?

My first big school project was an AIDS awareness program for the entire school. With the help of the Public Health Department and some personal friends in the field, we held the first session in Waterbury and in a Catholic high school. Thus it needed to be handled delicately and professionally, and it was. We were fortunate to have volunteers diagnosed with AIDS share their stories. You could hear a pin drop when they took the microphone. The students loved the program, and ultimately we received an invitation to appear on television. I was thrilled!

Every day I started my class by reading the newspaper with a focus on health issues, accidents, and risky behaviors. We covered what a DWI was and what numbers constituted a drunk-driving blood alcohol level. I felt my classes were interesting, especially when I started sex ed, and students who were not in my class asked to attend.

As we progressed into the fall, there continued to be turmoil in the family. Andrew started to rebel against Emily and speech therapy. She felt I was pushing him too hard. I acknowledged I was, and started to back off.

Laura's guidance counselor called me for a school conference. Laura had spoken highly about Mr. Wells, so I knew he liked her as well. He was a casual preppie, and I was immediately put at ease. I'm not sure if it was his ponytail or Birkenstocks.

"You're wondering why I asked you to this meeting. I like Laura, and she's a gifted student, but lately her work has become mediocre. She seems to be under pressure, and yet she has broken the barrier between the day students and boarders, which is not easy to accomplish. My concern is her choice of friends, many of whom are struggling with various problems."

"Mr. Wells, has Laura confided in you about her ... the problems at home?"

"No, not a word."

I thought, *Where should I start?* I probably went on to reveal too much information about our marriage in constant turmoil, James's drinking problem, and Andrew's accident, since Mr. Wells seemed speechless.

Laura's newest friend was Gerry, a girl from the Midwest. She was from an affluent all-American family, and her parents had been married for thirty years. However, Gerry was not a student but an unrealistic, spoiled child who lived in a fantasy world. She pictured herself an actress and marrying a rock star. Her vivid imagination complemented her country club lifestyle, and Laura was enamored by all this. And why wouldn't she be? Gerry's imagination helped Laura escape her dysfunctional family and temporarily leave behind the pain and suffering she dealt with daily as she watched the brother she loved struggle to survive, and her parents fight constantly as their marriage crumbled. Laura was always close to her father but felt a growing distance from him. Gerry helped to lighten the burden.

Laura began to demonstrate anger and frequent outbursts. I felt she needed professional help and made an appointment for her to see Dr. McMase, the psychiatrist I saw occasionally, who monitored my antidepressant medication. As usual, James disagreed, was negative and unsupportive. I told him, "I don't care what you think. I'm making the appointment and doing what I think is the right thing to do for her." And that was that.

Parents' Weekend was coming up at Westin. Laura was a member of the Glee Club, and there was going to be a special candlelight service, followed by a short reception. I was looking forward to the event and definitely attending. James was not. It was dawning on me that Laura, as well as Andrew, needed my presence and time. If only James would help, but he was nowhere around. He slept at home and that was about it. Laura's other good friend Haley and her parents invited us to join them for dinner after the reception.

Parents' Night was the same evening Andrew was going out for the first time with a group of his old friends. They were going to meet the girls at the mall. He was so thrilled and excited, but I think I was even more euphoric. As I got ready for Laura's concert, he was on his own to prepare for his big night. He stood in front of the bathroom mirror in boxer shorts, practicing his speech exercises with a tongue depressor. Taped to the side of the mirror were his speech instructions. Theatrically, he admired himself. "Not bad, kid, if I do say so myself!"

I walked by his room. "Andrew I'm leaving now. Have a great evening. You're sure I don't need to help you iron your clothes?"

Andrew was startled. The tongue depressor fell from his hand. "No, Ma. Ma and her radar. She was probably watching me too!"

I was thrilled to have observed his determination. Motivated, he continued his speech exercises for a few more minutes. Then he grabbed a pair of khaki pants and a pink button-down shirt and headed to the kitchen to iron them. It was a struggle, with one good hand and one that barely worked, as the material kept crumpling up, making more creases than when he started. He plodded along, determined to finish the job that took twenty minutes. Dressing and doing up buttons were a huge task, taking longer than planned. He was sweating and getting nervous as he checked the clock. He wanted to be ready and on time. And then the phone rang. It was Todd wishing him well on his big night out.

"Hey, can I call you back later? I'm late, not ready. Okay, I love you too, bro!"

Meanwhile, I sat relaxed in a dimly lit chapel at Westin, enjoying the Glee Club, reminiscent of all my years singing in choirs in Moose

Jaw. This, however, was no Moose Jaw. Between selections I observed a "couture" audience, which excluded me. The women, especially, were prone to talking and sounding like they had "leather lips." You know the type—nouveau riche who spoke as if they had a lemon in their mouth. So annoying. It was unfortunate that they seemed uncomfortable with who they really were and needed to pretend to be otherwise. I still wasn't sure who I was or where I belonged, but I was definitely comfortable in my skin. And that was probably painful for, oh so many!

When the concert was over, Laura came running to me. "So, Ma, how were we? Mr. Avers wants to know if I can go with the chorus to Austria during spring break. Wouldn't that be cool? That's where Grandma's from. I mean, it's my heritage too. Can I please go, Ma? Can I?"

I tried to avoid that discussion, as I knew that with everything going on, financially we would not be able to afford it. "You were awesome. I could hear you singing above the rest. So what are the plans for tonight?"

"We're going to dinner with Haley and her parents—is that okay, Ma?"

"Of course it is."

Haley's divorced parents were handsome, especially her father. He was this dashing, gorgeous hunk of a man—a tall, silver-haired professional fox—who I was sure could have his pick of any woman. These parents loved Haley and had obviously put their differences aside to do the right thing for her. In comparison, even though I was married, I thought how different and dysfunctional our two families seemed to be. I glanced over and watched Haley and her parents interact as they mingled in the crowd.

"Mom, you're staring at them."

"I'm really just wondering why it all looks so perfect when it's not, and yet they present such a united, happy harmony."

"Yeah, well, you obviously haven't been too observant. He's been eyeing every woman in the room."

Shocked, I said, "And how would you know who he's eyeing?" We both rolled our eyes and grinned. We were having fun and bonding. It felt good, even if it was at their expense.

Later, when we were all seated at La Foitina's Restaurant, Haley's dad eloquently stated, "Those two have really hit it off. Laura's a good influence."

"Thanks, they're both great gals. We're blessed."

Pleasantries were rampant as we shared our views on our daughters and their education, but the rest of our lives were a million miles apart. I shuffled my long legs and accidentally stepped on Haley's dad's foot. I was embarrassed. What did he think? I don't think he noticed. Good. Whew. Dummy Connie! And then—was I crazy? I felt something on my foot. Immediately I shifted my legs, but there it was again, and then a third time. He was playing footsie with me, all the while conversing about our wonderful daughters.

My face flushed, and I was fearful of eye contact. I rushed through dinner. "I need to excuse myself. It's late and I'm on call. You know—the *semper paratus* mode."

"Always prepared," said Laura. "Did you forget I'm taking Latin?"

"I'm impressed. I also took Latin at my high school in Moose Jaw."

"Where—did I hear right?" asked Haley's dad.

"Yup, my mom's from Moose Jaw. She's Canadian," Laura said.

I jested. "Thank goodness years ago when I left Moose Jaw, I had that Mountie escort and dog sled that got me from the prairies to Vancouver, to then hop a plane for Honolulu. That's where I met Laura's dad, and now we have this special young lady." How I loved the reaction from that made-up story. I kissed Laura, smiled, and bowed out, anxious to get home and check on Andrew's night out.

It was late when I got there. I could see a light in the family room. Andrew would be home by now. I entered the kitchen, kicked off my shoes, still laughing at the antics of the evening. "Andrew, tell me about your big evening out!" I poured a glass of wine and headed into the family room.

In a trance, he stared at the TV. He was still dressed in his pressed shirt and pants and polished orthopedic shoes. I was immediately confused.

"What's the matter, sweetie? Didn't you have a good time? Did you forget your money? Was it a bad movie? What?"

He continued to stare at the TV, not moving or speaking. Now I was concerned.

"Andrew, what happened?"

Sobbing, he broke down. "Ma, I waited all night. They . . . blew me off. No one called me. I'm hideous and ugly. No one wants to be seen with me."

In tears, I was vehement. "Don't ever say that—it isn't true. You are the most handsome and courageous young man I, and your friends, will ever know."

I knew he felt awkward because he walked with a limp, and that was why he worked so hard in PT, determined to overcome it. He felt once his gait was fixed, he'd look like he used to, before the accident. In reality, dealing with his deficits was just too painful for him, making him feel hideous and ugly. And fortunately or unfortunately, he could remember exactly how he had been before the accident. The boy who loved being at the center of attention and who dreamed of the Ivy League.

He was still very handsome. The accident had not altered his good looks, only his perception of himself.

I was furious. My heart felt stabbed and ripped open, my stomach sick. How on earth could anyone do this? And these were his friends? I wanted to call the parents, but I knew that would only make things worse. Did these kids have any idea of the emotional damage they had inflicted on my child? I wanted to hurt them and make them pay for what they had done to Andrew.

Soon I came to my senses and realized his friends were young and unable to understand or respond to the long-term ripple effect of the accident, and they also were struggling with Andrew's terrible catastrophe.

Later that week I met with my therapist and we discussed the evening with Haley's dad, and she concluded he was probably waiting for a phone call from me. I was so naive. "But, Rosemary, his ex-wife and daughter are friends of mine, and I'm still married — even though I'm no longer wearing my wedding band. I couldn't do that and live with myself. What if someone found out?"

"Connie, many people play by different rules than you do. I don't condone it, but it's reality."

I felt like a dumb blonde. James had often told me that he protected me from the real world. But that didn't change the fact that by November, I was at my wits' end with him. I could no longer live with the alcohol, and we needed to discuss the problem seriously and openly. He agreed that a weekend away would be a start. We made dinner plans and reservations for a hotel close by. I relished the idea.

Saturday morning, we left for Hartford and went shopping for everyone. A good start. But by afternoon he started drinking, and I was turned off. I had no desire to be intimate with an inebriated man. The weekend was a disaster, and we came home early, barely speaking.

"At this rate you're going to pull everyone into hell, Con!" James predicted.

I realized there was no more negotiating. Either James agreed to counseling or the marriage was over. For the first time he knew I was serious, and we made an appointment to see my psychiatrist, Dr. McMase, right after the New Year.

Christmas was around the corner. My parents sent us money to come to Canada and spend the holiday with them. James had just started his new job and felt he couldn't get away, so I made plans without him. He was stubborn, and I refused to beg. He would suffer the consequences without his family. Maybe that reality was what he needed. I was practicing tough love, hoping it would work.

We arrived in Moose Jaw, and my parents couldn't do enough to make our stay festive and fun. My mother constantly cooked, baked, and waited on everyone. The freezer was full of goodies, and everyone continually snacked. But my father drank more than he used to.

Andrew, however, was disruptive and put me in a nasty, stressed-out mood. My mother was patient and understanding, always giving him the benefit of the doubt, even when he looked her in the eye and lied to her. He was caught pounding nails in the basement bathroom but denied it. He set off firecrackers in the family room and burned the carpet. When he was caught with porn magazines, I went off the deep end. I had no patience and couldn't understand why he was being so disruptive in my parents' home, when they were being nothing but kind and generous.

Laura was also no prize. She was difficult, rude, and had a terrible attitude toward her cousin Tanya. Between her and Andrew it was constant havoc. When the rest of us went shopping in Regina, I refused to take Laura along.

Finally, my mother got wind of Laura's negative comments. Mom would never harm a fly, let alone confront her grandchildren, but at this point she verbally disciplined her. "Laura, you wouldn't speak to Grandma Kane like that, would you?"

"If I felt like it, I would, and it's none of your business!"

How dare she speak to my mother—her grandmother—in that tone? She would be grounded forever when we returned home. It was good that Todd was around, always enjoyable and never a problem.

He tried to keep Andrew and Laura in line, but it was no easy job. This family was slowly spiraling into hell as James had predicted.

We returned home and a somber, sober James picked us up at the airport. Later we celebrated Christmas with him and exchanged our many gifts. He cried. "It was awful without my family. I was going to fly up last minute, but the fare was outrageous."

I hoped all this would make him realize how important his family was and that he needed to give up alcohol totally. Perhaps this would all turn out for the best.

In January, James and I had our first meeting with Dr. McMase. I was in the waiting room reading a magazine, when James entered, wearing a suit, starched white shirt, and snappy silk tie I'd gotten at a discount store for three dollars. He was so handsome that he still made my heart thump. Even though he looked like Mr. GQ, I could tell he was very nervous.

Psychotherapy was uncomfortable, foreign, and out of his league. He was a sensitive man but found it nearly impossible to discuss his feelings openly. I blamed his difficulty on his mother, who had told him from the time he was an infant that he was an unwanted child. In return he punished her by refusing to speak until he was four, although he actually knew how, while she dragged him all over the Northeast from one specialist to another.

James opened his daily planner and handed me a piece of paper. On it was written, *Con, I love you more than anything in this world. I can't imagine life without you at my side. Love, James.* I was touched by the note. I smiled, patted him on the knee, and said, "Thanks, everything's going to be all right." And I truly thought it would be.

Dr. McMase introduced himself to James and nodded.

"James, why don't you come in alone first, and then I'll talk to Connie. Then I'll bring you both in together. Is that okay with you?"

Tentatively James responded, "Okay, Doc."

I waited outside, dying to hear their conversation. I even rolled up a magazine and put it to my ear to the wall but heard nothing. After what seemed like eternity, it was my turn, and then we went in together. James complained about my mood swings and disinterest in sex. My only complaint was the alcohol. Dr. McMase pointed out that in order for couples counseling to work, both parties must be substance-free. We agreed to meet a week later at James's convenience.

But the second meeting went nowhere, as James continually talked in circles, never bringing up his drinking. He felt alcohol played no role in our problems and that it was under control. Dr. McMase moved ever so cautiously with him, so as not to accuse or judge and scare him away.

By the fourth session, James showed up emotionally distressed, angry, and with a strong alcohol odor. He insisted the only reason he showed up was I had given him an ultimatum—that I was a schizophrenic and he felt Dr. McMase should be paying more attention to my problems than his.

"James, I can smell alcohol on you, and there is no way we can resolve any problems as long as you are drinking. I feel you need an inpatient treatment program, and one can be arranged with a simple phone call."

I added, "James, we have great insurance, and you can go to the best facility in the country. I'll support you through this with whatever needs to be done. Please."

He answered, "I don't need an inpatient program. I can stop on my own."

Dr. McMase pinned him down. "Okay, James, then what you are telling me is that you can remain alcohol-free on your own for thirty days?"

Defiantly, James said, "Yes, Doc, I can." Agitated, he stood up and walked out of the room.

And he did stop drinking.

It was now a fine balancing act between my job, Andrew, Laura, and James. At least Todd was settled and secure in college. I had saved one. Or at least I thought I had. I felt pulled constantly, trying to do the right thing for all of them, which left no time for me. Occasionally my friend Maria came over, or vice versa. And I talked and often walked with Liz. These were the only two friends who knew what was going on. I started power walking, which led to a personal wellness program that would eventually save my life.

One brisk January evening I said to James, "I'm going for a walk. Maggie's coming with me." I quickly increased my power walk into a run. My arms and legs synchronized as I breathed deeply. Suddenly I smelled a sweet floral scent. The faster I ran, the more intense the aroma became. It was impossible for flowers to be blooming in winter, but I smelled them. I forgot the stress at home and realized there was a part of me that was very much alive, and that if I continued to exercise I could become healthy and even enjoy life again. It was a runner's high, a euphoric experience in which my body produced endogenous opiates, which gave a sensation of feeling high. To me this was a sign from God on how to proceed and survive. And I could do this.

I walked into the house happy and invigorated, almost singing, "I'm home."

James looked at me quizzically. "Ma's taken her happy pills."

In February 1989 James lost his job. He blamed everything and everybody. A few days later I arrived home from work to find him in the kitchen with a beer in hand.

"James, you're drinking."

"That's right. That's what this is." He proudly lifted the can to show me.

I tried to remain calm. I had made up my mind I was not backing down. "At Dr. McMase's you said you could remain alcohol-free for thirty days."

"And I told you, Con, neither you nor Dr. McMase are going to tell me what to do."

I was boiling and then exploded. "I've had it. I can't take any more of this. It's over, James." I ran to the bedroom in tears.

"Get over it, Con, and go take a nap."

Instead I went out for a run and then stopped to see Maria.

"If you ever need to get out of the house, just come — alone or with the children."

It was difficult to wear a happy face to work, and my lesson plans were suffering. I decided to start sex education and anatomy, which I could teach without preparation. Already, two of my brightest girls had become pregnant after eighth-grade graduation parties. I separated the boys and girls, and started the class by asking the girls one relevant question: "Do you know where that penis has been? No, you don't." They all giggled at my frankness with the terminology. At parent conferences I was thanked.

Andrew, surprisingly, had adjusted beautifully to the new year. The guidance counselor, teachers, and home tutor enjoyed working with him and were in constant communication with me. In math he had a B+ average. The class worked on graphing, which was difficult, but he held his own. In Spanish he earned an A, English a B+, and in economics a B. He dropped biology because it was too difficult. Every day he attended the resource center for support from the learning disability teacher.

His teachers' comments were gratifying. His Spanish teacher wrote, "Andrew is a big help in class to other students who don't understand. He always participates and asks relevant questions. I am very lucky to be Andrew's teacher again. Keep up the good work." His political science teacher wrote, "He is working very hard. His grades have improved and probably will continue to do so." From the resource room came these comments: "Andrew is utilizing the computer and understands math much quicker. He uses his time wisely and always asks for help when he needs it." His geometry teacher wrote, "Andrew's effort is constantly good."

I now considered myself at a master's level for the PPT, and I came to the meetings prepared to work and ask questions about his program, the number of sessions he required, what they covered, how often, and how many hours per week. Most importantly, I requested a progress report from all the therapists and teachers, as well as open discussion. I needed to know his whereabouts every minute of every day. And I insisted it must all be written down. I had learned that far too well.

I was happy and felt the plan was perfect. However, at the meetings Dr. Jinnie never spoke directly to me or smiled. It was obvious she was not fond of advocating parents who were proactive and took matters into their own hands without her permission. And, yes, perhaps I was guilty of being too strong, but that was my job. I would put nothing on hold for Andrew. Time was of the essence, and all the time and effort we'd put in so far had paid off.

I was amazed that Andrew's attitude in school was so positive since James's drinking was again escalating. One afternoon I picked him up from school, and when we got home James was in a drunken half-comatose state, asleep in the family room. He tried to get up but could barely stand, let alone walk, and rolled off the couch onto the floor. Andrew took one pained look at him, and his right arm went into spasm, shaking. "I can't stand looking at you anymore. Every day you're drunk. You disgust me."

James wobbled from side to side in an attempt to walk to the bedroom, his pants nearly falling off. Andrew followed him, more agitated, and began shoving and pushing him. James held his hands up to protect himself as he fumbled and fell to the floor.

I said, "Andrew, he won't remember any of this. Leave him alone."

James flopped into bed. Andrew and I left. I redirected Andrew into the family room and tried to distract him from what had happened. It took a while before he was smiling again.

That was it. I would start divorce proceedings. I couldn't have Andrew subjected to this environment any more. If we continued, James would kill us emotionally and physically. It was time to stop the madness. I could deal with Andrew and his problems, but I could no longer tolerate James's drinking. The War of the Kanes had begun.

I involved two good friends who were attorneys, but James wouldn't listen to reason. So they gave me the name of a respected divorce attorney. I then got a court order to get James out of the house. And James's threat from the weekend we'd spent away, and from whenever I'd brought up divorce, echoed in my ears: "I'm warning you—if you pursue this, you'll see a side of me you've never seen before."

Then I received a letter from a home equity loan we had set up for Todd's college tuition. James had taken out half of the money. I called the bank manager, informed him what was going on, and closed the account. For days I was in complete shock. Was James capable of this behavior, or was someone giving him bad advice? And did they realize he had a child with a handicap? I was not backing down, not realizing how ugly it was going to get.

Reluctantly, James moved in with his parents. My sister-in-law, Trudy, acknowledged she would have thrown him out years ago. I was relieved to have her on my side. A few weeks later she called. "Con, James can't live with my parents. They're too old, and he'll kill them. You have to take him back."

"No, I can't!"

"Yes, you'll have to. That court order won't stick, and you know it."

I knew it wouldn't, but I needed him out, even for a short period of time, to maintain our sanity and to prove I was serious.

My mother desperately needed a break from my father's escalating drinking problem, so she planned a spring vacation to Acapulco, and asked my sister Pat and me to join her, all expenses paid. I was at my wits' end, so the timing was perfect, and friends would take care of Andrew and Laura. I would not divulge my present state to my mom or sister. The less they knew, the better.

In Mexico, the weather was sunny, and the Acapulco Princess Hotel was grand. We sunned, walked, shopped, and dined. But every evening I returned to bed early and wanted nothing to do with the nightlife. I was tense and ready to burst from the previous week's trauma. My mother and sister were astonished, as I was usually the life of the party, but they accepted this behavior without questioning me. After all, I was the *older* sister. For one who would never admit her age, I couldn't believe I even acknowledged this. I must have been in really bad shape!

I had decided to stay an extra day, so after waving good-bye to them, I proceeded to check out that night instead of the next morning. There was a huge error with the bill and I was left owing an enormous tab. I went to see the hotel manager and became so overwhelmed I started to cry. Then I advanced to hysteria and immediately returned to my room. Mexicans aren't used to Caucasian histrionics. I think the manager thought I was going to "off" myself, so he kept coming to check on me with a fresh supply of tea bags and cucumbers for my eyes, which were swollen like golf balls. He had never witnessed such a demonstration from a billing mix-up even though it was their error and was resolved. Little did he realize that I had been keeping the door to reality closed, but now, as I was about to return home, it had hit me in the face and erupted all over him. He offered me two free nights, "Because we have upset you."

I returned home to find that James had moved back into our house. I made an appointment to see my lawyer, and we served James with a subpoena.

When the sheriff came to serve the papers, I answered the door, showed him where James was, and then went to Laura's bedroom to hide.

The sheriff confronted James. "Mr. Kane, you must vacate this house. You'd better take some clothes with you."

"Yeah." I could hear James shuffling about in no hurry, paying little attention to the sheriff.

"Mr. Kane, you don't seem to understand. If you return here you'll be arrested."

Meanwhile, I was in Laura's bedroom, hiding under the sheets. I could hear James walking down the hallway. He opened the door, looked at me, and snarled, "You've gone too far this time, little girl!"

The sheriff was behind him. "Just keep moving, Mr. Kane."

I lay in bed trembling and terrified. Had I gone too far?

I thought James would go to his parents', but the following evening Dee called, screaming hysterically. "James never came home last night!"

I didn't respond.

"How could you serve him with a subpoena when he's treated you like a queen all these years? He's going through hard times, and you throw him out! You're a sick girl, Connie. If anything happens to him, it will be all your fault."

Click, the phone was dead. Momentarily I was frozen. Then I came to my senses. More than likely he was on a binge, but what if he wasn't? I called Rosemary, and she fit me in for a session.

The next day the phone rang and rang. Everyone was upset with me and worried about James. I explained I was divorcing him, but all I heard was, "Con, he loves you."

I knew he loved me, but he loved alcohol more. No one cared about what the children and I were going through. They just remembered the former James Kane, a kind, caring guy. They didn't know the present James Kane—the alcoholic in the advanced stage of the disease. Alcoholism is slow, insidious, and progressive. It continues over years and years with minor changes until finally it progresses to the final stages, characterized by the loss of health, job, and family. We were there.

The following Monday morning James showed up at the house, and he looked terrible. I let him in even though I knew I shouldn't. He had gone to a cheap hotel, binged, and crashed for three days. He said he did a lot of thinking and wasn't angry with me anymore and blamed everything on "poor legal advice." He wouldn't fight me anymore and was going to stay with his folks. A few weeks later he called me for a dinner date, to talk.

"Yes, as long as you're sober," I said.

Emphatically he replied, "Of course."

At the restaurant I sat down. He was shaking. Immediately I could tell he had been drinking. It saddened me to watch him go through such pains to try to do and say the right thing. However, in my heart, I also knew if we were to win this terrible battle of denial and alcoholism, I had to be consistent. Fighting for love was difficult. I addressed his drinking and he admitted he had been. "I was like a school kid getting ready for a date. I even cut myself shaving."

I looked at his beautiful face and smiled. "James, you're still a little boy and I love you, but I have to leave." He started to beg me as he walked me outside to my car.

"I've got motel reservations!"

"I told you no alcohol, and I meant it!"

He was angry and shouted for everyone to hear, "I don't know why you got married. You should have been a nun or a lesbian."

I watched him speed away, hoping he wouldn't hit or kill some innocent person. If he just stayed out of the house, I would not pursue the divorce.

Two weeks after our disastrous dinner date, as I drove through Middlebury, in the distance I could I see a jogger and could tell by the body movements it was Andrew. He was jogging four miles a day. I slowed down to greet his healthy, sweaty face. In return he was shaking, frowning, and scared.

"Ma, Dad came to visit. He was drunk and fell into the glass slider in the living room. I thought he was dead . . . We called Mum-mum and . . . and they took him to the hospital."

"Oh my God, Andrew, are you all right?"

"Yeah, I'm gonna finish running."

"Was Laura home?"

"Yeah."

"Oh, my God! I'll see you later." I sped home and rushed into the living room to find shattered glass everywhere. I shouted, "Laura, Laura!" There was no answer. A few minutes later she walked into the house with her godfather, our next-door neighbor Dr. Sean. I hugged her petrified, shaking body until she was settled.

Then I frantically called Dee. "How is James? The kids said it was terrible. They thought he was dead. Is he in the hospital? Is he okay?"

Dee was calm and sarcastic. "And aren't we the concerned one? James is right here with me. There's nothing wrong with him. He accidentally tripped. Don't make a mountain out of a molehill. Con, you're really sick! All these years he treated you like a queen, and you threw him out when he needed you most. This is all your fault. I don't know how you live with yourself."

Click. The phone went dead.

"Bitch." Everyone was traumatized and worried about James, and she had turned it around and made everything my fault.

The next morning James arrived at the house as the children were having breakfast and getting ready for school. He was remorseful and ashamed as he apologized to them. He was sober, sweet, and gentle, perfectly manicured, and holding a tape measure. "That's it. Yesterday really scared me. You're right—I've got to stop drinking, and I am, as of right now. I'm sorry for what I put all of you through. I'll measure the glass slider and have it fixed today."

I knew he was utterly serious and sincere at that moment. However, I also knew that unless he got into a substance-abuse program and was detoxed, there was no way he could stop drinking on his own. Mentally he wanted to quit, but physically his body would not allow him to. He measured the slider and walked over to me. "Con, could I come home for dinner tonight?"

"Sure, James. See if you can make it early to see the kids, around four?"

I optimistically looked forward to the evening. However, four, five, and six o'clock came and went, and no James. At eight o'clock the phone call came. "Con, I'm sorry. I started drinking at noon."

"I'm sorry too. Good-bye."

My job at Sacred Family was coming to an end. It had been a busy year with daily lesson plans, but being a nurse had made it easier. The only criteria the students had to meet in order to pass was to listen and partake in class. Two boys openly refused. I failed them both. Bad, bad Moose Jaw girl!

Andrew successfully completed his sophomore school year doing exceptionally well academically, even though his home environment was a disastrous roller coaster with the constant turmoil from James's presence. But of late, something was not right with him.

Laura finished her year at Westin, again doing mediocre work. Her friends there were gone, and I was happily rid of that influence until fall. She was still rebellious but got a job at a local yogurt shop, and I hoped that would keep her busy.

Todd finished his first year at Northeastern and came home for the summer. He had the same summer job as last year, as a handyman at a factory. His stable presence helped maintain some semblance of normalcy in our dysfunctional family.

I made it mandatory for everyone to be in counseling for the summer. Fortunately the excellent health coverage from my teaching at Sacred Family paid for everything. All this turmoil had to affect the children. Thank God I had Rosemary, and was often seeing her three times a week. The house was quieter with James living with his parents. He made no effort to spend time with the kids. Every now and then he came over, under the pretense of seeing them, but always ended up in the basement. I had supposed he missed tinkering in his workshop—how stupid was I?

Andrew was working, doing odd jobs for a wealthy bachelor who liked him. He continued his summer rehab program and saw Dr. Smine twice a week. This was less hectic for him, but a bit busy for me. But my teaching job was finished, and I was going to be home all summer with a project to wallpaper the kitchen. In the fall, when everyone was back in school, I would return to nursing. Until then, my job was Andrew and his success. That was one of my many mistakes. It should have been Andrew's, Laura's, and Todd's successes.

By the end of June, Andrew was paranoid, confused, unfocused, and irritable. I shared my concerns with Dr. Smine, who had noticed the same symptoms. He upped his sessions.

I was with Andrew constantly, except when I went to bed. I couldn't put my finger on what was going on with him, but I was suspicious that he was taking my car when I was asleep. He vehemently denied it. One hot afternoon as we were gardening, he paced nervously, attempting projects but unable to complete them.

Moments later, I saw my car going down the street. I ran into the house and frantically called the police, who knew the Kanes very well.

"It's Connie Kane on Green Road. Something's not right with my son Andrew, and he just took off down the hill driving my car, license plate C.KANE. I have no idea where he might be going, and you know he does not have a driver's license and is partially paralyzed."

Andrew would remain permanently partially paralyzed on the right side of his body. His right hand suffered the greatest damage, with a residual use of only about five percent. But with the body's natural ability to heal, and two years of extensive rehabilitation that exercised his muscles and helped to heal his brain's relearning process, his legs were certainly strong enough to engage and push a gas pedal and his hands could maneuver and turn a steering wheel.

Thirty minutes later, the phone rang. Pacing, my head swimming, I grabbed the receiver.

"It's Dee. Andrew just drove over here in your car."

"Thank God he's all right. I've been worried sick!"

"We'll bring him home." *Click.* The phone went dead.

Soon Dee arrived with Andrew in tow. Andrew said, "Ma, I don't want to talk about it. I'm sorry and just want to go to my room."

"That's okay, sweetie. You lie down and rest."

I tried to explain the situation to Dee. "Something's going on with him, but I don't know what it is. Even his therapist is concerned. I feel that soon he will be totally out of control. I'm frustrated and fearful." I began to cry.

Unconcerned, Dee changed the subject to James. "What is going on in this house? Are you giving James enough sex? I told him not to marry you."

Unprepared for her attack, my eyes went as wide as saucers. I scrambled for words. "Dee, I'm divorcing him if the drinking doesn't stop."

"Learn to live with it, Queen. Everyone else does!"

"Well, not me!"

"Now hear me—you'll never get this house or a dime from us. We'll put you on the street, and you'll be working the rest of your life!"

My nostrils flared. "It's time for you to leave!"

She started to push out the door. "And I want back the cut glass bowl I gave you."

"The one you gave us for a wedding gift?

"Yes!"

Under my breath I muttered, "you bitch." Without hesitation I went to the dining room, grabbed it, and shoved it into her hands. "Take it!"

Shocked, she stared at me momentarily, then pushed out the door. I went to my room and popped an Ativan. As soon as my turbulent state calmed, I called Dr. Smine to apprise him of the recent events, and to ask him if he could see Andrew.

He told me, "Bring him in at three thirty."

I tiptoed to Andrew's room, where he lay staring at the ceiling. "Sweetie, I've made an appointment for you to see Dr. Smine today. You'll feel better, and we'll get to the bottom of this."

He started to cry. "Why is this happening to me? What's causing it?"

At Dr. Smine's office, I tried to relax in the waiting room even though my heart was bleeding. Ten minutes later Andrew bolted out of the session. Dr. Smine followed behind, wide-eyed and dazed. Andrew's behavior was bizarre, and he was escalating.

"I'm not coming here any longer. He's gay!"

I was shocked.

"Please call me later, Mrs. Kane."

Where was this coming from? Perhaps Andrew just needed to go home and relax. On the way home he lay with the front seat reclined, his eyes twitching but closed. At home he seemed once again empowered. He eyes darted back and forth at me, oddly piercing into me. His six-foot frame towered over me, and his right hand was red, shaking in spasm.

"I can't take this. I can't take this anymore!" He paced about the kitchen and put his hands over his ears to block out some voice he seemed to hear. Then he stopped and stood in front of the butcher block table and grabbed a large knife.

I shrieked in terror, "Andrew, please put the knife down. I'll take you to the hospital now. We'll fix it. I promise. Please put the knife down!"

He was deaf to my pleas. He took the knife, aimed it over his wrist, and sliced across the veins, once and then a second time.

I gasped in horror as I watched the blood oozing from his wrist drip slowly onto the butcher block.

Chapter Nine

June 1988–November 1989

EN ROUTE TO MEMORIAL HOSPITAL, I was speeding yet cautious, if that's possible. Andrew was emotional, unmanageable, and confused, and I feared he might open the car door and jump out. Fortunately, the hospital was only fifteen minutes away.

I pulled up to the emergency entrance, and a security guard approached. I tried to remain calm. Without Andrew's awareness, I motioned with my eyes about the gravity of the situation—that he could escalate and cause more of a crisis. I shuddered at the blood-soaked towel wrapped around his wrist. It appeared the wound had stopped bleeding. Perhaps only a few sutures would be necessary. However, it was obvious that Andrew's thought processes were severely wounded. I wasn't sure how this could have happened under my constant surveillance. Where had I gone wrong?

After jumping out of the car, I positioned myself in front of the security guard so Andrew could not see the terror on my face. I whispered, "My son needs help." I motioned to the bloody towel wrapped around his wrist. "Can you please carefully escort him into the ER? I want to run ahead and speak to the triage nurse, alone. I know her. I'm a nurse and work here in the OR. My son just made a suicide attempt, and we need to see a doctor immediately." My voice was tense and pleading, but it was the look of fear that must have quickly alerted him to call another security guard. Andrew was led into a small cubicle.

In the ER, Andrew was disoriented, in a constant state of aimless activity, agitated, delusional, and paranoid. It appeared that he was responding to auditory and visual hallucinations. I was terrified and didn't know what was going on, or how all this related to his brain injury. I did know we desperately needed help. After he was sutured up, with no damage to any tendons or nerves, and after what seemed like hours, a psychiatrist finally showed up. He tried to perform a mental status evaluation, but Andrew's psychotic state made it impossible. He could not explain his feelings and remained guarded. "I don't know, I don't know. I don't think I should be speaking to you." His speech was incoherent and unintelligible, but he clearly denied being suicidal. He was not dangerous, even though at one point he bolted out of the cubicle, only to return moments later.

The psychiatrist diagnosed him with organic brain syndrome—a general term used when a diagnostician is not sure what is happening to the patient. It is a diagnosis for psychosis induced by brain changes in which the patient's character is changed. He becomes less stable and more irritable, and has frequent, angry outbursts. Gradually he deteriorates, and sooner or later memory, comprehension, and orientation are affected. The cause could be alcohol, narcotics, syphilis, poisons, chronic infections, encephalitis, or brain tumors, among others.

On July 6, 1988, at three a.m., almost two years to the day of his accident, Andrew was admitted to the Adolescent Psychiatric Unit. Even though I was fatigued, my focus was totally on Andrew. I'd forgotten to be tired as I was escorted to a small conference room. Andrew was exhausted and taken to his room. I was surprised at his compliance as he hobbled down a hallway. This was so unfair. When was he going to get a break? When would God finally hear my prayers? Or was there a God? Sleep would overcome him, and in the morning his situation would look better and brighter. Yes, it would.

In the conference room I sat with the admitting nurse, whom I knew from Middlebury. She avoided eye contact and pretended she didn't know me. "Excuse me, Mrs. Post, we know each other. Our children have gone to school together for years. We were all just at confirmation."

She looked awkward and foolish all at once. "Oh, Mrs. Kane, I didn't recognize you."

Right—I'd changed my face for the occasion. I sat fidgeting in the chair, pondering her inappropriate behavior. What or who would be taking care of my Andrew? Was this the best place for him?

The next day I arrived and met with the team. I advised them that they had to be careful with medication, due to his sensitive and compromised central nervous system, which was already altering his gait. He did not remember how he got to the hospital, and due to his rapidly fluctuating emotional state was considered a fall risk and put on one-to-one supervision.

Over the next few days, the psychiatrist evaluated and tested Andrew. He found him to be psychotic with impaired memory, and poor attention, concentration, judgment, and insight. His IQ was lowered. I felt it much too early to evaluate IQ, but they had their own protocols. Andrew's treatment plan was to attend individual and group meetings and to have a complete medical workup: blood, urine, chest X-ray, EEG, brain CAT scan. The psychiatrist would review his files from Newington Children's Hospital, Region 10 high school, Daview Rehabilitation, and notes from his private psychiatrists. Andrew was started on Haldol for psychosis and Benadryl for sleep. I was relieved that they were so thorough.

On the third day, he became aggressive and struck an employee in the eye. I was shocked. This was atypical for him—he was nonviolent. For his own safety, he was put into soft restraints. The team felt that the least amount of stimuli was imperative, and restraining him in a quiet room would help his agitation and unstable emotional state. However, he was terrified and yelled, "I want to call my mom. I haven't seen her, and I'm afraid she's dead. Where is my mom?"

The doctors changed his meds continually, unsuccessfully. One minute he was too sedated, almost comatose, rigid, sweating, and only able to grunt. The next, he was manic and out of control. The nursing staff and I were very concerned. When he started yelling, "Someone is trying to kill me!" the doctor called me in, hoping the sight of me would help allay his fears. When I arrived, I was stunned at what confronted me.

There was my baby, lying in bed, his arms and legs in thick leather restraints, as if he were awaiting crucifixion. Hadn't he been scorned and jeered enough? He was sound asleep, heavily drugged, and in worse condition than when I had left. He was sweating and almost naked from continuous restlessness. Momentarily, he roused, unable to speak, responding only by nodding his head. Occasionally, his eyes would open and roll almost involuntarily to stare at the ceiling. Watching him was agony, and my heart raced with every breath I took.

The staff requested that I stay only for a short time, to reduce stimuli. I trusted that they knew best, yet cried all the way home. What would I tell Todd and Laura? How would they react? They were dealing with enough pain, and this might be way too much. When I did discuss Andrew's condition, they told me they had caught him smoking marijuana and sneaking alcohol. I blamed myself and couldn't imagine how I had not noticed, wondering what more I should have done.

I was later told that my in-laws, Dee and James Sr., showed up at the unit, but because of Andrew's serious condition they were not allowed in. Dee staged one of her demonic scenes, causing the staff to gather.

"How dare you tell me I can't visit? We're his grandparents. Who's in charge here? I want to speak to them right now." As they left the building, Dee shook her cane at James Sr., who was at the receiving end of her wrath. I learned later that the staff then quietly made bets on her ability to drive carefully as they watched her hobble to her car. In the driver's seat she started the car, jerked it into reverse, and then screeched out of the lot. The staff dubbed them "the Bickersons."

Then James came to visit, clearly drunk, and created another scene. "Mr. Kane, it is strict hospital policy that anyone suspected of using drugs or alcohol will not be allowed on the unit. We can smell alcohol on you." Security was called, and he was escorted off the premises.

The behavioral team met every week to discuss Andrew's issues: coping with alcohol and marijuana use, acute psychotic condition, potential for injury of self, family dysfunction, and the importance of physical mobility. His level of social stress, with the addition of his brain injury, soared his rating to "extreme." They requested a family session. A sober James did attend but didn't participate. I was just happy he was there in body for Andrew.

A weekly visit was all James could manage, even though he lived five minutes from the hospital. I hoped he would visit more often, as the staff felt it therapeutic for Andrew to see him. But then James was heard sabotaging plans and programs, causing confusion and frustration for Andrew. He would say things like, "You don't need that medicine, Andrew. Don't take it."

During my time away from the hospital, I did a great deal of soul searching. I concluded that if I had divorced James years ago, Andrew would not be going through this now. I felt the impending divorce was causing most of his stress. But I needed sanity.

When I visited during Andrew's second week, he thought I smelled "fishy." The staff explained that someone had heated up scallops, but he was unable to process this and became more upset. "My mother never showered, and she's polluting the air on the unit. Ma, how could you not shower? You're embarrassing me, and I think you better leave until you're clean."

I left in tears. He was getting worse. When I returned home, I watered the schefflera plant and broke down just looking at it. It continued to grow healthy—green and vibrant. It was if the plant was telling me that in time Andrew would also grow healthy, and I was not to give up.

That evening Todd and Laura went to visit. Andrew continued to obsess. They were shaken to witness their brother's behavior. The nurses tried to console them and explain what was going on.

"What's going to happen to him?" Todd whispered to Laura, his eyes glazed in tears. That was enough for them. They couldn't take seeing Andrew so out of touch with reality and needed refuge away from this crazy house that was now their brother's home.

Eventually the team conferences became more positive, as Andrew's doctors discontinued the Haldol and started him on Trilafon. His thinking was clearer, and he was able to sit up and read a newspaper, but still needed help bathing and dressing. He continued to say, "My mother's going to die and leave me." On a positive note, I no longer smelled fishy. Whew!

One crisis followed another. While brushing his teeth, he squeezed the tube, and the cap popped into his mouth and he swallowed it. Within seconds he was in respiratory distress, his lips blue, but was saved by the Heimlich maneuver. The cap was expelled, and immediately he was taken to the ER, where an ear, nose, and throat specialist examined him for throat trauma. He had no permanent injury but would be hoarse for a few days. A few minutes after the incident, the nurse called me at home and relayed the details. "He's okay and will be back on the unit shortly."

I was drained by the call but made a quick trip to the hospital just to see him and make sure he was okay.

My life was in a constant state of crisis, and stress continually churned internally. How much more could I take, and what was all this doing to my heart? I had already been put on hypertensive medication, but I needed an extensive physical to make sure I stayed healthy for this ordeal. I'm sure, *many* thought a psych evaluation would be more on target!

Once again, Andrew had come close to death, but later that day when he asked me to join him in a game of Ping-Pong, I knew it was a cue that he was recovering.

A nurse called me later and said, "Mrs. Kane, you'll be proud to know that at our closing group discussion, Andrew thanked the community for all the care and concern he's received."

That was the wonderful Andrew we all loved.

By the third team meeting he had improved, was less psychotic, and was responding positively to the medications. It was still a constant balancing act between his physiological and psychological issues, and he was still overmedicated. I was concerned that through all this trial and error, the doctors were using him as a guinea pig, due to their lack of TBI knowledge. TBI had only been diagnosed in the 1980's, so this was new to many, which frustrated me. I wondered what our next step would be and was concerned about his speech and physical therapy programs being put on hold. I felt his improvement was too slow and there was no discussion of discharge, probably due to the fact that I had great health insurance.

At the family sessions, Andrew was unable to participate and show insight into the family dysfunction, and he minimized the effect it had on him.

James had his alcoholism and need for sobriety addressed, to which he responded, "No one tells James Kane what to do. I won't be attending any more witch hunts."

Laura tried to visit Andrew often. She just wanted the brother she loved back and viewed his hospital stay as temporary, but it frightened her.

Andrew's loss was difficult to understand and endure. Physically, he was the same. But emotionally, sometimes he was the same and sometimes he wasn't. Part of him was gone and dead, yet we could not grieve the loss because part of him was alive and the same. The more we learned about TBI, the more complex it became, but we would never stop trying to comprehend.

For James and his family, their denial and dysfunction was almost pathological.

By Andrew's fifth week he had better self-control and only sporadic signs of psychotic behavior, and he manifested no visual or auditory hallucinations. But he was depressed and in no way back to his baseline. Even though he was cooperative and steady on his feet, he was not ready to come home. The social worker and I felt it was time to check out TBI facilities. The hospital had gotten him through the crisis, but it had become merely a holding area. He needed a specialized program to regain what he had lost.

Meanwhile, Dr. Smine called to say he was concerned by Andrew's social isolation, confusion, and insecurity, which seemed to stem from overwhelming family issues. He pointed out that these issues would affect his adaptation for improving future academic and social skills, and that we'd see a stark contrast to the gains he'd made.

There were few TBI facilities in our area that included psychiatry, rehabilitation, and education. Could Andrew have a mental illness? If he did, I would be furious with God. There were so many decisions to make, and it was all up to me. I was loathing James for not visiting or helping. He appeared not to care, and I pitied his utter lack of self-control. But on the other hand, his attempts at sabotaging Andrew's progress drove me wild. James felt no sense of obligation and was certain I would take care of everything. After all, I was a nurse. But he forgot I was a mother first.

I was elated when the social worker found an excellent TBI facility called Highgate in New Hampshire, but it was very expensive and five hours away. She contacted them, and they were immediately interested in Andrew and said they would drive or fly me up to visit the facility. I was driven up, and on the way I read over the packet provided for me. On the cover was a photo of a young teen boy and girl working in a beautiful greenhouse that overlooked a plush green field and manicured trees. Inside was a photo of an Olympic outdoor pool, flanked by two large pristine New England saltbox-style buildings. Highgate encompassed two hundred acres, with small client houses nestled among the trees on a beautiful spacious campus in the White Mountains. It offered a healthy, homelike environment for children, adolescents, and adults who needed to rebuild their lives after head injury. There was a barn with cows and horses, dogs, and a state-of-the-art gymnasium that combined physical and occupational therapies.

The Highgate philosophy was that therapies such as physical, occupational, and speech need not be in a structured setting but could be accomplished as well—if not better—on various areas of the farm (depending on the activity and the program). This encouraged me. It seemed the program was tailor-made for Andrew.

During the tour, I was informed that when I came to visit Andrew, I would be put up at a nearby bed and breakfast, all expenses paid. By now I was salivating. Highgate was owned by a large corporation and considered the leader in head-injury rehabilitation in this country. I wanted this program for Andrew, but knew it would be a long shot, requiring battling insurance for the funding. The cost would amount to twenty to thirty thousand dollars a month, and in 1988, this was a tremendous amount of money. What was I going to do?

When I returned home, I walked early in the morning, tried to be optimistic, and saw Rosemary regularly. I would go to Mass daily and pray, *Please, God, make this happen—he deserves it. Are you listening, or do you even care anymore?* With all the turmoil in our lives I think the only way my strength endured was due to my strong belief in God. I never believed he wasn't always there for me.

The summer was almost over, and I hadn't even thought about a job. Andrew's predicament was taking a toll on me, and I was again gaunt. A friend of mine compared my so-called great legs (the reason James married me) to skinny chicken legs.

There wasn't a minute for anything but Andrew. I met often with the social worker who struggled daily with the insurance company. Andrew had to get into this program—it was the only one of its kind in the Northeast. For weeks we battled our insurance company to convince them that he met the criteria for admission. I called and begged every doctor I knew to call the insurance company on his behalf. And then we waited.

Meanwhile, at home, Laura had begun hanging out with a bunch of kids I wasn't totally comfortable with. She had a curfew, but I was exhausted and often in bed before she was home, so wasn't sure when she got in. I questioned her about her activities, but this always led to an argument. She was angry and secretive.

In one of his more lucid moments, James called her. "I know you're smoking marijuana, and it's going to stop now—do you understand?" When and how he came to that deduction was disturbing to both Laura and me. We wondered if he might have the police watching the house. Many mornings he had breakfast with them at the local diner. He never seemed to be working and just hung around nearby, even though he was living in the next town with his parents. Neighbors told me they'd seen him cruise the neighborhood. He seemed to be stalking us and the house. I began to feel I was in an Alfred Hitchcock movie. James had always subscribed to the philosophy of nonviolence, but he appeared to be very close to the edge and somehow knew too much of what was going on with us. I called the phone company to check the line to see if the phone had been tapped. They emphatically told me no. I believed them, but it was all very strange.

All the while, I was still contemplating the divorce. I knew I could raise my kids and handle all the family responsibilities alone, and it would be easier without James and his drinking, but between Andrew, Laura, Todd, and the insurance, it was overwhelming. I needed to get a job and still have enough time for Andrew. We had no savings—James had always relied on his parents for our retirement. We were supposed to grow old together, wrinkles and all, and retire back in Hawaii. Tears streamed down my cheeks. I felt totally abandoned.

Then I got the call from the social worker. "Andrew's been approved for funding, and you can take him to Highgate immediately. We did it!"

"No, *you* did it. We're forever indebted to you." Her words were a gift of relief. *And thank you, God. I'm sorry—I really never doubted you.*

Laura joined me on the five-hour drive to New Hampshire. En route, Andrew was quiet and docile, and appeared drugged and robotic.

On arrival we were met by staff members. Andrew would be living in a house with six other clients. He would have his own bedroom and bath, but that didn't seem to impress him. He was sad and depressed, his eyes glazed.

"Ma, you're gonna stick me so far away that no one will be able to come and visit me."

"I'll be up every week, and we'll explore New Hampshire together. But I can't speak for your dad." After a thorough orientation, a weary Laura and I left for the bed and breakfast Highgate had arranged for us. I slid between the fresh sheets. Sleep was a priority. I grabbed my trusty companions—my tranquilizers and rosary beads—popped an Ativan, and started to pray. Someday life would be normal, and I wouldn't need to rely on medication to sleep. Today was a gigantic start. Slowly my eyes closed, and I began to flow softly into a peaceful valley. I think I said two Hail Marys, and the angels finished the rest.

The next morning we stopped to say good-bye to Andrew. He was pensive and unsure of himself. He stared at me ambiguously with his beautiful brown eyes that pleaded for me to take him home, but he never uttered a word.

I told him, "I'll be back in one week. I promise."

Somberly, he answered, "A week is a long time, Ma."

"Honey, you're gonna be so busy, the time will fly. Promise me you'll work hard. Remember, this is only a minor setback. You'll be back on target before you know it. I love you."

As we approached the car, Laura grabbed my hand. "Dad is such a jerk. He never even came to see Andrew to say good-bye."

I didn't like to hear the children talk about their dad like that. It was all right for me but not for them. "Laura, your dad is a sick man."

The drive home was an opportunity to talk. She and I had been distancing. She had always been Daddy's little girl and now rarely saw him. I couldn't be a father, yet I desperately tried to be all she needed. She was still the baby, caught in the middle to constantly witness the family dissolution. I kept reassuring myself that she was strong and smart. I was so stupid.

"Mom, how does Dad seem to know everything that's going on in the house?"

"I don't know. I phoned the telephone company, and they assured me the phone is not being tapped. Your father is friendly with the local police . . . maybe they're helping him."

Three days later my mother called to tell me my dad was hospitalized with a rare blood condition. The doctors were not optimistic. I called Dr. McKenzie, the director at Highgate. "Tell Andrew I had to see Grandpa. He's sick. But I'll be back as soon as I can to see him."

Then I flew home to Moose Jaw.

Fortunately, my dad had been sent to the University Hospital in Saskatoon and within a week was stable. I returned home to discover that James had moved back in. I walked into the family room, where he was resting on the sofa, and said, "James, what are you doing here?"

"I'm in my home, and you're not keeping me out."

It was obvious he'd been drinking. At that moment it became clear. It was over. Tomorrow I would call my attorney and finally proceed with the divorce. James had made his choice. Now I was making mine. He would only drag me down, and I could no longer support such a burden. My energy would focus on my three children and myself. Thankfully, I didn't realize the power—like that of a 747 jet engine—that I'd need to propel me through this, or I might have changed my mind. But James would no longer keep this family hostage and dysfunctional.

A family is like a dangling mobile—everyone hangs in balance together. When one member abuses a substance, it causes the mobile to wobble and throws the rest of the members off, making them unbalanced and crazy. James would no longer be allowed this control.

I'd get a job—I was a nurse. James would help support the children. Everything would work out. I was optimistic we would work it out. After all, a girl from Moose Jaw doesn't give up.

The next morning my positive attitude was shaken when Dr. McKenzie at Highgate called. His usual pleasantries were guarded and hesitant. "Mrs. Kane, there was an incident yesterday. Andrew was in the resource room, became impulsive and excitable, and ran toward the window as if he was going jump out. Before we knew it, he darted to the stairs and threw himself down one flight of steps." I was numb.

Dr. McKenzie continued. "We've had him fully examined, and he has no physical injuries. The psychiatrist will be here next week to see him, but for now we've put him into more restrictive housing with additional supervision."

The next day I drove to New Hampshire and checked into the bed and breakfast. I was stunned to hear that the proprietors had already heard of the incident, and they were just as shocked to hear Andrew had done this. Highgate would now not allow Andrew off the property, so I visited and observed all day long. We walked around, talked, and then had lunch on the patio overlooking the majestic White Mountains. This was a tranquil spot. The staff was still assessing Andrew and designing a personal program for him—the usual physical, occupational, and speech therapy, in conjunction with a computer and school program using materials sent from Region 10 high school. Everything was perfectly in place, and when I left, I was reassured that Andrew was on the right road. Thank you, God!

A week later when I visited Andrew, I was taken aback when he pulled out a wad of bills—more money than I had left him with. "Where did all that come from?" I asked.

"I've been working, doing gardening mostly, and they pay me."

I saw red, but concealed my feelings. "Andrew, I've got to check out something, I'll be back in a few minutes, okay?" I went directly to see Dr. McKenzie. I marched into his outer office and told the secretary, "It is vital that I see Dr. McKenzie immediately." Without hesitation I was in his office. He was a professional, in his midthirties, good-looking, and well dressed. Smiling, he made me feel comfortable.

I tried to be polite and diplomatic, even though my breathing was agitated. "Dr. McKenzie, I have a copy of Andrew's program, which includes all the details of his therapeutic plan here at Highgate. But I'm concerned this program doesn't seem to be in place."

He stood and adamantly denied the accusation.

"You see, Dr. McKenzie, Andrew's been doing yard work and gardening, and getting paid by you. That's fine in his leisure time, but he's here for therapeutic physical and emotional rehabilitation, not gardening, and when he returns home he'll finish high school and eventually be college bound."

Dr. McKenzie's face drained of color when he picked up the phone to call each therapist. It was true. Andrew had not attended one therapy session. "Mrs. Kane, I am so sorry. I'm going to fix this right now."

I continued. "I'm very disappointed that no one is monitoring what is going on here."

"Don't worry, Mrs. Kane, they are now."

"Good, I'll be up next week and every week until he's discharged, and I expect an accounting for every day he's here."

After kissing Andrew good-bye, I drove off the grounds, noting the expanse of the facility. It would be very easy for patients compromised with head injuries to skip therapies if the staff were not acting responsibly. I think I made it very clear what my expectation was, and that Dr. McKenzie was to be held accountable for every therapist there. After all, that's what he got paid the big bucks for. Insurance was paying thirty thousand dollars a month for therapy, and Andrew was going to get every penny's worth.

At this point I didn't own a car. James had registered both cars in his name, so when he lost his job and his company car, he took mine and left me with nothing to drive. So I looked and then bought a new car, signing all the papers in the same day. Since I was in the process of a divorce, I had no money and no job, but I did have the gift of gab, and now a brand-new red Taurus. I thought I was the cat's meow.

The ink was not even dry on the loan papers when somehow James found out about the new car. Now I was positive that the phones were tapped. Emphatically, I again called a supervisor at the phone company, and they said they would send a specialist over. When he arrived, I voiced my apprehension and got a judgmental glance. I didn't care. I knew something was wrong. I followed him down to the basement, where he shone a flashlight on the ceiling beams. He didn't say a word—he just kept following well-hidden wires and looking at me, shocked.

"I've worked for the phone company for thirty-five years and never seen anything like this. This guy sure wants to know what's going on in this house. You're tapped. In fact, you're tapped in several places. There are tape recorders all over this basement. Your ex has been switching the location of the taps so they are well hidden and the exact spot of the break in the line can never be found. I'll remove all this stuff, but if I were you, I'd call the police. This guy could be a psycho and dangerous. If he's resorted to this, who knows what else he's up to."

He handed me the tape recorders, six in all, and a tangled mass of wires. He was right—who was this psycho? I certainly didn't know any more. Later that day I watered the plants in my house, paying special attention to the schefflera that was growing by leaps and bounds. In the dining room, I found a voice-activated tape recorder in the buffet cabinet. Why was I so stupid not to see all this?

The restraining order didn't hold up and James was back home. I called my divorce attorney. She was concerned for my safety and contacted James's divorce attorney. I had moved into the den permanently, and late that same night I heard James come home. I waited until I thought he was asleep, then tiptoed down to the bedroom, took his keys, and went out to his car. I opened the trunk and found a large box with more tape recorders and cassettes. I was sickened to see all this.

I grabbed everything and locked it all in my car trunk. I snuck back into his bedroom and placed his keys where I had found them. I returned to the den and put my car keys under the pillow, along with a paring knife I had grabbed from the kitchen. At this point I was uneasy and afraid of what he might do. I needed him out of the house and the divorce done. And since the restraining order wouldn't hold up, I begged my attorney to move as quickly as possible.

In October we had a pretrial date to order him out of the house. Todd and Laura joined me at the hearing, ready to testify against their father. That was probably a drastic move, but I could not survive much longer if he remained. In addition to both of our divorce attorneys, Bill Jones also showed up to try to help. It was difficult, since he was a friend to both of us. I welcomed his presence, as he tried to deal with James. He was struck by the gravity of the situation when he saw Todd and Laura there.

James entered the court dressed to kill, briefcase in hand, and inebriated. He waved and winked at me and the children as if this were a game and he was the ringmaster at a carnival. Bill immediately took him aside to try to talk some sense into him. James had told his lawyer that I was independently wealthy, and claimed he had left me a check for a hundred thousand dollars, which were out-and-out lies. The man was going crazy. I didn't have a dime. Only his mother had money.

Bill and James's attorney took him aside, but he was agitated and walked away from them. They cajoled him into a private room and returned minutes later to find my lawyer. The three attorneys talked as James disappeared, carrying his briefcase. He returned later, more intoxicated than before and furious with his divorce attorney for trying to evict him from his home.

I think the thought of losing his home was too much for him. He probably remembered building his home—his castle—in his spare time, as it came alive with tastefully designed rooms, fireplaces, an adjacent greenhouse for growing orchids, and a Japanese rock garden that in summer hosted live fish. His greatest project was a master bedroom and bathroom suite with a huge sunken tub, gold-plated fixtures, and a fireplace crafted with handpicked fieldstone rock that he had gathered from various places and loaded into the trunk of his car.

James's mentor as an adolescent was his uncle Randy. He spent every Sunday learning how to fix and take care of Randy's properties. Randy had molded James into a creative and talented man. Unfortunately, those words described him as he had been in the past. Sadly, Uncle Randy died of a heart attack while James was in the service. James would have listened to him, I'm sure.

Both attorneys explained the severity of the situation to James. We were next on the docket. When the case was called up, the lawyers did all the talking, and the process was over in five minutes with no one testifying. The judge ordered James out of the house by November 10, 1988. I prayed, *Thank you, God. I don't know how much more I could have taken.*

We had won the first round on the road to the divorce—if this was winning. But no one wins in a divorce. Divorce is the death of a relationship, good or bad, and death is not a winner. Lawyers won or lost, but that didn't matter, since they still got their fees regardless of the outcome.

Now I needed a job. It was emotionally difficult for me to return to the OR at Memorial Hospital, so I accepted a position at St. John's Hospital in Waterbury. I had worked in the OR there when I was first married, and now accepted a part-time position in the Psychiatric Unit. I loved psychiatric nursing. Little did I realize when I received the silver medal in psych nursing when graduating from Moose Jaw Providence Hospital that the specialty would be my mainstay for the rest of my life. And I was confident I could do this job. The supervisor was supportive with my requests to see Andrew midweekly. This was a prerequisite to my accepting the position. I had made a promise to visit him weekly and would keep my word.

On Columbus Day weekend, Todd joined me on the trip. Andrew was now permitted off the premises, and we explored the surrounding towns, outlet stores, miniature golf course, and biking trails. We stayed at a scenic inn overlooking a beautiful lake, all at Highgate's expense. I was trying to maintain some semblance of normalcy in our lives. As I pulled my car out of the parking lot and crashed into a metal dumpster, I realized how stressed I was. With great pleasure, Todd drove. When the weekend was over, we dropped Andrew back at Highgate. We were melancholy, and I sensed Todd was uneasy. Unfortunately, I depended on him too much, and later would become aware that he had not entered adulthood unscathed.

Reflecting, I admitted my life was total chaos. I found peace in just coming home and staying home. But I was grateful for my life and children and felt it would get better. Andrew was improving but still not himself or back to baseline. I was in constant discussion with Dr. McKenzie regarding his medication, hoping they'd eventually wean him entirely off the drugs.

Finally the day for James to vacate the house had come. He was unemployed but constantly in and out of the house. I thought it best that Laura wasn't around when he left, so I took her with me to visit Andrew. It would also be beneficial for us to spend some quality time alone, as we were constantly at each other. She was struggling at school, and it showed in her grades. I had picked her up one night and found her alone in the library, staring into space. She looked exhausted and sad. I didn't approve of her friends, and she was reluctant to bring them home. As much as I loved her, at this point I was finding her increasingly difficult to like.

"My friends are scared of you—you're so strict. I'm not allowed to do anything or have any fun."

I listened to her but stood firm. I believed in right and wrong, black and white, no gray. As a responsible parent, I believed I had to pass that on to my children, which was difficult and often precluded being a friend. I think at times she hated me.

We drove to New Hampshire, picked up Andrew, and tried to have a fun-filled weekend. But there was paranoia in his eyes, no smile, and slow responses. Laura was so patient with him, and for three days we entertained and cajoled him in a desperate frenzy, hoping to have him snap out of it but not sure what "it" was. We drove home utterly exhausted, but returning to peace was my focus.

James would be forever gone, and I could finally crawl back into my old bed.

Tentatively I drove into the empty driveway. I was relieved James was gone and it was over, but when we entered the kitchen, I stopped in my tracks. My head and stomach shook. Something was wrong. Things were missing. "Oh my God, Laura, we've been robbed!"

I dashed to the family room. Furniture, lamps, figurines, pictures, and random items were gone. Frantically I ran from room to room, and Laura followed behind. It was the same everywhere—until I reached the master bedroom. It was completely stripped, with my clothes strewn in heaps on the floor, my jewelry resting on top. I was speechless, and felt like my blood had drained out of my body. I muttered, "This is no robbery. It's the work of James Kane."

Laura hugged me. "Mom, you're right. Dad's a jerk and pretty sick to do this, but you've got Todd, Andrew, and me. It'll be okay. You'll see."

"I can't believe your father is capable of this—someone is brainwashing him. He wants me to stop the divorce and he does this? What's going on in his brain? Or maybe there's no brain left." We sat quietly, and then Laura went to bed.

I was dazed. The clearer the picture became, the more incensed I was. I went to the living room and took stock of the pillaged room. My tears had stopped, but an internal rage was building. Did he think he could come in here and take what he wanted? If he wanted a fight, it was a fight he'd get. And I wasn't playing to lose.

I stalked around the sunken living room like a panther looking for prey, needing a physical release from the fury inside. There was a ten-foot railing on one side of the room that I had always hated. I flew down the stairs to James's workbench, grabbed a sledge hammer, and returned. Positioning myself, I began swinging the hammer into the railing. After the first few cracks, Laura came running out of her room shouting, "Mom, for God's sake, what are you doing? You're losing it! You're scaring me!"

Puffing from exertion, I said, "Laura, I'm okay. Really, I am. I've always wanted to get rid of this railing, and now is the time. This is therapeutic for me. Go back to bed. I'm just about finished." What I didn't tell her was that each swing was intended for her father. When the last bit toppled over, I felt triumphant. I also had another plan.

I called my friend Maria and confided in her. Then I told her I was about to do something drastic and illegal. If anything happened to me and I was only allowed one phone call from jail, it would be to her. I told her to then call my attorney. And to please take care of Laura, Todd, and Andrew. "Say a prayer for me. I'm petrified, but I'm fighting fire with fire."

Late that night I drove to Dee and James Sr.'s house, where James was living. His parents were presently out of town on vacation. Feeling like a criminal, I tiptoed down the dark driveway to a lighted basement window. Kneeling in the pachysandra, I peeked in the window and saw the stolen goods. Quietly, I backed away, opened James's car door, and grabbed the garage door opener. Yes!

I returned home but barely slept that night, checking the clock every hour. I paced as I dressed. I couldn't eat. Then I left when it was barely light out. I parked a block away from James's parents' house, just far enough to see the driveway and garage. In a matter of minutes, I saw James leave the house, drive away, and head out for breakfast as he routinely did. I had spent all night planning my strategy. There was no turning back now. The assault was commencing, the general in charge.

I drove into the driveway, pressed the garage door opener that I had taken the night before, and *presto*—the door rolled up. I opened my car doors and trunk; proceeded to the basement; and grabbed our tables, chairs, lamps, and pictures. When the car was full, I headed home and feverishly unloaded so I could go back for more. I was edgier than on the first trip, but continued. On the basement window sill were three Royal Daltons figurines that James had received from his mother. I grabbed them and gently put them in the front seat. He treasured them, and I would use them for collateral. I unloaded the car but didn't have the guts to enter the battlefield a third time. We could fight over the rest of the stuff in court. I was shaking. I would make a terrible criminal.

I ran to Maria's to tell her what I'd done. We were mute. Slowly we began to snicker, laugh, and then break into hysteria. We needed a stiff drink.

At noon the next day I received a call from the Waterbury Police Department. "A Mrs. Kane in Florida has reported a break-in at her home, and she's accused you."

"Do you have any witnesses?"

"No, we don't."

"Officer, Mrs. Kane is my mother-in-law. I'm still married to her son but in the process of divorcing him. He's an alcoholic and lives with her. That poor woman—I'm sorry to hear that she was robbed."

Now I was petrified. What would happen to me? I phoned my attorney to tell her what I had done and how scared I was. "Good for you," was her comment. "They can't do anything to you. They didn't see anyone. No one knows anything. You're still married. Don't worry."

If James returned to try to take the stuff back, I'd call the police and have him arrested. I replaced the furniture where it belonged and took a nap. I was exhausted.

I was paranoid with every phone call, thinking it was the police calling to arrest me. My crime from a few days ago was still fresh in my mind when a few days later the phone rang at four o'clock. I was relieved to hear Dr. McKenzie's voice.

"Mrs. Kane, it's Dr. McKenzie."

"Hi, how are things at Highgate, and how's my man?"

"Mrs. Kane, I don't know an easy way to put this. There's been another incident . . . Andrew stabbed himself in the abdomen."

Chapter Ten

November 1989–February 1990

I FELL AGAINST THE WALL and slid to the floor.

"I'm sure Andrew will be all right," Dr. McKenzie told me over the phone. "He's leaving by ambulance for the hospital in nearby Foxtown. They're waiting for him, and he'll go directly into the OR, where the surgeon will assess the situation. We should have more answers in an hour."

I took a deep breath. "Please tell me what happened."

"While the staff and clients were preparing dinner, Andrew was cutting up peppers. The next thing they knew, he plunged the knife into his abdomen. Fortunately, it was a small knife, so it couldn't have gone too deep, but he was bleeding quite heavily. You can imagine the panic and confusion that followed."

"Dr. McKenzie, I'm coming to Foxtown. Please find me a place to stay. I'll be ready to leave when you call me back. Is there anything else I should know?"

"Right now, I can't think of anything. I'll call you if I do."

Dazed, I placed the phone down. The barren room was closing in on me. My heart was heavy as if I were under a ton of bricks. I was in no condition, emotionally or physically, to drive, so I called Maria.

"Hi, it's me, I need a huge favor. Can you please drive me to see Andrew? He's in a hospital in Foxtown. He just stabbed himself." I broke down and sobbed. I could always count on Maria. She would be over in an hour. Thank goodness Todd was not home and Laura was spending more overnights at Westin.

Ninety minutes later the call came. "Mrs. Kane, I'm Dr. Barth. I just operated on your son Andrew. He's resting in recovery and in no danger. Fortunately, the knife did not puncture the peritoneum, so none of his internal organs were touched. By tomorrow he'll be out of bed walking around. He's young and healthy. He'll probably be out of here in three or four days. I understand you're coming up. Please have me paged as soon as you arrive."

Physically Andrew was out of danger, but emotionally was another issue. Did he hate himself that much that he wanted to kill himself, or was another disease surfacing with voices telling him to harm himself? I was desperate to sort this all out, but now the priority was getting him out of the hospital and back on track in a safe environment.

Foxtown, New Hampshire, was a quaint tourist town in the summer, but in November it was dreary and desolate. The hospital was small, all on one level. Maria and I entered the front door, saw no one, then proceeded down a hallway. To the staff, Andrew had a minor injury. To me, it was permanent and vital. We were dealing with life and death, and I was terrified.

I called out, "Hello, is anyone here?"

"I'll be right out." A pleasant middle-aged woman appeared. "Can I help you?"

"Yes, I'm Mrs. Kane. My son Andrew just underwent surgery. I'd like to visit him briefly, please."

I was taken to his room. The door was ajar, and I pushed it open to see Andrew sound asleep. Next to him was Steven, a staff member, also asleep in his chair. He woke up startled and began to apologize, to reassure me of his attentive vigil.

"Oh, Mrs. Kane, I can't leave the room. I need to watch Andrew every minute."

"It's okay, you don't need to leave. I just want him to know we're here and that we'll be back in the morning." I walked closer to his bed and stared at his beautiful face, so peaceful. I stroked his sweaty forehead and brushed back his thick curly hair. Slowly he opened his groggy eyes.

"Ma, you're here."

"Yes, sweetie, and I brought Mrs. Hall. It's late, but we wanted to see you. Go back to sleep. Everything will be fine, and we'll see you tomorrow morning. I love you, Gigi."

"Me too, Ma." He turned over, closed his eyes, and fell asleep.

Maria and I walked through the hospital. "Thanks for coming, for driving, for everything. I never could have done this alone, and I have so few people to turn to. I'm losing all my friends, and it's my fault. I just don't have time, and they have no time for me and this continual saga. Maria, you are a wonderful friend, and I'm blessed by your support."

Maria just shook her head. "I don't know how you do it and keep it all together." I linked my arm in hers and we left.

We arrived at an inn to lovely accommodations and were instructed to charge everything to Highgate. Their kindness made a terrible situation easier, but sleep taunted us. I shared my stash, and we both resorted to an Ativan and hit the pillows. Ah, sweet sleep!

The next morning we arrived at the hospital by nine a.m. The staff had changed. I tried to persuade the attendant to leave so I could spend some personal time with Andrew. But he informed me he was not allowed to leave for even a moment. When I insisted and stated I would be responsible for anything that happened, he reluctantly left. Andrew was asleep, his forehead sweaty. I dampened a face cloth and gently mopped his brow. He slowly opened his eyes and stared at me with that haunting, horrible paranoia.

"Ma, it's their fault. They shouldn't have left that knife out for me."

"Andrew, it's okay. Dr. Barth said you're going to be fine—there's no internal damage, and you're going to be as healthy as a horse. You will get better and forget this ever happened."

He brightened up. "Mrs. Hall, I'm glad you came. You're one of my mom's best friends, aren't you? And how's Christopher?"

"You know Chris—he does what he needs to do and says, 'Mom, don't sweat it.' I've never known anyone as laid back as him."

"Why didn't he come up with you?"

"Andrew, Chris is away at college."

He seemed puzzled. "Chris and I are going to get an apartment together ... someday ... Ma, I'm hearing the voices again. They make me nervous and confused. I can't think straight. I take so much medicine, and it's making me crazy. Ma, do something."

"I will."

At that moment his case manager, Rob, arrived. He was clumsy, blinking rapidly. He wanted to speak to me in private. "There are hospital papers that need to be signed. Andrew is eighteen and legally should be able to sign, but he's paranoid, and we may have a problem. Can I ask for your assistance?"

"Sure, Rob, anything."

"I'll wait until the nurses have him cleaned up and moving. We're keeping staff with him round the clock to ensure his safety."

By evening, when the anesthesia had worn off, we witnessed Andrew in full-blown psychosis. He was a frightened boy who trusted no one—not even me. For two days we begged, pleaded, humored, and cajoled, but his paranoia kept him from signing the hospital release papers.

I called James to come up and help, but he refused. So far he'd made only one trip, stayed thirty minutes, and left. The staff wouldn't allow him to take Andrew off campus because he smelled of alcohol. Rob had told me about the incident, and I could only imagine how it tormented Andrew, increasing his feelings of abandonment. I wanted to be both a mother and father. Though I knew it was impossible, I'd have done anything to fill the gap.

Rob nervously took me aside. "Mrs. Kane, I think you need to look into conservatorship for Andrew. Maybe it will only be temporary, but at this point he's not competent to take care of himself. You've probably never thought about this, but he's eighteen, and legally someone has to be responsible for him."

I called my friend Jack Lew, a probate court judge, who was well aware of our family issues. After I explained the situation, he said, "Connie, I'll fax the conservatorship papers right now. Call me if I can do anything else. Good luck."

"Thanks a million. I'll keep in touch." I turned to Maria. "Okay, pal, it's time for dinner." We found a corner in the inn dining room, ordered cocktails, and began to relax. I talked nonstop, constantly on the verge of tears. "Maria, is he ever going to get better? Does he want to die? Did I do the right thing putting him here? Why is God punishing us? Will I ever have a life?"

Maria gently reassured me. "Connie, you are the best mother I know. You've devoted your life to your children, and soon it will get better. You can handle this trial."

I smiled. "Yes, but it's one hell of a road test."

Dr. McKenzie left a message for me to see him before I returned home. I entered his office, my head throbbing, not paying attention to his somber demeanor.

"Please sit down, Mrs. Kane. Can I get you a cup of coffee, some water?"

Squinting, I said, "No thanks, I just want to be on my way." I didn't have any energy left for pleasantries.

"Mrs. Kane, due to this second suicide attempt, Highgate regrettably feels that we are not presently the best facility to take care of Andrew. This psychotic phase needs constant monitoring in a safer environment. The layout and openness of our facility does not permit the safety that Andrew now requires, and his welfare and continued success would be better met at another facility."

A bomb exploded inside me. "Dr. McKenzie, I've been through this before, searching and searching. There are no such facilities!"

"Andrew's case manager, Rob, is presently exploring options to help you. Meanwhile, Andrew will stay at Foxtown Hospital. We've made private arrangements with the administrator, and we'll pay for his stay until you can find another facility. We'll also have staff members within arm's reach, twenty-four hours per day, to maintain his safety."

I was mute, my legs like jelly as I wobbled out of the office. I would again need to comb the country and play the insurance game to find a facility that could help Andrew, if indeed such a facility existed.

In a week it would be Thanksgiving. My mother had already planned to come, and the timing was perfect. I'd need her support, as I seriously pondered how much more I could take.

Thank God for health insurance. My carriers were wonderful. In fact, one case manager had recently called to ask if they could do anything for other members of the family. I couldn't believe my ears. "Thank you so much, but I think everyone is doing fairly well." Or so I thought!

I needed a personal secretary to handle the insurance paperwork, spending hours tracking bills for thousands of dollars, to make sure anything not covered by one policy was covered by another carrier. I constantly murmured, "Thank you, Tish, and the Archdiocese of Hartford, for my teaching job at Sacred Family. Your health-care plan has carried us through."

In the midst of this, I received an overdue bill from Newington Children's Hospital. Dr. Jinnie at Region 10 refused to pay it, until my attorney Bill Jones called her. At this point I would have taken her back to court in a minute. It seemed she was hell-bent on making my life more difficult than it already was. But she'd taught me how to compartmentalize my thinking. I put all her negativity in a box, closed it up, and stuck it in the back of my brain, leaving room in the front for only the positive. I guess I should have thanked her, but not today. I stayed resilient, focused, and one step ahead. After all, I was a girl from Moose Jaw.

A few days later, Highgate's case manager, Rob, called. I detected an uneasy tone.

He'd found a facility in Massachusetts that was setting up an adolescent TBI program. Immediately, I drove up and was met by a director young enough to be my daughter, high-spirited and all smiles. I liked her right from the beginning. It was a very small facility, but that was okay as long as it did the job. However, as we toured, it quickly became obvious that all was not well. The physical therapy room was empty and sparsely furnished with outdated equipment, and the furniture was old, dark, and ready to be tossed. As we strolled the hallways, we only encountered contented graying residents in wheelchairs or on walkers. It resembled an old folks' home, which was reinforced by an awful smell of urine. The facility's ranking was now severely compromised.

"Andrew is eighteen. How many clients do you have in that age group?"

"Uh, well, the closest one is thirty, but we're geared and ready for a younger population."

"Thirty is very old to an eighteen-year-old."

"I have three teenagers on the waiting list."

"I'm sure they'll do fine here, but it's not right for Andrew. He's unique in so many ways, but thank you for your time."

"But the tour isn't over, I haven't—"

"Thank you very much, but it is. I have a long drive home." I marched out. I would never put my Gigi in a place like that—never.

I called Rob to relay my assessment. And he had found another facility on Long Island that might meet Andrew's needs. It was a brisk but sunny morning as I once again ventured into unfamiliar territory three hours away. I came upon an institution-like gray weathered building. The entrance was cold, dark, and overly formal. Things needed to rapidly perk up. I breathed deeply, in and out, my foot tapping out of sync. I was seated in a small reception area to await the arrival of Dr. Dan Shinitski, a short, bald-headed man in a gray suit. Oh my, his suit matched the weathered building. Was that deliberate? He was cordial as he explained the program, through a heavy accent and maze of evasive verbiage. There was no doubt I was present in a prominent program that involved extensive rehabilitation and psychotherapy. Was I lucky!

On our tour we roamed through several floors, and I got a better look and feel for the layout. There were few clients around, and the equipment in use was also outdated and worn—nothing like Highgate. There was lack of structure and continuity to the groups I witnessed, and I sensed more nonprofessionals than professionals.

"And, so, who does the psychotherapy?"

"Oh, I do all of it."

"Hmm, and how often and how long is each session?"

"Once a week, for twenty to thirty minutes."

"That's it? And who would Andrew talk to between sessions?"

"We have excellent resident counselors trained specifically in prophylactic and psychological intervention."

"Good, so they have college degrees?"

"I maintain a rigorous training program."

"Oh, so you are the trainer?" I knew Dr. Shinitski was getting annoyed with me.

"Yes, I work very closely with staff, and they are very skilled."

Condescendingly, I said, "Yes, I'm sure they are."

I couldn't imagine anyone in psychotherapy getting better by talking to Dr. Shinitski. If I, who was alert and oriented (at least I thought I was), had difficulty understanding his English, how would a psychotic patient comprehend anything? It was not a judgment—just reality. I felt this place was only a holding area. In fact, I wouldn't leave my dog, Maggie, here. I was polite and thanked the doctor. He told me he'd get back to me in a day. I could see the dollar signs dancing in his eyes when he glanced at the insurance funding. He thought it was a done deal.

When I arrived home I immediately called Rob. "You're going to have to do better than that. It was a horrible, dreary dungeon. I was waiting for Nurse Ratchet to barge in. There's no way I'll ever put Andrew in a place like that." He knew I wasn't happy. There was a dead awkward silence.

"I'll discuss this with Dr. McKenzie and get back to you."

"Thanks, Rob."

Rosemary gave me the name of a facility in Virginia. It was far away but worth a call. I spoke to the director at length, explained my dilemma as he listened patiently. Then he passed on this wonderful advice.

"Mrs. Kane, did you like Highgate? Did you feel it was a good program?"

"Yes, once we got the kinks ironed out I thought it was great. I was up every week to check in and watch them like a hawk."

"Then tell them you want Andrew to stay there. Make them provide staff to constantly watch him. You told me they advocated a lot of one-on-one—make them live up to their philosophy. If they give you a hard time, threaten to sue. After all, he did get hurt while in their care. They're responsible for the incident, and you'd win any legal battle. I'm sure they don't want to enter into a lawsuit as it would entail investigators and prosecutors checking into their entire program, files, and finances. One never knows what one might find. Make them accountable for their purported role, as a leader in head-injury facilities."

His wisdom struck a chord. I wanted to hug this man I did not know. "Thank you so much for opening my eyes. You've no idea how much you've helped me."

After I composed myself, I called Dr. McKenzie at Highgate. I took a deep breath and said, "Hi, it's Connie Kane. I've just returned from visiting the last facility on Long Island you suggested, and I really want to thank you for all of your help, but I wouldn't put my dog there."

I took a deeper breath. "I want Andrew to stay in your program—after all, you're the national leader in head injury and neuropsychological intervention and have advocated one-on-one treatment and care for your clients, and"—I took an even deeper breath—"on the advice of my lawyers and the fact that Andrew was injured while in your care, we still think you can provide the best care and program for him."

There was a very long uncomfortable pause, and every word that followed was measured. "I see . . . but . . . we'll need time . . . to hire and train staff . . . it might take a while."

"That's okay—take all the time you need. My mother, the children, and I will be coming up to spend Thanksgiving with Andrew at Foxtown Hospital. I'll be over to see you, and we can discuss the details then. And can you please set up accommodations at the inn for all of us? Thanks so much."

I got off the phone and hugged it. Then I danced like a rocket down the hallway. It worked! *God, you are watching.* I went to water the tall, beautiful schefflera plant and smiled at it. "Now I know why Andrew bought you. You're resilient, like him."

When we arrived for Thanksgiving at Foxtown Hospital, Andrew was walking around like nothing had happened. His psych meds had been changed, and he was happy to see his granny from Moose Jaw, as well as Todd and Laura. We never heard from James or his family. I met with Rob to review Andrew's new plan. They would start with a 2:1 protocol—two people within arm's length of him—then a 1:1 protocol, and then back to regular supervision. He would continue all his therapies and schoolwork but could not leave the grounds. I was agreeable to the plan, but saddened by the reality that he would not be returning home for a long time.

Christmas was four weeks away, and I advised Rob that Laura, Todd, and I would be coming for the holidays. Highgate flew us there and provided a rental car. Our arrangements were made late, so we were put up in a grungy motel used by deer hunters, but at least we were together, and that was all that mattered.

On Christmas Eve, we gathered at Andrew's cabin dressed for the festive occasion—me in a red corduroy dress and Andrew in green corduroys and a beautiful green-and-raspberry sweater we'd bought at the Ralph Lauren outlet store. The other clients wore jeans and T-shirts. We waited for their families to arrive, but it soon became obvious no one was coming. I was stunned that anyone would leave their loved ones here alone for the holiday. I hadn't fully grasped the concept that Highgate *was* their new home and they would never return to their families. Andrew was different, and I never doubted that he would come back to us.

On Christmas morning, Laura, Todd, and I went to Mass to give thanks for all we'd been blessed with. When we returned to the cabin, there was no frivolity, so we attempted to lighten up the place. It was awkward for Andrew with staff hovering over him, but we carried on as if they weren't there.

Todd had bags of gifts. "Merry Christmas, dude." He and Andrew hugged hard.

Laura noticed Andrew's new duds. "Whew, look at you. Hey, snappy outfit, Brother!" A compliment from she who wore an Indian skirt and baggy sweater. She was going through the grunge hippie phase. I should have been happy it wasn't tight jeans and leather. Where had I gone wrong with her dress code? I surmised that the King of Jordan's daughter, who was also a student at Westin, was not dressed in this fashion.

Christmas was a special time — the birth of Christ — and we were going to celebrate even in the confines of this restricted, unnatural setting. It was for Andrew, and he was the center of attention opening gifts. But then there was a knock on the door. It was the mother of another client, Danny, who arrived with two huge bags of presents. Todd jumped up excited and called to Danny. "Your mom's here."

Danny entered, looking bewildered, "Where?"

"She was at the bottom of the stairs with some gifts for you."

But then she disappeared.

"Maybe she went out to park her car." Todd went outside and saw a car slowly driving away. Shaken and sick to his stomach, he returned. "Mom, I can't believe she just dropped off the gifts and left without saying Merry Christmas to her son. That is so cruel."

"I know." But I kept quiet. We hadn't heard from James either.

Danny left the gifts in the hallway and scurried back to his room, alone. I thought one of the staff should go check on him, but they were too busy filling their faces with fresh shrimp cocktail.

Laura asked Andrew, "Have you heard from Dad?"

"Yes, he's in Florida with Aunt Trudy and her family. Said he'll call later. He knows you're all here. Aunt Trudy wants to talk to Ma."

I had no use for any of that family. They ignored us and didn't care about Andrew, and lived their lives like nothing had happened. I loathed all of them, but had expected more from the cousins Tina, Cane, and Anita. In spite of the fact they were Notre Dame graduates, they were selfish, dysfunctional people.

Midafternoon, the phone rang. It was James. He conversed with the children and then asked to speak to me, which I did for their sake and the Christmas spirit. He was apologetic.

"Con, if I hadn't gone to Florida, I wouldn't have made it through the holidays. I want you to stop the divorce, please. I'll be back in Connecticut in a week. Call me so we can go out for a pizza and talk and resolve everything."

I wanted to believe him, but his total estrangement throughout this crisis was the clincher, and I was not calling him. We were on the docket for February third of the next year, and I was on course to divorce him.

The next day a few more client family members showed up at Highgate. I found it difficult to deal with their apathy. Did they think that having a brain injury also injured your heart, and you no longer had feelings? Not only were these clients rejected by society but by their loved ones as well. It was cruel. Animals got better treatment.

Later we headed home. On our way to the tiny airport I felt the weight of three emotionally draining days. I looked forward to a reprieve, a few days at home. Our flight was called, and we walked onto the tarmac to the plane. I knew I was in trouble when the man taking the tickets was also the pilot. I was ready for a package of pretzels. I checked out the tiny plane, walked up the stairs, and entered the minuscule eight-seat cabin. I took the seat in front, breathed deeply, then gasped and shouted, "I can't breathe! I'm suffocating." I jumped out of my seat, and ran outside and down the steps. "I'm claustrophobic and can't fly in that little plane. I will die if I have to get back in there."

Todd and Laura stood by the door. "Mom, come on, stop it. You're scaring us!"

I was in a full-blown panic attack. "I'm sorry, kids, but I can't get on that plane, I'll rent a car and drive home."

The captain was patient and kind. "It's only a thirty-minute flight to Boston. We're going to give you a few moments and then try again. If you sit in the very front row, I'll open the curtain so you can see the stars out the window in the cockpit."

"Mom, I'll give you my Walkman," Laura said.

"And we'll sit on either side of you and hold your hands the entire way," reassured Todd.

Obviously, the children realized this was no joke and that I had a serious problem. "Okay, I'll try, but I don't know if I can do this."

"Come on, Mom, you can."

Cautiously I reentered the cabin and deliberately took my seat. Laura put her headphones on me, and I seemed okay. The captain opened the curtain to the cockpit and closed the plane door, and we were ready for takeoff. I stared forward out the cockpit window and focused on the black sky dotted with stars, the music in my ears, and the grip of my children's hands. *Only thirty minutes—I can do this.* The Ativan I popped was beginning to take effect.

As we landed, I took stock of what had happened. Was I losing my grip with reality? Was claustrophobia only the beginning?

A week later I received a call from a friend who had seen James in Florida. "He was out of his mind drunk the entire time. His family's afraid he's having a nervous breakdown."

"Who has time for a breakdown?"

And later I received a letter from James. It read:

> *Con, your letter doesn't make sense, must have been on your happy pills. I was willing to forgive and forget because of your mental state. You could have made a call to stop the divorce. I know you've got the kids programmed against me, but I'll change that. I'm making a list of things I want out of the house. If you get nasty, we'll go to family court. I guarantee you I will win! I still love you with all of my heart. I only blame you because you thought you were doing the best. As Mother Teresa would say, "You miffed it." I'll never forgive Maria for giving you the money for the lawyer; it's like giving someone a gun to kill their family. I know you're on medication and can't think straight. And if it wasn't for Liz and Maria egging you on, we'd still be together, or maybe the three of you still prefer your "ménage a trois."*
>
> *Highgate informs me that Andrew is doing better. They get a twenty-percent success rate, and he will be one. I wrote him and told him his main goal is a high school diploma. It's like I told you, he's not coming out of there any better than he went in. Unfortunately, you ran out of love for him and me about the same time. Someone said, "She's found God, but doesn't realize she's still on earth."*
>
> *Con, I just reread this letter and only want to say that it would hurt too much to see you. I can't be where you are at any time.*
>
> *All my love, James*

It was sad. The man was crazy. I couldn't wait for it to be over — only a few more weeks.

I was working three days a week and every other weekend on the psych unit at St. John's. That schedule allowed me time to visit Andrew. During my initial interview with the head nurse, I openly told her everything that was going on in my life.

She commented, "It's amazing you are still so positive."

"I'm trying. I thank God for continued strength. My ultimate goal is to somehow change the world's negative perception of TBI."

I was not, however, overly positive in regard to Laura's new boyfriend, Alberto. Even though his father was a highly respected doctor at New York Presbyterian Hospital in New York and his mother a Spanish contessa, I was downright suspicious about him. He looked sneaky and disheveled, with hair halfway down his back. I couldn't believe my beautiful, bright child had brought this oddball home to meet me. When Alberto arrived, I invited him to dinner. I made spaghetti, which appeared to be a challenge for him. He ate as if the fork and spoon were obsolete tools, allowing the spaghetti noodles to continually drop out of his mouth. Dinner could not be over too soon for me. I anxiously awaited the moment Laura drove him back to the bus station. I relaxed, did the dishes, and was shocked when she returned home an hour later with Alberto still in tow!

"Gee, Mrs. Kane, I missed the bus."

Under my breath I murmured, "I'll bet you did!"

He called his parents, and I spoke with his dad, a patient man, whom I could tell had suffered trials and tribulations with this child. It was obvious that Alberto's irresponsible behavior added unwanted stress to the family vacation, since they were flying to Spain the next day at noon. I reassured him that I would personally put Alberto on the first bus in the morning.

Alberto was a bright child who got involved in drugs, and now his parents faced many difficulties finding a school that would accept him. He was enrolled in an expensive private school in New York, but was doing poorly academically. When I observed him, all I saw was an adolescent who had chosen to fry his brain. I didn't want him around Laura, but for some reason he was the light of her life. I was worried sick and wondered what on earth they had in common. This courtship was packed with fire, and she had no idea of the ravages of flames.

I knew if I criticized him it would make him all the more attractive to her. Her behavior was already challenging, her mood frequently changing and angry. She didn't seem to care about anything, and her grades were mediocre. She was on an unstoppable, spiraling, out-of-control roller coaster. Was it Andrew, the divorce, the estrangement of her father? Whatever it was, she was on overload. Would it ever stop for her, and if so, at what price?

Foolishly, I thought her strength and stay at boarding school would help, but instead she was getting worse. I didn't know where to turn to help her.

The divorce proceedings were moving quickly, and the first day in court was the worst. I stood in the waiting area, cordially saying hi to attorneys we had socialized with, chatting about their wives, their children, their normal lives. In turn I was aching. James showed up late, already high, and by the end of the day negotiations had gone nowhere. Again, Bill Jones, our lawyer friend, was called in for help.

"Con, he thinks if he makes this tough, you will realize you can't do it on your own and will stop the proceedings."

James's behavior only propelled me forward more furiously. He was totally unreasonable, did not want to give me or our children anything, and argued continually with his lawyer. At one point he was so inebriated, it looked as if he was going to hit his lawyer.

A day later he called and asked if we could meet for breakfast. I was favorable and relieved. I assumed he'd rethought how little we'd resolved in court, not to mention the attorney fees we were both amassing. My attorney empathized, charging me a flat fee, and would not add any extra for all the supplementary time and work. The only negotiable assets we had were the children and the house, so it should have been simple. James was overheard saying to his lawyer, "In five years when all the dust has settled, we'll be back together." Dream on!

At seven a.m. I walked into the diner. It took only one look to know he'd been drinking. I should have left, but desperately wanted to make this divorce amicable, so I stayed. Big mistake! In minutes he was shouting, berating my attorney, attacking her character and personal life. Then he moved on to Andrew, maintaining he was only getting worse because "you stuck him away to get rid of him." He ended his tirade with "The whole family is going to hell in a handbasket, including Laura, and it's all your fault!" Everyone stared. He continued to shout as I fled to my car.

The following weekend I drove to Boston to visit Todd for Parents' Weekend. Regardless of the pending divorce, I was determined to spend quality time with him. He was happy, doing well in school, disciplined, and hardworking. I loved his friends, who genuinely cared for one another and someday would be an asset to any community. Their parents were hardworking folks who loved their children, and everyone was still married to their original partner. Again, I was the oddball.

Todd had one request. "Mom, please don't embarrass me by saying how handsome I am."

"I'm never going to change, will always be eccentric, and will forever tell you how wonderful you are. You're going to have to learn to put up with me. I can't tone down." He would forever be insistent on trying.

I had needed a boost, and the weekend did it. I never revealed how volatile things were at home—the less he knew, the better. At least one of my children didn't need to live the insanity that Laura and I experienced.

At home I was sleeping in Andrew's bed, as I had no money to replace the one James had taken from our bedroom. One night I awoke to the piercing sound of someone furiously banging and pushing on the glass slider door, trying to force it open. I was afraid the glass was going to break and the door crash open. Terrified and paralyzed, I was unable to move to call the police. I prayed the intruder would leave, and finally he did. When I heard a car door slam, I peeked out to see James drive away.

I was at my limit with the harassing and abuse. His presence in our lives was detrimental. He swore too much and called Laura a drug addict. Todd phoned him to ask how to fix something, and he refused to help, which sent Todd into hysterics. This was the James no one saw. He saved the hurt for his family. It was payback for the impending divorce.

It was only a matter of time before the case of Kane vs. Kane came to court. After being ordered out of the house on a court order, James showed up drunk twice—to visit the children, he said. I called the police, and one of his police buddies showed up. The three of us argued. The officer and James against me. He refused to leave on the grounds that it was still his house. The chauvinistic police friend took his side.

"You're not divorced, and a man can visit his children in his home."

I was furious with this male-bonding garbage. I'm sure they had commiserated about how hard James worked for twenty-two years, only to be dumped by a psychotic bitch who continually complained about his drinking. In James's distorted perception, he was the victim and I was the dragon lady. But I didn't care what people thought of me. I was not in a popularity contest and would continue with the help of professionals to do what was right for my family.

We were on the docket for February 16, 1990. I tried not to look at James as I took the stand and answered the usual questions.

"Do you think your marriage has broken down irretrievably?
"Yes."

"Is there any hope of reconciliation?"
"No."

"I believe, Your Honor, the parties will stipulate to irretrievable breakdown."

James's attorney concurred. "Yes, Your Honor, so stipulated."

Laura was seventeen, the only minor involved. We agreed to my having sole custody and reasonable visitation for James. He hadn't worked in six months, so I provided medical insurance and we divided the cost. We never discussed Todd or Andrew. I was positive he would want to help pay for college and help Andrew when he returned home from Highgate. I was stupid and dead wrong. We would be forced to deal with the reality of James's total abandonment of the children, and to watch his family stand by and back up his decisions. I would soon discover the power of profoundly dysfunctional family genetics.

I did not request alimony, and relinquished claim to James's pension and any joint accounts he had with his mother. All I wanted was my home and children, which I got. I was responsible for the mortgage and home equity loan and a payment of twenty thousand dollars to James after five years. He would have to pay bills we had incurred as a family. I was relieved—it was all over. Or so I thought!

There were Laura's tuition bills. I had signed the school papers; therefore, he was not legally bound and refused to pay. As for the other bills and furniture, the attorneys suggested we come back in two weeks. The judge viewed it differently. "We shouldn't leave something like that hanging, and I'm not in the habit of entering partial judgments on dissolution. Go down to Family Relations and discuss it."

Later James agreed to pay a third of Laura's tuition bill but would not negotiate on anything else. I wouldn't push for further resolution of the rest because I wanted the divorce over and done that day. I agreed to a good-faith resolution. I was a fool, but at four o'clock that day I gratefully heard: "The court will order that this marriage be dissolved."

I wasn't prepared for the emptiness I felt as I left the court. My attorney and I hugged. She said, "It's finally over. Good luck to you and your family. When things are easier, think of getting involved in changing the divorce law with regard to children with handicaps."

I nodded my head. It was the end of the day and the end of an agonizing era. I walked outside, my vision blurred by tears. My body was numb, incapable of thought or feeling. I had three days off from work, which I desperately needed. Laura was at Westin, and I would visit her later. Then I would drive to Highgate to see Andrew. Things would get better.

I arrived home exhausted and sleep beckoned me. I welcomed the solitude to close out a cruel world and slept for three straight days. My kidneys must have entered lockdown mode, for I didn't remember ever getting up to use the bathroom.

The next Monday I returned to work with a huge weight off my shoulders. I would now try to put our lives back together. I knew the only way I could ever be peacefully happy was to ultimately forgive James. In order to heal, I would have to stop hating. Right now though, I was still bleeding, and it was going to take a long time. But, I mused, you can eat an elephant if you do it one mouthful at a time. My work was cut out for me. I would learn to turn the other cheek, hold my head high, look people straight in the eye, and once again make our house a warm and loving home.

That evening I went to Westin to pick up Laura. We needed to work on and resolve issues that were tearing us apart. I desperately wanted our lives to be normal and loving. As of late, she saw me only as the "heavy," the controlling mom. At school I found an angry, disheveled girl who vaguely resembled Laura. In the car, I tried to make small talk, but she refused to communicate with me, as if I were the enemy.

When we arrived home she made a beeline for her room and slammed the door. I knew I wasn't perfect, and maybe the divorce had made my behavior less so, but now I was ticked off. There was no reason for her attitude, and I wouldn't tolerate it. I knocked on her door.

"Laura, what's going on? We need to talk."

"Just stay out!"

I slowly opened the door and tried to reason with her, but she was irrational, volatile, and ready to explode. It was like looking at a poisonous snake hissing in my face.

"Just leave me alone and get out!"

I grabbed her hands. She flailed, and soon we were both hitting each other.

"Get away from me! Just get away, you witch—you're crazy!" She grabbed my hands, dug her fingernails in, and drew blood. I let go when I saw the blood. She then pushed me out of her way, picked up her backpack, and ran out of the house. Stunned and limp, I fell to the floor and curled into a fetal position, wailing, "Please, God, just let me die!"

I cried myself to sleep and woke an hour later, not knowing where Laura was but assuming she had gone back to Westin. I decided to let things simmer down. In a few days I went to see Andrew.

The following week, Betsy Fugowa, Westin's assistant headmaster, called me in for a conference. Laura entered the room, obviously still angry, and sat as far away from me as she could. Her beautiful bright eyes were faded and sad. Her once cheery and happy face held a flat, vacant stare.

Betsy began. "Mrs. Kane, I've called you and Laura here for a very important meeting. This is difficult because I like Laura—she's a bright student who will fulfill her dreams and aspirations in the future.

However, it has been brought to our attention that several of our students are smoking cigarettes, using drugs, and drinking alcohol. During a room check of suspicious students, we found loose pieces of notebook paper that revealed disturbing information about Laura. I told her we suspected her of drug use, and that she would be required to undergo a urine test."

My heart pounded furiously straight to my brain, and I didn't know if I was hearing right. I was in total denial that Laura might have a drug problem. She was too smart, in school full-time—often boarding—with no money. I remembered James had referred to her use of drugs. He must have heard her conversations when he had the phone tapped. And then it hit me—last summer the kids were growing plants in the greenhouse—a science project, they told me. I was proud. Weren't they the best, still yearning to expand their minds, even during their summer holidays? And James had come over, seen the plants, and pulled them out, hollering at me that I was letting the kids grow marijuana.

I was shocked and had no idea it was marijuana. It was just a live plant that grew in glory and majesty to become pretty, green, and lush, all due to my responsible watering. How nice of me, I thought. How really stupid of me. This Moose Jaw girl was still naive.

Betsy continued. "Laura's urinalysis tested positive, as well as that of several other girls. Her friend Alberto has also been accused of selling drugs. And it has been brought to our attention that Laura has made other drugs available to other students."

I was numb and devastated.

"Until this matter is fully investigated, we are requesting that Laura immediately withdraw from Westin."

Chapter Eleven

February 1990–June 1991

LAURA BOLTED OUT OF THE room. I tried to grab her, to hug her and hold her and reassure her that everything would be all right, but she pulled away as if she loathed me. My heart pounded in terror. *What do I do now? Where do I start?*

Betsy sensed my anguish. "She's been seeing John Herald, our resident therapist. I'll call him now."

The words were stuck in my throat. "Thank you."

I wanted to cry for her and, yes, for me. How much more could I take? Was that selfish of me when she was so fragile and nearly broken? I just wanted someone to hold and comfort me, if only for a few seconds, but I was alone, facing another dreadful giant.

There was a cloud of doom hovering over me and my home. No wonder people distanced themselves from me. I couldn't say I blamed them. It was as if I were infected with a malignant, contagious disease. I wouldn't wish this sentence on anyone.

Effective immediately, Laura was now priority and not Andrew. All this was so unfair. We'd had more than our share of trauma, and maybe I was to blame. I had put my head in the sand last summer when she was hanging around with kids I didn't trust. But I didn't want to take her support system away. I didn't know what bothered her more—losing Andrew, her father, the divorce and abandonment, or all of the above. Laura's life had evolved into a battlefield on which she was tired of fighting, so drugs were her retaliation and peace. I understood all this, but it needed to be fixed immediately.

I was in communication with the other parents whose daughters were involved, and was shaken by the reality that they were not so concerned. No one saw the life-or-death danger, or the road to destruction that their daughters and my Laura were on. The only solution was to put her into the best drug rehab program I could find. I would do everything to save her life, even though now she hated me and would fight my decision. I still had excellent health-care coverage, which included in-patient treatment programs for up to two months.

To avoid conflict, I didn't consult with James. It had only been three weeks since the divorce. I would inform him after she was in a program. I contacted John Herald, her therapist at Westin, and we found Silver Acres, a rehab program in Carmel, New York. Laura met with John at his office in nearby Woodbury immediately. In shock, I sat in the waiting room as she went into John's office. Later John called me and told me about their session.

"Laura, we've always been open and honest, right?"

"Right."

"You're a gifted young woman with the world at your feet, and you've had more pain and suffering than most people will know in a lifetime. But right now you are on a road to destruction, and it has to stop before it kills you. You need to get into a drug program, and your mom has everything in place. I know you think she is too controlling, but she's also been through a lot, and right now her only priority is you."

They went back and forth. Laura's eyes were glazed with tears. "Okay, I'll give it a try. I'm not saying I'll stay or I need it, but I'll try it out."

The drive to Silver Acres was pin-drop quiet. Laura was dazed and sluggish. Her school friends acknowledged she was experimenting with drugs, but I didn't know if it was marijuana, acid, cocaine, or all of them. I quivered at the reality, afraid to speak for fear she would misconstrue my intentions and provoke a scene. But she seemed textbook high on marijuana, exhibiting all the signs of drug use: interference in muscle coordination and reasoning skills, long-term memory loss, vision impairment, diminished school performance, no motivation, and low self-esteem. I remembered teaching all this to my students at Sacred Family. Where had I gone wrong with my own daughter?

The ride seemed like an eternity, and I sensed she was getting anxious. Was she in drug withdrawal? "So I smoked a few joints—big deal. Everybody does it. I don't have a problem. I'm too smart. Todd and Andrew both smoked and you didn't put them in rehab."

When we reached Silver Acres, I didn't utter a word and fearfully parked in the no-parking zone. She stared at the building and slowly got out.

"There are no bars on the windows."

I panicked. *Is she having second thoughts and going to run? Then what will I do? Who will I call? Please, God, just get her inside.*

She headed to the front door and never looked back at me. Was this intentional, to avoid seeing tears in my eyes, along with the despair and agony on my face? Then she turned around.

"Mom, the only reason I'm trying this is because I respect you and John Herald. I'll stay a few days, and then you can come and get me."

I remained quiet. I had learned not to argue. The admission process went quickly. I yearned to hold her and say, "Everything will be all right. I love you." But immediately a counselor appeared and whisked her off. I returned to the car and sobbed. A few days later I received a letter from her.

> *Dear Mom,*
>
> *Now that I've been here four days, I know how everything works—how the counselors observe you and how the system operates. I know what they are thinking and what they are going to say. I got your letter yesterday. Thank you. It was nice to get mail. I'm giving you until Monday until I do something drastic. Mom, be reasonable, what were you thinking when you stuck me here? Come on—I'm a teenager who smoked pot occasionally, and all of a sudden I'm some drug addict who needs eight damn weeks of rehab? I don't have a problem. All I needed was for Westin to say, "You're getting a urinalysis, and if your usage doesn't decrease, you can't go to school here anymore."*
>
> *I know you are concerned, Mom, but this is a little much. This place is for people addicted to crack, cocaine, heroin, and alcohol. They're going to make pot legal soon—it has no harmful effects and little lung damage. You've been overprotective since Andrew's accident, and I don't blame you, but this time you've gone too far. I am a tremendously confused girl whose life seems to be crashing in on me.*
>
> *You and John misled me into thinking this place was for troubled teens. There are no bars on the windows, and it is quite easy to escape. Don't make this a problem. I have inherited your strong-headedness and know I shouldn't be here, and I refuse to stay. If I don't hear from you by Monday,*

> *I'm going to have to do something. When you get this letter, call Silver Acres and tell them you are coming to take me home.*
> *Laura*

Three days later I received another letter.

> *Mom, I just spoke with my case manager, and she has informed me that if they discharge me from this program, you will send me to another place. If they discharge me, it means I don't have a problem. I think you are afraid because my problems have to do with your problems, and you don't want to face them. Stop pretending and playing games. Sooner or later you're going to have to face the truth. I think that's really shitty of you!*
> *Your daughter, Laura*

Due to her strong denial of a drug problem, we scheduled an intervention. After two hours of anger and more denial, she walked out. The staff informed me they would not keep her if she did not acknowledge her drug use. I begged for John Herald's help for a second intervention. He agreed, as did three of her friends from Westin, whom he prepared for this meeting.

Finally, she broke down and opened her soul to the pain that had disturbed her for years. She whimpered, her body shook, and she erupted into tears and then loud sobs. She rose from her chair and embraced John and her friends. Everyone cried, but to me they were tears of joy, almost symbolic of a baptism for her start on a road to wellness and recovery.

I was scheduled to work three days at St. John's, visit Andrew for three days, and see Laura on Saturday—the only day visitors were allowed. When Laura called and asked James to come and visit, he said, "My heart is broken, and I cannot bear to be in the same room as your mother."

Laura was on her way from numbness to being alive again. She told him, "Please, Daddy, love me. I love you." But her cries were in vain. James was inhumane. I was livid.

Back at Highgate, Andrew had graduated to regular observation. I still drove up every week, and we had our first unchaperoned visit. I mentioned to Dr. McKenzie that Andrew wanted to come home for a visit. Two weeks later he did. The weekend ran smoothly, and he was almost too perfect, controlled, and agreeable. I basked in every moment. It had been nine months since he'd been home, and I had my sights set on him returning to start his senior year at Regional School District 10 in the fall. Prior to Andrew's home visit, James had seen him at Highgate twice and stayed thirty minutes, but was not allowed to take him off the premises because he had been drinking.

Laura's rehab program was coming to an end. She'd worked hard and learned a lot. She had placed James on a pedestal that had been slowly shattered, and she was terrified he might die from drinking. Her education profile stated she was an exceptionally talented young woman, had maintained an A average in all subjects, and translated *Winnie the Pooh* into Latin. Her test scores placed her beyond twelfth-grade ability.

She was anxious to return to Westin in the fall for her senior year, not knowing that the disciplinary council had already expelled her.

"There is no drug use at Westin," Joe Crabb, the headmaster, maintained.

When I originally received the letter of her expulsion, I was outraged. Laura had been condemned and crucified without a hearing. How could they penalize her because she went into rehab to save her life? She had a disease and should be admired for her courage, not blamed for the school's refusal to deal with its substance-abuse problem.

I was sure the headmaster was behind all this. He was old, out of touch, and ignorant with regard to addiction and substance abuse. I decided I would fight his decision and call in legal help from my lawyer, Bill Jones, even though I wanted her out of Westin. Bill and I met with Joe Crabb, but his decision had been made. I dropped the idea of a lawsuit—it would take time, and we had none. Laura needed to get into another school now.

At Rosemary's, I reclined on the couch. "I'm completely drained. In a few weeks Laura will be discharged from Silver Acres. The last four days of her rehab program will be a family forum, and it's very important for all family members to attend. It'll be too much for Andrew, but Todd's coming home from college, and I begged James to attend. I'm sure if I promise him a quickie, he'll make it. Who knows—I might even enjoy it, if I put a bag over my head."

Rosemary and I giggled like teenagers. But all too soon the silliness of the moment was gone. "Sometimes the pain is so heavy I feel I'm sinking and would be better off dead, but who would take care of these children that I love more than myself?" *I just need a break. Please, God.*

"I think we need to up your antidepressant again, and I need to see you twice next week."

"Okay, but I need to scoot to Region 10 for a PPT meeting for Laura. She'll be starting there soon." And now, having deservedly earned a PhD in PPT meetings, everything went perfectly.

The week of the family forum, Laura had spoken to her dad, who still accused me of ripping the family apart. I could hardly believe my ears when I heard he would come if I drove. No problem—I would do anything to have Laura involved with Laura at this crucial point. Well, almost anything. I picked him up and complimented him on how nice he looked. Then I focused the conversation on Laura and the boys.

At Silver Acres, we were directed into a small room with six other families I had bonded with over the past seven weeks. They knew our family dynamics and were nonjudgmental of James. The situation offered absolutely no opportunity for him to sneak a drink. When he walked across the room with a cup of coffee, his hands were shaking as if an earthquake were under his feet. One of the counselors asked to meet him privately, and at the end of the day I heard him say, "I won't be attending any more sessions. I have to work."

It was an out-and-out lie.

On the way home, he started yelling in the car as I drove, "Those counselors had one hell of a nerve, trying to get me alone in a room and zero in on my drinking. They had no right infringing on my personal life. It's none of their business. They even had the nerve to say it was Laura's idea. Those places are all the same—minding everyone's business but their own."

I tried to maintain my composure. "James, Laura's had eight weeks of substance-abuse education. She loves you very much and is afraid she's going to lose you. Your presence is vital to her recovery."

"Yeah, well, she'll get over it."

If I hadn't been driving, I would have ripped his carotids out of his neck. Why did I keep hoping this man would see the light, be a parent, and stop causing his children so much pain?

Ten minutes from his mother's house, I could hardly wait to dump him out.

"Con, can we go for dinner?"

I was at a boiling point but kept it hidden, just in case he changed his mind and would return to Silver Acres tomorrow. "Thanks, James, but I'm really bushed. Maybe some other time."

The next morning Todd and I showed up for the family forum at Silver Acres. Laura came to greet us and appeared much happier. She hugged Todd. "Where's Dad? Is he driving himself?"

Todd was hesitant. "Laura, he's not coming."

Momentarily she froze, and then ran out of the room, sobbing. I explained to the group what had happened, and we continued on without James.

By the end of the third day it became obvious to all that Todd was at a breaking point. His body shook, his face reddened, and tears streamed down his cheeks. He gasped, unable to speak as the counselor rushed and knelt in front of him. She consoled him and instructed us to form a human chain. Then Todd lay down on the human chain, supported by the hands of the group, and was bounced up and down the chain. This allowed him to break down the barriers of control and give in to trusting the members in the group. He was able to open up and discuss his feelings. The human touch from caring people creates a sense of security, trust, and peace.

On the last day of the family forum, it was Laura's turn to talk. She participated in a role-playing exercise and chose a kind man to play her father. It was difficult for her to look at him, and she twirled her hair nervously.

He began by saying, "Laura, I love you."

She rocked back and forth and whimpered, her eyes full of tears. I sat in the circle, agonized by her raw, aching pain, while trying to control my own battle of emotions, my heart and soul ripped open and bleeding.

After a few moments, in a meek, quivering voice she began. "Dad, I love you. I worry about you all the time. You were always there for me. You always had time to listen. I was your special little girl. I miss you so much and don't understand how you could leave me." She gulped a breath. "What have I done that you don't love me anymore?" She wept openly. "I'm afraid you're going to leave me forever and die from your drinking."

The counselor hugged and held her. Todd and I were mute, our lips trembling. The group cried as they watched Laura grieve the death of her relationship with her father. She was broken and bleeding. Could she be saved?

In the four days of the forum, the group had shared their deepest and most intimate fears. Could our children make it in the real world now? After discharge, every patient had a continuing treatment plan. Laura would attend The Center for Living, twenty minutes from Middlebury, as well as ninety consecutive days at Narcotics Anonymous and Alcoholics Anonymous.

As well as seeing my therapist, I was going to once again try Al-Anon. Maybe it would help. Dammit, we were all going to do better! Things weren't going to change overnight, but at least we were moving forward—one minute, one hour, one day at a time.

Laura was ready to come home, even though the treatment team felt she might do better going to a halfway house for a few months. Bidding farewell was upsetting but happy. There was so much uncertainty in her life, and so much had changed.

On the way home we dove directly into the future with an afternoon PPT meeting at Region 10 high school, where Laura would finish her junior year. She was tense at the thought of a new school, new friends, new curriculum, and all the world knowing she had just come out of drug rehab. It was a valuable meeting, except for the fact that James was missing. I made sure that her detailed educational needs, as well as the huge support system we discussed a few weeks ago, were in place.

You can imagine how thrilled my public enemy, Dr. Jinnie, was. Andrew and his issues were one thing, and now with Laura's, I'd be at school twice as much. I could already feel the love.

After the meeting, the school counselor asked me to stop by while Laura was getting a tour. He closed the door, and before he could get a word out, I reached for a tissue and started to cry.

He said, "You know, you're doing more than most. A lot of parents would have given up by now. I can only try to understand what you're all going through. Please tell Laura my door will always be open for her, and don't hesitate to call if you have any concerns. By the way, how's Andrew?"

"I'm hoping he'll start his senior year here. It's still up in the air."

"It's time your luck changed."

"You're right. Maybe it will now, thanks." I sat in the car waiting for Laura. *God, you heard the counselor. Please, I need my luck to change. Isn't it time?* I leafed through some of the paperwork from Silver Acres and found a small notebook that was given to me by some of the group members. I began to read it for the first time.

> *Dear Connie,*
>
> *Your family is very lucky to have you as their mother. You have courage and strength to deal with the problems of life. This is a rare quality. Feel good about yourself.*
>
> *Love, Joan*

> *Connie,*
>
> *You have been an inspiration to me—so centered, sensitive, and open in the face of adversity. I know Hemingway was talking about men when he said this, but you have "grace under pressure." Your presence has been a gift.*
>
> *Love, Evelyn*

> *Connie,*
>
> *I think in some language "Connie" must translate to inspiration. I only hope that in my own life I can be as strong as you. To face what you have, and still be as wonderful a person, is quite an accomplishment. Thank you for your strength and support over these weeks.*
>
> *Much love, Lucy*

I pressed the notebook close to my heart, then quickly put it in my purse, as Laura was heading to the car. This book would be a wonderful source of encouragement when I hit the low points on this difficult journey.

Then finally, there was a ray of hope. The assistant headmaster at Westin, Betsy Fugowa, contacted me. She disagreed with headmaster Joe Crabb and believed Laura should be able to apply as a new student for her senior year. She recommended Laura complete her junior year at Region 10, do summer work to complete Latin, and then take a placement test. Then she should contact all the other teachers and write a full statement about her reasons for wanting to return and her commitment to remain drug-free. Determined, Laura did all this but the bitter verdict came down. Joe Crabb overruled and was vehement. "Laura can never enter Westin again."

I met with Betsy, but she was powerless to change Crabb's decision. Two weeks later she resigned her position. Actually, I was happy Laura wasn't returning, but she was once again shattered. She wanted so badly to graduate from Westin. It had always been her dream.

July Fourth was almost upon us, and Todd, Laura, and I were going to Nantucket. Finances were tight, so we would backpack, bring food, and all stay in one room at a B and B. When we arrived, the beautiful, familiar Nantucket skyline greeted us. I was sure this was a cheery omen. Nothing could touch us here . . . or so I thought. As we walked into town, Todd and Laura rolled their eyes while I prattled on about wellness. "All this walking, biking, and hiking will yield a cardiovascular reward."

"Yes, Mother," they respectfully moaned. Under their breath they said, "I hope she's done."

But I wasn't. "We haven't survived to this point on luck, and can't dwell on problems. Your main focus must be to take care of *you* first. If this isn't your priority, you are useless to those you love. A good night's sleep is core. A rested, energized person thinks clearly, regardless of the crisis. Poor sleep puts your day in a deficit, causing the rest of the day to be an uphill battle. Exercise gets the endorphin juices flowing and increases energy, a gift you give to yourself. And with healthy food, the body is a fine-tuned engine."

Todd and Laura just rolled their eyes.

While browsing in one of the shops, we were completely unaware that Trudy and her family were coming directly toward us. We hadn't seen or heard from any of them since the divorce four months before. Not a word when Laura was in rehab. When I saw Trudy, I immediately pictured a letter she'd written prior to the divorce, listing half the silver, china, crystal, and antiques that she felt James should have. I remember my lawyer being exasperated with her meddling and saying to me, "If you're going to divide that stuff, the kids should each get one-fifth, so they'll have a plate to eat on at Thanksgiving."

And now there she was, right in front of me, three feet away with hubby, Dean, and son and daughter, Cane and Anita. She looked trapped and shocked and walked over and hugged me and the children. We started a pleasant conversation. Cane said, " hi", then disappeared. Anita stood like a statue, and Dean—showing his true colors—turned away, unable to face us and walked out of the store without uttering a word to his niece and nephew. I was livid. It was clear that Trudy, Dean, Cane, and Anita considered themselves divorced from James's children as well.

Trudy informed me that James was back at the cottage, still heartbroken since the divorce. I knew the kids wanted to see him, so they called.

"Dad, we're going to dinner—Mom included—and we want you to join us. Please, Dad."

"It would be too hard for me, but why don't you kids bike out to the cottage?"

They did, but returned earlier than expected, with Todd visibly shaken. "Mom, it was awful. Nobody talked to us, and we weren't offered anything—not even lunch. It was like we were intruders. We couldn't wait to get out of there. What have we done wrong?"

"You haven't done anything wrong. Your dad and his family are . . . just not well, not thinking clearly. They'll get better."

On our last day we spent our time surfside, riding the waves. No one mentioned the other side of the family. The minute we got on the ferry back to the mainland, I was asleep. The cardio challenge had done me in.

August was a hectic month. James and I were back on the docket. I received an updated list of more items he wanted from the house. I was positive his family had egged him on, and they would not rest until they had stripped us bare. In retaliation, I refused to give him anything. The family relations officer announced she saw no resolution between the two of us, to which James replied, "Now you can see why I divorced her, can't you?"

"Excuse me, but I divorced *you*."

I heard rumors that Dee had bought him a business, and that he had a girlfriend. I wasn't prepared for my ambivalent feelings and was damn annoyed he had time to start a new life.

Also, Andrew would be coming home for his senior year at Region 10. Joy to the world! There were many powwows over his discharge from Highgate, but I was firm—it was time. He'd been there a year, and it had cost the insurance company $300,000. He was the only one who was discharged that year. I wasn't surprised, because no other client had an excellent program like Andrew's, and no other parents were there weekly to monitor their children. It was easy for Highgate to bill for services not rendered, but I naively trusted and believed that most people were honorable. I would again be proven wrong. Would I ever learn?

During one of my last trips to Highgate, Andrew and I were moseying around the grounds when Dr. McKenzie approached, a big smile on his face. "Mrs. Kane, Andrew, I have some very exciting news. Remember a while back I mentioned that PBS was doing a special on traumatic brain injury? I submitted Andrew's success story, and we've been chosen for the show. They're helicoptering in a producer, director, and crew for a day of shooting. It's scheduled for the week before Andrew leaves. You've worked hard and it's paid off. It's a big step for you and TBI."

Andrew smiled and nodded his head. "I told you I'd do it."

"Mrs. Kane, they want to interview you as well."

Elated with the news, I arched my eyebrows and beamed. "And well they should." Finally I was going to be in the movies! I wondered if my right or left side was best for the camera.

Andrew laughed it off. "My mother sometimes . . ."

A good sign—we had not lost our sense of humor.

The day for filming arrived. Most of the shooting revolved around Andrew, who looked handsome in khaki shorts and a pink button-down shirt. He talked about the hardship of going to school, coming home, and sitting around, but mostly about the loss of his friends. He described the onset of his depression and the realization that he needed help when he was at home, alone, and lying on his bed, and when, in his head, heard people laughing at him. He spoke of the hurt he felt being estranged from his father, recalling the devastation he experienced when I threw him a birthday party and James didn't call or show.

I was amazed at how at ease I was during my interview, especially when I had to recall the accident, the roller coaster, the psychological damage our family had suffered, and the fact that James was no longer at home.

The shoot was over. As I drove home, my mind was completely absorbed, overcome with emotions. I barely saw the flashing lights and trooper behind me. I pulled my car over, and as the trooper approached the car, I broke into tears.

"Officer, please, let me explain." And then I went on and on and on . . .

He listened, surely regretting he'd ever stopped me. "Put the car on cruise control so you get home in one piece."

No ticket. Ah, most people are good. And a Moose Jaw girl always respects the law.

A week later I brought Andrew home. He was both anxious and proud to show me a letter.

> *To whom it may concern:*
>
> *It is with pleasure that I write to express my observation of Mr. Andrew Kane at Highgate Rehabilitation Center. For the past six months Andrew has been in charge of weighing and stamping mail at our facility under the direction of his job coach. This part-time job was an integral component of Andrew's rehabilitation plan and a very important function for the facility, which has over three hundred employees and clients.*
>
> *Andrew's job performance was exemplary, as was his dedication to arriving on time and working until the job was completed. On many occasions he demonstrated creative problem-solving and the ability to plan ahead and develop contingency methods to meet his responsibilities. He was cheerful and extremely polite to people as he worked in a highly trafficked area. I feel he has the ability to expand his work experience if given the opportunity. He will be a most valuable employee.*

I was overcome with joy.

September arrived. It was the first day of school for Laura and Andrew entering their senior year at Region 10. I was up early, and had the day off, so planned to make a big breakfast and drive them to avoid a bus schedule as well as everything else. They should have been relaxed and happy, but I knew they weren't. At least they had each other.

Being a morning person, I headed down the hallway and knocked on Andrew's door. He was already up and dressing. "And don't you look handsome, ready for your first day?"

"It takes me so long to get dressed, and I'm already late. Would you please tie my shoelaces?"

I knelt down. "Of course, I will. Getting into the routine is hard. You'll be fine in a few days. Would you like pancakes or French toast?"

"Ma, you don't have to make my breakfast. I'm capable of doing that."

"I know you are, but today I'm the chef. I'm a working gal now, and won't be here most mornings."

"Okay, French toast with Grandma's special syrup."

"You've got it, my man."

I continued to Laura's room. "You up, Laura?"

Before she could answer, I began singing with intensity and theatrics a song they'd heard since nursery school. "School days, school days, dear old golden rule days. Reading and writing and 'rithmetic —"

"Mom, stop singing. It's too early."

"Time to get up, Miss America. The limo leaves in forty-five minutes, and I want to get to Mass after . . . on time."

I think all this was more difficult for Laura, but I knew we'd survive these obstacles with increased strength, grace, and prayer.

That afternoon I had a session with Rosemary. "I'm drained by the continual pain in their eyes. I think Andrew is wrestling with his deficits. We've been working on that five-year calendar and only have a year to go. He thought if he worked harder than most kids for five years, he'd be exactly how he used to be. The reality is frustrating him, and the biggest problem is that he remembers exactly how he was before the accident. He was handsome, voted most popular, made every team, was always picked first to caddy by the big tippers, always had cash in his pockets from his odd jobs."

I was in tears. "And Laura—I'm not happy with her attitude or friends. She's very unhappy, so young, and has lost so much. Damn that James—we never hear from him or his family. We all see our therapists and will be better, but . . . somehow the thirty-two-ounce bottle of Kahlua I brought back from Mexico is empty, and I know I didn't touch it."

We just stared at each other, then I changed the subject. "I think I'll call James to see if he'll talk to me. Maybe he'll listen and see the kids, now that everyone is home."

James and I arranged to meet at his favorite morning diner, The Oaks. I hadn't seen him in four months and remembered that awful scene the last time we met. He walked in, and to my amazement was well-groomed and sober. I wished it could always have been this way. I realized I still loved this man. I hesitated and then seductively asked, "So how's your purple passionate penis?"

He nearly choked on his coffee. "You always know how to cut to the chase, don't you, Con?"

"Yes, I haven't forgotten. James, I desperately want us to be friends. Our children need both of us. I wish I knew how to be their father, but I don't. They love you very much, and want you to be part of their lives."

"Con, I told you when you started this divorce you would see a side of me you weren't going to like, but you wouldn't listen. I don't mean to hurt you, but if I can't have the whole package, I don't want any part of it."

Glaring, I replied, "These are your children, your flesh and blood. They've been through hell!"

"I'm sorry, but that's the way it has to be."

Unprepared for this blow, my face blanched. I bit my tongue. "You bastard, I hate you." He picked up the paper and read it as if nothing had happened, as if I wasn't there. I got up from the table shaking and sick at heart.

My mother informed me my dad's health was deteriorating and he wanted to take all of us, including my sister and her two children, on one last big holiday to Hawaii for Christmas. Everyone was excited. But I was even more so. I was anxious to share the lure of the islands that had beckoned me to move there when I was just twenty-one years old and a newly graduated nurse. I would show my children where their dad was stationed and where I used to work and live. I fantasized about the hypnotic aloha spirit, and returning to my home and friends of long ago and yearned to share that tender passion and enchantment, the place where my American journey began many years ago.

Hawaii was a tropical paradise. At Queens Hospital on Liho 111, a medical floor where I worked, I had met the most fascinating group of patients. The British ambassador was a patient, and when he was released he held a huge party at his home in Kahala, to which he invited me and my roommates. We parked our wreck of a car far enough away so no one would see it and have to valet it. Then, donned in cocktail dresses and big smiles, we entered the party and blended in quite nicely and rather easily.

Another patient from New York, who attributed his life to the care he received from the nurses, bought us all leis to wear while at work. He then took us out on the town. A priest, who was also grateful to the staff, brought in gold crosses for us.

One day, to earn extra money, I worked across the street at The Kaiser Center. I was asked to admit a patient by the name of Kaiser. One of the nurses in my class was Kaiser, so I knew the name and thought nothing of it. After I admitted Mr. Kaiser, he mentioned that he was going out to a cocktail party later. I smiled and then informed him, "I'm sorry, Mr. Kaiser, I'm not sure if that will be possible within the protocol and policy for the hospital, but not to worry. I will check it out and get back to you." I found his doctor and told him what had transpired.

He looked at me almost stunned. "Miss Gross, do you know who Mr. Kaiser is?"

"I'm sorry, I'm afraid I don't."

"Well, Henry J. Kaiser owns this hospital and half of the island."

And then my mouth fell open. "Oh, *that* Mr. Kaiser. Right. I'll be back in a minute." I went directly to Mr. Kaiser's room. He was standing looking out the window, in deep thought, I surmised. "Mr. Kaiser." He turned around. "I just wanted to say, have a wonderful evening tonight." I smiled at him.

He very calmly smiled back. "And you too, Miss Gross."

I walked out of the room and breathed a huge sigh. Working in Hawaii was one constant adventure.

At Christmas our family arrived in Maui for sun, surf, and frivolity. Todd was maturing into a responsible young man and spent a lot of time talking with Granny. She shared with him the fact that when her son Earl, my brother, had passed away, he had a sizable death policy that he had left to her. That was why she was spending so much of it on her family, in order to create wonderful memories.

We spent a day visiting one of the nurses I used to work with at Queens Hospital. Her family wined and dined us and took us snorkeling. She impressed the kids by doing the hula. We reminisced about people we knew: the resident who loved to surf; Robin Cook, who became a best-selling author; and Mrs. Gibson, whose artwork became internationally famous. We talked of the fun we had working on Liho 111. She knew James and liked him. And then, when Andrew was not around, she addressed me frankly. "Tell me about Andrew and James." As I related everything, her mouth dropped open wide. She went into shock.

Another day I took the children to Waikiki on Oahu, where I used to live, and to Queens Hospital, and then to Tripler Medical Center, where James had been stationed. Hawaii was where it all had begun so beautifully, and I had not forgotten.

After celebrating New Year's Eve in grand style, we ended an enchanting tropical vacation. My father attributed the enormous bill to my expensive choices and tastes. So unlike a simple Moose Jaw girl.

It was now 1991, the start of a challenging new year for the Kanes. Todd was finishing his junior year at Northeastern, and Laura and Andrew were graduating from high school. Then the guidance counselor from Region 10 called me in for a meeting. He was concerned that Andrew was slacking off and Laura's grades were falling. Both were unmotivated.

Discouraged, I confronted Andrew.

"Ma, I'm tired of all of this. I don't fit in anywhere. I'm older than most kids, have to go to special classes, and have no friends. You expect me to be perfect and I'm not. And I can afford to slack off. I only need three credits to graduate."

"Andrew, you are special. I've told you that from the time you were born, and since your accident I realize it even more. I'm sorry if I'm pushing too hard. I'm just a mother, and I'll do anything to make your dreams come true."

"I think it's time for me to take care of myself. I want to do my own laundry, ironing, and cooking. I'll still have time for my schoolwork."

I said okay, but I was worried that this would be too much. He'd also started a part-time work program with IBM and liked the idea of wearing a shirt and tie. At first it all went well, but then came reports of minor infractions of policy rules and stories of his being argumentative.

At home, Laura witnessed his frustrations. "Andrew, the kitchen's a mess, the ironing board is out, there's food all over—do you want me to help you?"

"No, I've got to learn to do it alone." There were tears in his eyes. Andrew was stubborn and determined to prove he was independent and ready for college.

With help from Dr. McMase, Rosemary, Todd, the guidance counselor, and the team at Region 10, we discussed that a college environment might only set him up for failure and that a local community college would better suit his needs. I enrolled him at Mattatuck for the fall. He was unhappy with the decision.

Despite this, he applied for a college scholarship from Newington Children's Hospital, and without my help he won. I'd hoped this would boost his spirits and ease his anxiety, but I sensed it was the upcoming graduation dance that was unnerving him.

He'd invited a German exchange student, and she'd accepted. This was his first date since his accident, and he was sweating. The day for the dance arrived. It was a beautiful June evening. Todd graciously provided the car service, and Andrew held his date's hand like the gentleman he was. Focused on walking perfectly straight—no limping allowed on the special night—his gait was a little slower than usual. His date ran inside the auditorium in the midst of a flurry of excitement. Everyone was euphoric, while Andrew stood watching in the doorway alone, trying to find his date. However, she was never to be seen again. He tried to comprehend what had happened as he turned away. Staring vacantly, his face drained, ghost white. She had dumped him.

He went outside, gasping for air, and wandered around aimlessly, hiding in shame in the dark. Somehow, he got home eight hours later.

I had worked an evening shift, came home, and went to bed late. The next morning I tiptoed by his room, and the door was still closed. I smiled to myself, assuming he was still sleeping and didn't disturb him. I walked by the tall schefflera plant in the hallway, "And good morning to you; you're looking well." I could hardly wait to hear all the details, and I loved that German student for helping Andrew realize what a wonderful young man he was. I'd have her over for dinner and put on a spread soon.

It was midday before the reality of what had happened unfolded. If I didn't pop a major blood vessel then, I never would. How could anyone be so cruel? This rejection was another brutal blow to his already delicate ego. I was furious at the entire world. Didn't anyone care about him? *God, are you there at all?*

Within a few weeks I was on my knees praying and sobbing. Something was not right. Andrew was showing signs of paranoia again. How could this be? I contacted his therapist, Dr. Smine, and took him in for an immediate assessment. Obviously psychotic, Andrew was uncooperative and refused therapy. When we returned home, he was highly agitated. His behavior had escalated, and he was shouting mindlessly. Dr. Smine called me to say that he had made plans for Andrew's admission to the Wellness Center in Hartford, but getting him there was the problem. Todd and Laura both tried to talk to him, but to no avail. His psychosis was in charge. I called and begged James to help us, but again he refused.

Meanwhile, Andrew played me. "Maybe I'll go. Maybe I won't. Maybe I'll go later."

I patiently played along, hoping he'd finally agree, but by midnight I was exhausted. His adrenaline was pumping him up. I started to call the police, but when he overheard, he really went off. I hung up the phone, hoping to resolve this on my own. He paced around the kitchen, and before I knew what was happening, he headed for the butcher block, grabbed a knife, fled to his room, and slammed the door shut. Oh my God, not again! Please not again!

My fingers trembled as I dialed 911. Terrified, I shouted, "This is an emergency. Connie Kane, Green Road." The very name validated that it was a serious problem. "My son Andrew's sick and out of control. Send help—no sirens please. He's got a knife in his hand!"

"They're on their way, Mrs. Kane."

Chapter Twelve

June 1991–November 1991

I DROPPED THE PHONE AND flew to Andrew's room. The door was ajar, and all was still except for my pounding, racing heart. Half dazed, I peeked in, fearful of the horror that might face me. A terrible vision entered my mind, and I quickly dismissed it.

I scanned the room. Andrew lay motionless on his bed, staring at the ceiling, the knife resting on his desk. The demons of paranoia surrounded him, and I was momentarily thankful for their distractions. He was unaware of my presence as I snuck to his desk, gently grabbed the knife, and tiptoed out.

My heart thrashed inside me. My hands were ice. My face flushed. I wanted to cry, but my tear ducts were frozen. I was losing ground. An ominous aura had taken over me and the house. I slapped my face and was jolted back to reality.

The police arrived and called an ambulance. Thank goodness for a small town where everyone knew everyone's business. Even though I was alone in trying to remedy Andrew's problems, everyone witnessed his struggle and still knew that he was a genuinely wonderful young man.

As Andrew ambled down the hallway to the kitchen, I started to call Dr. Smine, but once he saw the police, the pleasantries were all over. "What are you doing here? Did my mother call you? She's trying to control my life, and I'm sick of it!" He was agitated and escalating, his pupils dilated and right arm in spasm.

Calmly, I said, "Yes, Andrew, I called them. You scared me when you grabbed the knife. I think you need to go to the hospital, just for a little while."

"No more fucking hospitals!" With increased rage he grabbed another knife and wildly fled down the hall and outside to the patio.

The police chief called for backup as he scrambled out of the house. "Andrew, I've known you since you were a little boy. You played on my Little League team. I know you wouldn't hurt yourself or anyone else. You're scaring your mom, and you know she loves you. Just give me the knife, please."

Andrew pulled the knife closer to his chest, stood very still, and stared into space. No one spoke—we all froze. Then he started to rotate his head as if he was gazing up to the heavens and someone was calling him. Slowly, he extended his hand and gave the knife to the policeman. An ambulance and another police cruiser arrived with two EMTs.

"Come on, Andrew—let's get into the ambulance. We're your friends, and we'll stay with you." Taking every precaution, they called for another volunteer, well aware of the physical threat posed by an emotionally out-of-control individual.

It was now pitch black as I got into my car to follow the ambulance to the Wellness Center. Through my tears I glanced at the clock. It was after one a.m. My thoughts—strange that I could still think—were chaotic. The neighbors would be going to bed after listening to their police scanners, imagining the terror that had once again taken place. All the floodlights were on, the police activity visible to all. And Andrew, that wonderful Kane boy who fell from a swing, who nearly died, now has more problems than ever. I could hear their pity. "Poor Connie Kane carries such a burden, and then there's that alcoholic husband." At that moment I wanted their pity as I sobbed uncontrollably, sinking into despair. Would Andrew ever be well? Would he survive the trauma of the accident? Did he really want to kill himself? Was it all too much for him to endure?

I finished the admission paperwork and was directed to the building where Andrew would be staying. The Wellness Center had a wonderful reputation as a facility for celebrities and the very wealthy. I heard that a member of a famous family was in residence, which meant it must be a top-notch place. And thanks to my excellent hospital insurance from my job on the psych unit, Andrew was covered 100 percent for this facility.

When I arrived on the unit, Andrew was with the on-call doctor. The man wore baggy jeans and a sweater, and wrote frantically, unaware he would soon have volumes. After the admission intake, an exhausted but calmer Andrew was taken to his room. I kissed him and watched him go down a hallway, shoulders slumped, defeated. I glanced at my watch. It was four thirty in the morning. I desperately needed sleep.

The next morning, I returned drained but eager to discuss Andrew's treatment and to make sure he was being cared for properly. I rang a bell outside the large door of the Wellness Center. When the door opened, I was greeted by an obstinate young man about twenty-five years of age. He was annoyed and impatient, and before I could speak, he rudely snapped at me. "Visiting hours aren't until six p.m."

"I'm Mrs. Kane. My son Andrew was admitted early this morning."

Obstinate Boy with major attitude interrupted me. "And I repeat, visiting hours aren't until six p.m."

"Excuse me, but I spoke with Dr. Krause, and he's expecting me."

"Wait a minute." The door slammed shut.

Obstinate Boy with an attitude and I were doomed for major confrontation. Preparing for battle, I took several deep breaths. I work on a psychiatric unit, and this is not the way to treat people. I stood very tall, shoulders back, chest out. The taller I was, the better to intimidate.

He probably believed *this* opposite sex was old, weak, and should be put down. He hadn't encountered Connie Kane from Moose Jaw. The door opened again. It was obvious that Obstinate Boy's divine right had been trampled on. He barely looked at me.

"Follow me."

I followed him to the nurses' station.

"Wait here. His nurse will be just a few minutes."

Obstinate Boy continued on, most likely determined to control the next important situation. Everyone appeared to be very busy. They acknowledged me with quick glances but continued on with what they were doing. Of course I knew that discussions and collaboration were important, yet I felt the appropriate and professional response would be polite acknowledgement of my presence. I questioned their common courtesy.

The quality and integrity of caring for patients must include family, social, psychological, and spiritual needs. All this was critical to Andrew's success, and I questioned if this group met that criteria. I was growing restless with the negative aura. It was not healthy or therapeutic. I had expected superior treatment from this facility. I was terrified and at the mercy of the staff—even an eye gesture or half smile would have been welcomed. I always had a gut feeling, an immediate instinctive sense, about hospitals, and I was usually right. And now I was having second thoughts about this place. Did I make a mistake bringing Andrew here?

Finally, a nurse appeared. "Hi, Mrs. Kane. I'm Andrew's nurse, Beth. Let me explain, please. Since Andrew threatened to harm himself, we have him on suicide precautions to ensure his safety and the safety of those around him. He must stay in his room, which is stripped of everything that can hurt him. He will be observed every fifteen minutes. At this stage, we usually restrict visitors, but Dr. Krause okayed it. Please don't stay too long. Rest is imperative, and we've just medicated him. Thirty minutes."

And to myself, I said, "I'll stay as long as necessary to check on Andrew and this facility. This is not a social visit."

Grinding my teeth, I followed Beth to his room. Andrew was asleep. The room was depressing and needed a major update. I had expected a more therapeutic, healing environment, especially with the international reputation the center had.

Feeling our presence, Andrew opened his beautiful brown eyes. "Ma, why did you put me here? They want me to take medicine again, and you know what that does to me. This time you made a mistake!"

His pleading pulled my aching heartstrings, and I questioned myself. Did I do the right thing? I felt alone against the world and hoped this was the right place for him.

"Please tell me, Andrew—have you been smoking pot or drinking? I'm not angry. I just need to know to help sort this all out."

He shouted, "No, Ma, I haven't. Why do you always think the worst? Why is this happening to me again? I'm sick of hospitals."

"I know, and so am I. You've had a lot of stress this past year, and maybe I've pushed too much. Please take the medicine to get rid of the confusion and voices."

"It makes me sleepy."

"That's okay for now. You need to rest. I'll sit with you. You're not alone, my Gigi. I love you."

He closed his eyes. Quietly I walked around the room. In the bathroom, my eyes caught sight of his electric razor and cord. I rifled through the drawers and found his belt. I glanced at my watch, and it had been more than fifteen minutes, and no one had come to check on him. This was unacceptable. Very controlled and gently, I said, "Honey, you rest, I'll be back in a minute."

I stormed to the nurse's station, only to be intercepted by Obstinate Boy.

"Excuse me," I said, "I need to see Andrew's nurse."

"She's in group therapy and can't be disturbed."

"Then I'd like to see the head nurse."

"She's also in group. I'll let you out—your thirty minutes are up."

"My ass the thirty minutes are up! I want to see the administrator of this hospital, and I want to see him now!"

"I'm calling security to have you removed."

"Call them, and just let one of them try to remove me. Now make that call to the administrator. I'm suing you and this entire facility!" Under my breath, I muttered, "Stupid, stupid boy!"

Soon a middle-aged man entered the unit. Obstinate Boy immediately went to speak with him. I glared at both of them until the gentleman came over to me and extended his hand to shake mine.

"Mrs. Kane, I'm Dr. Krause. Please come into my office."

I was still fuming and wondered if my nostrils were smoking. "This is a lovely room, much nicer than my son's." The doctor stared at me and acknowledged my obvious displeasure. "Are you the administrator of the hospital?"

"No, I'm the unit head. Can I help you?"

"I certainly hope so. My son's razor, cord, and belt should have been stripped from his room, and he has not been monitored every fifteen minutes for suicide precautions. If he really wanted to kill himself, it would have been a done deal. And furthermore, I don't like being treated like an out-of-control dimwit by a pompous twenty-three-year-old. Or whatever age Obstinate Boy is. I'm a registered nurse on a psychiatric unit in Waterbury. My son is my most cherished treasure."

I watched Dr. Krause's posture stiffen.

And I continued. "I'm Andrew's conservator, and until he gets clearer, I don't think it's a good idea for his father to visit. James will sabotage all plans for recovery. He's an alcoholic."

"I understand your concerns, and I will personally handle this matter. Please feel free to call me anytime, and I'm very sorry for all of this. Be assured it will not happen again."

Even though I'd exploded and got my point across, I still wasn't convinced this place was safe. Psychiatry as a discipline was yet not expert on TBI. Even though Andrew presented with the symptoms of psychosis, it was all connected to his TBI. Medicating him was difficult due to his compromised central nervous system.

"Thank you, Dr. Krause." I left his office, and standing outside were two security guards.

"What are you doing here?" Dr. Krause asked.

"We got an emergency call from Tim that a highly agitated female needed to be removed."

Ah, Obstinate Boy had a name. "Dr. Krause, I want Tim's full name. I am reporting him to the hospital administrator. He should not be working here. A prison system might be more in his league. He is nasty, negative, and rude."

"Mrs. Kane, we are in process of downsizing. People are restless, unsure of their positions."

"Uncertainty is not an excuse for bad behavior, Dr. Krause."

As I walked to Andrew's room, a nurse ran quickly in front of me. She rifled through Andrew's drawers and bathroom, removing the potentially dangerous items. It had taken only a few minutes for the word to get out. And soon I would again be dubbed "Meddling Witch," or "Meddling Bitch." And that was okay. I wasn't there to win the Miss Congeniality contest.

Meanwhile, medicating Andrew started with the usual trial and error. I arrived a few days later to find him in bed with a wheelchair parked beside it. "Hi, sweetie, how are you?"

"I don't know. They're doing all kinds of X-rays and tests on me."

I thought, *I bet they are . . .*

He whispered, "Ma, I've had a few accidents. The meds make me so sleepy that I forget to go to the bathroom. And I'm falling and can't walk. The voices are gone, but the doctor told me I need a special place to live. Ma, please take me home."

My heart was heavy as he begged to return to the serenity and peace of his own room, to his personal space and his private memories of what could have been, and away from the present, which bewildered, tormented, and frightened him.

"Andrew, don't worry. Of course you're coming home with me. Where else would my Gigi go? Hey—you're starting college in six weeks."

He looked relieved and smiled for the first time since admission. "I love you, Ma."

"Me too. I need to talk to your doctor, I'll be back in a minute." At the nurse's station I saw Dr. Krause. "Andrew's on too much medication, and it's created more problems."

"Yes, Mrs. Kane, I realize that now. But it will take a few days for the drugs to get out of his system. We're also doing an extensive medical workup."

"Thank you very much. Andrew won a scholarship from Newington Children's Hospital, and a special luncheon is being given for him next week. Any chance?"

"I'm afraid not."

I was hoping for a miracle, for Andrew deserved this recognition, but now I would go alone. That was my norm, and I was used to it. I walked back to his room and watched as he slept peacefully. While he was here, I would have time to organize the other parts of my life — Todd and Laura. Todd was having headaches and nosebleeds. Somehow his nose had taken a wrong growth turn and had curved noticeably to one side. He needed a septoplasty, or nose job. He'd also sprained his ankle and had to see an orthopedic specialist. We were all still in therapy, and the bills were piling up.

I received Andrew's final PPT from Region 10, and Dr. Jinnie infuriated me. She reported that Andrew was hospitalized due to "senioritis," not depression, as stated by the professionals at the center. What the hell was senioritis? Did she think I called the police at one a.m. for a social visit? I might be desperate, but not that desperate! We had battled for too many years, and now I needed to put her out of my mind. I had done what needed to be done for my children to get ahead, ever grateful for my town taxes that included the Region 10 school system and all the extra special services they had provided for Andrew and Laura. Both had received their high school diplomas, and we had moved on and were finally finished with Region 10.

At the center, Andrew was starting to clear. The team had agreed that James should not visit, but when I learned he and his new girlfriend had been there earlier the same day, I was livid. I checked with the charge nurse, who had no explanation of who had let them in and accepted no responsibility. I asked her to call Dr. Krause and she refused. "It's his day off."

"He told me to call anytime with a problem." When I threatened to contact the hospital administrator, she made the call. Dr. Krause was the only one who practiced any sort of follow-through, and asked to meet me early the next day. He felt Andrew was ready for discharge since the psychosis had disappeared but some paranoia remained. I didn't agree, but Andrew wanted out so badly, I went against my better judgment. Andrew was discharged after being there thirty-nine days.

At home I walked on eggshells, as he'd be all alone during the day. Todd, Laura, and I were working. Maria, who was a stay-at-home mom, offered to help keep an eye on him, but by the end of the week he was confused, irrational, and running uncontrollably through the neighborhood. My gut feeling had been right. He'd been discharged too soon and needed to be readmitted. But he adamantly refused to go back. I sat at Maria's and worked out a plan. With Chris and Todd's help, and the doctors on board, we would first take Andrew to Hunter Hospital. Once there he'd be assessed and then transported by ambulance back to the center. First though, we needed to get him in a car and to Hartford.

When I told him that Hunter Hospital was on Asylum Avenue, he theatrically arched his eyebrows. "I don't think I like the sound of that." Then he laughed. Chris and Todd chuckled.

He entertained us while keeping us hostage. After hours of pleading, we convinced him to go with Chris, Todd, and Laura. I drove alone and at the hospital relayed a history to the psychiatrist.

After the initial assessment, a new psychiatrist told me bluntly, "Mrs. Kane, I think you need to accept the reality that Andrew should not return home. He cannot take care of himself and needs full-time supervision at a facility that can provide that."

I was stunned, my mouth frozen. (Many would have loved that to be permanent.)

I replied, "You don't know Andrew. When he's at his baseline, he's totally independent. I will not institutionalize him. He's going to start college in six weeks." I didn't blame the psychiatrist—he'd only seen Andrew at his worst. And Andrew would prove him wrong.

In August Andrew was discharged from the center with everyone in agreement. He would do a partial-day program and was discharged on Trilafon, Amantadine, Tegretal, and Elavil. This worked for now.

Three days later he also started to see his former psychiatrist, Dr. McMase, whom he regarded highly. Dr. McMase served as a stand-in for James—who was certainly no stable father figure, now dating and a man about town.

Meanwhile, the insurance company screwed up bills in the thousands of dollars, and I was constantly in Human Resources, filling out papers and contacting doctors to explain Andrew's disabilities, dates, assessments, treatment plans, etc. It was a nightmare but it did get resolved.

Together, Andrew and I visited the community college where he would attend that fall. I was pleased that a special counselor was set up to help him. I then stopped by the campus nurse's office to introduce myself.

"Hi, I'm Connie Kane. My son Andrew is starting here next week."

"So you're the mother of that very special, handsome boy."

My head cocked like a poised, proud peacock. I beamed from ear to ear. "Yes, I am."

"I'm very happy to meet you. I've dealt with a wonderful TBI specialist, Jack Sarnelli. Andrew might benefit from seeing him."

"Thank you, I'll keep that in mind."

"If I can do anything to make this transition easier, please don't hesitate to call."

I was relieved. This small college would allow constant surveillance, and he'd do fine. I reminisced momentarily. It wasn't Princeton, but that was a dream from the past. Andrew would go to college. This was a start, and that's all that mattered.

At the end of September, he was still seeing Dr. McMase, who called me. "Connie, did Andrew tell you anything about our session today?"

"No, and I don't ask. That's between you two."

"Halfway through the session he asked me how I thought he was doing, and I told him, 'very well.' He then informed me that he'd stopped taking his medication the day after he got home, six weeks ago. I told him that obviously he didn't need it and should throw it away."

I was elated, since I had been uncomfortable with the antipsychotic drug regime. He was not a psychiatric patient. Like a Rockette, I danced into the family room upping the volume on the stereo. "I know you can do this, Andrew!"

I was momentarily interrupted when Chris, Maria's son, walked into the room. "Wow, some moves, Mrs. Kane. Wish I could do that, but this pulled muscle is still bothering me."

"Chris, you better get that looked at—that's been going on all summer."

"I will. Is Laura around? We're going to jam before she leaves on her trip." Chris was close to all my children, and I'd nicknamed him my third son. He had taught Laura how to play the guitar, using a guitar I had given him. I listened as they played their guitars in the family room, and it warmed my heart and beckoned me to join in as I sang harmony, alone in the kitchen. I think all this meant that, finally, everyone was settling into their designed places. As I walked down the hallway I checked the soil in the schefflera plant, "Oh my goodness. I am sorry—I'll get you a drink. You are quite beautiful today."

Laura shouted, "Ma who are you talking to?"

I smiled. "To our good luck charm and symbol of survival, the schefflera plant."

Meanwhile, it was fall, and Todd had returned to Northeastern. James refused to help with tuition. I dipped into a retirement fund from work I had contributed to. I thought of pulling Todd out of college, but he'd had enough turmoil in his life, and his friends were wonderful. I'd always find the money for my children. They were important; money was not. I'd learned that the hard way. And I'd always be able to sleep at night, knowing I'd done the best I could for them.

Laura, who had decided against college that term, was traveling cross-country with a girlfriend. I was not overly concerned, because I knew she would eventually pursue a degree. She was too smart to sit around and do nothing. She had learned to enjoy the finer things in life, and knew they didn't come free. Not every child went directly from high school to college, and since Laura's life had not been the norm, I didn't expect her to follow the average modus operandi. However, I was not prepared for the obstacles that would come with this choice.

The following Sunday, Maria called me. "Con, that pulled muscle Chris has is getting worse. Would you go to the ER with us?"

I was more than happy to help my best friend. "I'm ready right now." We went to Memorial Hospital, and upon examination they found nothing wrong. They advised him to return for X-rays if the pain persisted. Chris accepted this and we went home.

I loved Chris, remembering how he'd hug Todd when they were babies. And when Todd saw Christopher coming over to play, he'd get so excited, but wasn't able to say his name. "Fuffy coming, Fuffy coming." We would bring Chris on vacations as part of our family. And when he stayed for dinner, he got the Waterford crystal because he had beautiful table manners. Since the accident, he had gone out of his way to include and accept Andrew without judgment.

Four weeks later Chris returned for X-rays. Frantically, Maria called. "They want to admit him immediately. He has a mass in his abdomen."

"Oh my God, Maria, it can't be. I'll be right over." I clutched my chest and needed a few minutes to myself. *God, this can't be happening again. It's only been five years since Jill.* When Maria's third child, Jill, was eighteen, she died of Toxic Shock Syndrome. There had to be a mistake. Not twice in the same family.

I visited Chris the night before his surgery. He appeared his usual stoic self with not a care in the world. I put in a call to a good friend, a nurse anesthetist, to keep an eye out for him. The next day at work on the psych unit, I took my break and ran up to the OR. I had worked there and was still good friends with a lot of the girls. They had been wonderful to me when Andrew was in the hospital. Pat, the supervisor, greeted me with a smile.

"Are you back for a job? There's one here for you."

"Not yet, Pat, I'm still enjoying psych. Of course, no one's ever sure if I'm a patient or staff. You'll love this—last week Dr. Harkey came to see a patient on the unit. Now, you know I've known him for years, I take the kids to his clinic all the time, so when he entered the unit and barely looked at me, I knew something was wrong. Bad hair day, I thought, and forgot about it. A few days later my friend Liz went to see him and he said to her, 'Liz, I saw your friend Connie Kane the other day. Poor thing, she's a patient on the psych unit at St. John's—not a wonder with everything she's going through.' Liz burst out laughing and said, 'Bob, she works there.'"

Pat laughed. "You're such a ditz. No wonder he thought you needed to be locked up."

"Thanks." Suddenly the laughter stopped. "Pat, you know why I'm here."

She got up and closed the door. The mood turned formal, and I was uncomfortable. An aura of doom filled the room. "When they opened Chris, they ran into trouble. The cancer has spread. We've called in several other specialists."

I shrieked and trembled. The tears stung down my cheeks.

"His mother will need your help—you're strong. If I can do anything, please, do not hesitate to call."

How on earth could this happen again to such wonderful, good, Christian people? Five years ago they lost a beautiful, healthy daughter after being ill for only two weeks. Maria and her husband Ed were the salt of the earth, never talked about anyone, never judged, went to church constantly, and practiced kindness. That was who they really were. Maria was my role model, and I wanted to be like her. It was hard enough for me to practice my faith with all I was going through, but now this. How could God do this twice, in the same family, to two perfectly normal, healthy children? How on earth could I be of any help, when I was also in such pain?

And there was Chris, the perfect, always smiling patient. He never complained and was always thankful for everything. He was the closest to an angel I would ever know.

Chris died two months later.

Chapter Thirteen

November 1991–September 1992

And now to tell the children Chris had died. What would I say? I called Todd first.

"Hi, Mom, it's early. Is everything all right?"

"Todd—" And the words got stuck.

"Mom, you're scaring me. What's the matter—is it Andrew?"

"It's Chris. You just saw him, and he was doing well, and he came home from the hospital, but . . . he died this morning." There was a dull silence. "I'll call you later . . . I love you."

All I heard was whimpering and sobbing. "Okay, Mom."

After a half-dozen phone calls later, I found Laura. I said, "Hi, I should be working for the FBI. Can't believe I found you."

"Mom, I'm in Boulder and want to go to school here. It's so beautiful. I'm waitressing, so will be here for a while."

"Laura, I have some bad news . . . are you sitting down? Chris . . . has died."

"Oh my God, Mom, what happened?"

"He had cancer. I should have told you sooner, but he was improving and I didn't want you to worry—you're so far away and alone, and then everything happened so quickly, He came home, but he died this morning. I wish you weren't alone. Come home for the funeral."

She sobbed uncontrollably. "I'll call you back."

I was in the kitchen when Andrew entered. All he had to do was take one look at my red, swollen eyes.

"Ma, what's the matter?"

I grabbed him and held him tight. "Chris died this morning." We had danced with death too many times.

Andrew wept and kept repeating, "It can't be. Not Chris." He was angry. "God, why are you doing this to all of us? It has to stop!"

I called James. He was at his girlfriend's, so I spoke to Dee. "Something terrible has happened." I broke down crying. "Chris just died."

"How terrible. That family has been through so much."

I went into the details slowly, with a heavy heart, barely able to get the words out, not knowing what or how to say the words. "I want to bring Laura home, and was wondering if James could help me with the airfare. Last minute, it will be expensive."

"What good will it do, bringing her home now? It's too late."

I stammered, "Dee, she needs to say good-bye. Chris was like a brother to her."

"Do what you want, but don't expect any money from James."

I slammed the receiver down. She was just a nasty, nasty woman!

At the funeral home, I watched Todd and Andrew, both pallbearers, as they faced an insurmountable emotional struggle. Maria had instructed the casket be left open for Laura, since she was arriving that morning. She finally got there a few minutes before we left for the church.

Later at the gravesite, the crowd began to disperse. As we walked to our car, Todd was red faced, visibly angry, and then exploded. "I'm never going to speak to Dad again for not showing up. How could he do that to Chris?"

"Todd, your dad's a very sick man."

"Bullshit, Mom. I'm tired of hearing that. This time there is no excuse. I've had it with him!" He cried, kicked the ground, and flailed his arms wildly.

I think Todd had such a difficult time with Chris's death because subconsciously he was also mourning the death of his relationship with his father. Thank God that when he went back to school he had friends that were a great support system.

In January 1992, Andrew passed all his first semester courses at Mattatuck Community College, but he wrestled with the social aspect. He used to be Mr. Popularity and had complete control over his social life. All that had changed. I hoped the second semester would be easier. He started seeing Jack Sarnelli, the TBI specialist in Cheshire recommended by the nurse at Mattatuck, and also continued with Dr. McMase.

I was unrelenting and clashed continually with the insurance company, which wanted to deny benefits. I pointed out that their reasoning was unacceptable, inappropriate, and not in Andrew's best interests. I had several professionals submit letters on his behalf regarding the importance of continuity of care for his well-being and for him to reach his future goals. The battle continued, positioning me in a permanent fight-ready mode. I refused to accept no. All these battles served as the groundwork for my PhD in unrelenting advocacy, and I would strive only for magna cum laude!

As Andrew entered the second semester at Mattatuck, he appeared evasive. I chalked it up to his living at home alone, and me being the center of his social life. I fully understood his frustration and hoped the experts could help him. But a call from a guidance counselor at the college told me otherwise. Andrew hadn't been in school for the past three weeks.

I was shocked. He left the house every morning with his ride. Where was he all day? And how could he blatantly deceive me? What would become of him with his handicap without an education?

I called both his therapists, who knew nothing about his quitting school, and then I waited for Andrew to come home.

A car door slammed, and he entered the house, a book bag slung over his shoulder.

"How was your day at school?"

"Good."

I stared at him. "The guidance counselor called."

"Ma, I can't go to school now. It's too hard. I need help with all the classes. I have no friends. You sent me to a community college, but Todd could go away to a nice college and have nice friends and live away from home. That's what I wanted, but, no, I'm stuck here alone."

"Andrew, you were in a hospital in July and August, and going away would be disastrous for you. A large campus, dorms, no friends, and no TBI support would put too much pressure on you. It's okay to start small and then go big when you're ready, but that's not now."

"I'm not going back. I've been working so hard since my accident that I need a break. I've had it."

"You're right. Maybe you do need a break, but what are you going to do?"

"I'll get a job."

I was discouraged and heartsick. What type of job could a nineteen-year-old handicapped boy with a hemiparesis and only one good arm find? There was no bus service in our neighborhood. I left for work at six thirty a.m. I couldn't drive him. Desperate, we needed help.

Laura returned from her cross-country trip and was working at a yogurt shop and doing some babysitting. She was heading to Nantucket to work for the summer with no mention of college. I tried to be patient but was concerned. She seemed content with menial jobs and virtually no money. She adored the Grateful Dead and always found a way to attend their concerts. Sarcastically, I thought, *right — she can afford the Grateful Dead because she's given up shaving her underarms and legs and doesn't spend money for shaving supplies.* That hippie look drove me crazy, but I had learned that I needed to pick my battles. I tried not to hound her too much and prayed that God would keep her safe and that soon she would see the light. Even though I had questioned God, and his purpose and plan, I felt that my daily prayers and weekly Mass attendance gave me strength to continue on during life's darkest moments. And perhaps God had instilled in Laura too many gifts, which made it difficult for her.

I spent a lot of time contemplating my life, thankful for the support I'd received from my faith. It had molded and enhanced my character, but since the divorce I was uncomfortable at Mass and with receiving the sacraments. I was not perfect, but I was a good mother and had been a faithful wife. I had wanted the marriage to work, but James's genetic predisposition and dysfunctional upbringing hadn't allowed him to participate in a healthy, committed relationship.

I didn't blame him or his family; it was just the reality of the situation. But I needed peace, freedom from the stigma of divorce, and to not feel as guilty as I did. I was brought up attending Catholic schools from first grade to nursing school. Our lives revolved around the church, and we never knew anyone who had divorced. It was a foreign subject that was never discussed. We were a family of strict Catholics and attended Mass weekly, on Holy days, and daily during Lent. I loved celebrating the special feast days, the processions and carrying of flowers in the month of May to honor and crown the Virgin Mary, the beautiful organ music, and the choir singing. I still remember singing in Latin "Tantum Ergo, Panis Angelicus" and trying not to cry hearing "Ava Maria." No one forced me to attend; I wanted to. So even at a early age, my faith was foremost in my life, comforting me and developing in me those values, morals, and principles I professed and instilled in my children. I always felt peace, support, and comfort inside a church.

But since the divorce I felt a bit paranoid, as if everyone looked at me and judged me for not staying in the marriage and making it work, which as youngsters we were always taught to do. And now, here I was—a terrible divorced woman—and what kind of job was I able to do, raising a child with so many special needs?

Being educated by nuns and always having them around actually made me contemplate becoming a nun at one time. That, however, was short-lived, and I'm sure my spontaneity would have gotten me thrown out and disgraced forever—never mind the shame it would have brought on my parents. I remember when my senior class went on retreat prior to graduation and I—the only one—brought a six-pack of beer. I had purchased the beer to share with my classmates and to offer them a bit of respite, but I was found out and in deep trouble. Not only was it sacrilegious, but I was the valedictorian for the graduating class. When we returned to school after the weekend retreat, Reverend Mother addressed the senior class and spoke of my despicable character, pointing out that I could not represent the class as the valedictorian. The class was asked to vote again on who would represent them, and once again I was voted the most outstanding graduate. I really was a good person, just a bit feisty. However, it left

Reverend Mother in a state of shock, wondering what this world was coming to.

I'm sure she remembered the day I showed up for school with purple hair, and she immediately sent me home with orders not to return until the purple was gone—she told me it clashed with the school uniform, and if God wanted me to have purple hair, I would have been born that way! The entire box of Nestle hair rinse I had used gave me a punk-rock look. I was so before my time. Ha! But my mother and dad were not impressed with my feisty spirit. They feared it would jeopardize the tuition they could not afford to pay in cash, and which they instead paid with bags of potatoes from our garden. And they were adamant that I receive a Catholic education.

Maria and I spent hours talking about the divorce and how awkward I felt receiving the sacraments. I knew the only way to once again find peace at church was to have the marriage annulled. I wrote to the archdiocese and started the process. In a month I received the paperwork. As I read it, important facts were quickly addressed.

> *Annulment does not affect in any manner the legitimacy of the children, property rights, inheritance rights, etc. It is simply a declaration from the Catholic Church that a particular union, presumably begun in good faith and thought by all to be a marriage, did not, in fact, give rise to a perpetual bond. There is no attempt in these proceedings to impute guilt or to punish persons. On the contrary, the purpose is to serve one's conscience.*

I would complete the marital history form and see where I stood.

> *If, at the conclusion of the entire process, the decision is in favor of nullity, a fee of $350.00 will be asked of the person who introduced the request for a study. However, if one*

> cannot afford to pay all or even part of the fee, a simple explanation to the Tribunal will insure that the case will proceed, free of charge.
>
> At no time should financial considerations discourage any person from exercising the right to receive a just hearing from the Tribunal. One's ability or inability to pay a fee in no way affects the progress or outcome of a request.

The materials made it clear that "a radical defect must be present from the beginning." We had a case. I wrote about James's unstable, unhappy childhood: his mother who spoke openly about not wanting to be pregnant or to have him; his alcoholic, unfaithful father who had no time for him; and his only sister who proclaimed she loved him, only to use every opportunity to take advantage of him, taking for herself his personal and home items, especially when he was inebriated. It was a terrible, sad story, but it was reality.

I kept a notepad on me at all times, documenting facts about the marriage whenever I had a minute. If I got the annulment, I could return to church and practice my faith without feeling like the scarlet woman. This was important to me. I needed it for my peace of mind, and I felt I deserved it.

One day at a garage, having my car tuned up, I sat in the waiting room and wrote feverishly, not noticing that John, the mechanic, had entered.

"Mrs. Kane, were you in an accident?"

Shocked, I answered, "No, why do you ask?"

"We've got your car on the lift. I want to show you something."

I followed obediently and couldn't believe my eyes—the front undercarriage of the car was mangled. Did I run over a curb and not realize it? Was I under so much stress that I was zoning out?

"John, what do you think happened?"

"Does anybody else drive your car?"

"Only my daughter, but she's been away."

"Well, someone did two thousand dollars' worth of damage."

I gasped. "I don't have that kind of money."

"Don't worry—let me see what I can do with the warranty and insurance."

I was beginning to doubt my sanity. I remembered running over a curb when I'd left the supermarket one day. That was probably when it happened—a stupid mistake on my part. Or had Laura done it? But she'd tell me, wouldn't she? I never, ever, suspected Andrew. What was done was done, and I couldn't dwell on it. I needed to get back to work on the annulment, which was now my focus.

I returned home with a repaired car and found Andrew gone. But he'd written in our communication book: *Mom, went for a walk; have a sparkling day!*

Walking daily was his norm. He'd pack a lunch and be gone most of the day. I wasn't sure where he went, but he was all too visible, and everyone in town knew and liked him. No one would ever forget the accident on the swing. He was often picked up by friends and the local police and given rides to the pizza parlor, pharmacy, library, or deli. I assumed he couldn't get into too much trouble during the day, just hanging around Middlebury.

It had been almost five years since the accident. So I thought it might finally be time for *me*.

Sherri, another nurse, and I joined a singles club. It was then I came to the realization that I was somewhat attractive, but to men over seventy, twenty years my senior. They thought I was great.

One gentleman finally spoke to me and said, "I can't believe you don't have a man in your life, and you've been divorced five years and haven't dated?"

I never got into the details of my life for fear it would have blown them away. I simply answered, "I've been busy raising my children."

Then I got the look: something must be wrong with her—big issues. Maybe she's gone to the other side.

To start, Sherri and I attended a singles mixer, and since I had taken dancing lessons from Mrs. Wilson in Moose Jaw, I was Ginger Rogers looking for Fred Astaire (certainly showing my age). So I sat waiting to be asked to dance, but sat and sat and sat. I felt like I was sixteen again, at a church social. It was uncomfortable then and still was now. Reality hit me in the face that I was free but no one wanted me. And I had thought I was such a gem! I had a lot to learn, but already hated the singles scene. Maybe now was the time to join the convent. Moose Jaw girl, get ready.

During that period, I met Tim, my very first date, who asked me to a church social. I brought Sherri along, since she knew Tim and he found her entertaining. Big mistake! We arrived late and sat in the front pew. I listened and hung my head in amazement. The speaker had a monotone voice and deliberately paused after every three words. I lost composure and peeked at Sherri as her eyes rolled. We began quietly laughing, shaking the pew up and down. Tim nudged me, not sure what was going on. We were out of control. Tears rolled down our cheeks. Thank God the speaker finished.

We then went down to a kindergarten room for a group discussion, the chairs appropriate for little people. Sherri was a tad heavy and afraid her chair might break, and I was having a hard time tucking my long legs under my tiny chair. Tim deliberately maneuvered between us. The group facilitator introduced the topic "ownership of your new single life." Several women voiced difficulties balancing their checkbooks and taking on home projects. My difficulties were far greater. At that point Sherri took over the class.

"Look—get a grip. Go out and do things. Tell yourself you can do it, and you will. Last week I wanted to organize my closet. I went out, bought one of those closet organizers, read the directions, and did it."

Tim gave me "a long disapproving look" several times, and I'm sure he was embarrassed. The finale was a social hour. Somehow one of my heels got stuck in the floor, and my body lurched back, causing my beverage and cookies to go flying onto the blouse of a woman Tim was chatting with.

That was my last date with Tim, and I was through with dating forever! And strangely enough, the woman with the blouse predicament became Tim's wife! Hmm . . .

I received a letter from the Tribunal on the annulment. My case was going forward. They contacted James for his take on the courtship, marriage, and breakup. His response made him appear totally deranged. On the first page, he crossed out my name and wrote *nut*. Where the judicial vicar signed his name, he wrote *and girlfriend*. And where the notary signed, he again wrote in *girlfriend*. On the second page he responded to the questions: Did anyone advise you against this marriage? *Everyone.* What caused the separation? *Personality change on part of wife.* Do you wish to cooperate with these proceedings? *Void.* Is there a convenient time for you? *When I die.* He listed his three contacts as *God; Blood, Sweat, and Tears;* and *Heaven on Earth.* And signed it *John the Baptist.*

I think that wrapped it up for me. The following week I received a letter from James.

> Connie, I will never forgive. Thanks for making me, and everyone I told, laugh. I will not make a mockery out of the church by responding to this. I will not perjure myself as you did under oath in court. At that moment you became a bitch. Good luck, but I doubt God bless.

P.S. Afterward you can become a nun, which you should have been, because a man to you is only money, not love.

In the envelope he included a copy of an advertisement for a commercial heavy-duty hand cleaner that showed two hands scrubbing, and wrote this note on the ad: *You'll need this the rest of your life, but you'll never get the dirt off.*

I surmised he was not handling the annulment well, which surprised me, since he never went to church before we married and was a Catholic in name only. I remembered Laura's confirmation, when he arrived home minutes before we left for the church and smelled like a brewery, embarrassing the children and putting us all on edge.

By this time, Andrew's activities were beginning to wear on me. We disagreed constantly. I never knew where he was. He roamed around, had no job, his life purposeless.

One night a friend called me, concerned. "Connie, I don't mean to alarm you, but I was driving on Route 188. It was dark, and I nearly hit Andrew. I just didn't see him."

A coworker then told me, "I saw Andrew on the highway hitchhiking. Luckily the police picked him up and gave him a ride."

We had an appointment with the Department of Rehabilitation Services to see if they could help him find a job, and I'd made an appointment to see Dr. Sarnelli to inform him about this downward spiral. Andrew viewed this as my wanting to control him, even though the truth was quite the contrary. I wanted him to have his own life and fly, as my other children had, so I could have mine.

"If you don't shape up, you're not going to Todd's graduation," I said. "You're not ruining it for everyone, including your grandmother." I felt unappreciated. My expenses continued to mount, and I was exhausted but had enough energy to work two jobs—at St. John's and back at Memorial OR per diem to get more hours. I often worked nine or ten long days straight without a day off, but I was making ends meet.

Todd's graduation weekend began at the Boston Park Plaza. My mother had flown in for the graduation of the first grandchild, and it was an excuse to also see Andrew and Laura. Whatever the festivities, my mother always wanted to check on Andrew's progress. And she was always the first one to make excuses for him.

I popped bottles of champagne and we toasted. "Congratulations, Todd, on your finance and business degrees. We're all so proud of you."

He opened the little blue boxes from Tiffany's. "Ma, it's too much. You shouldn't have."

I hoped he'd always have the engraved silver money clip and key chain holder to remind him of this day. Nothing was too good for Todd—he was my rock.

On the other hand, Andrew and Laura were driving me crazy. They fought constantly, were rude, ran all over the hotel, and sat outside their rooms on the floor, acting like bratty, spoiled children. I was ready to snap but kept it inside. I didn't want my mother to see how close to the edge I was. I honestly felt like giving up on them, but I wasn't a quitter like their father. It would get better, hopefully, before I died.

Back at Northeastern, Todd received his diploma, and when the services were over, James appeared out of nowhere. He wouldn't face me or my mother, but I was happy he was there for the children. Soon thereafter, Todd was offered a job and started a sales training program with an orthopedic company. He would embark on a demanding professional journey.

A few weeks later, I sat in Dr. Sarnelli's office working on a behavioral contract for Andrew. I was stressed to the max. His life appeared to be heading in a dangerous direction, and I was petrified. I'd gone to the Department of Rehabilitation and met with Dave

Brown, a social worker who was doing back flips trying to help Andrew. He brought in the director, Lois Gallo, to assist. She understood Andrew's frustration. They would provide educational assistance or training or both. But Andrew wanted an apartment and a job, and until that was available he was content to stay home. He was determined to work and live independently. I didn't see this as even a remote option.

Dave Brown provided Andrew with transportation to and from his therapist, so I was not hovering over him all the time. But soon he refused to go. I met with Dr Sarnelli alone, trying to remedy the behavioral plan. It was not working. Andrew continued to sleep until noon, be gone all day, return home late, and stay up into the early morning hours. We were like two ships passing in the night. I was also suspicious that he was drinking, as he roamed around town charging all sorts of things to my name.

The owner of the pizza parlor asked him to stay away. The local restaurant where he used to work wouldn't allow him on the premises because he had shown up drunk and disorderly.

One morning I got ready for work at five thirty. Andrew was asleep, his room a mess. I walked through the house, viewing the signs of his presence—a disorderly kitchen, cans strewn in the family room. I was sleep deprived, stressed to the max, and facing a sixteen-hour shift. I was uncertain of what lay ahead. Todd was home and later called me at my work.

"Mom, I'm in the ER with Andrew. He got into a fight at Scotty's Restaurant and needs stitches in his hand. Apparently he owed Scotty money, and Scotty wouldn't let him charge anymore, so Andrew started a fight. Scotty's not going to press charges because he understands Andrew's situation and really likes him, but Andrew can't go back to the restaurant."

Andrew was using his handicap to manipulate the generosity and kindness of friends. It enabled unsafe and inappropriate behavior, which was becoming a vicious cycle. I feared for him and didn't know how this was going to end. I couldn't provide a safe monitored home environment because I needed to work, and didn't have the resources to provide him with the daily structure and behavior management he required.

Now Dr. Sarnelli was my only hope. He did a neuropsych evaluation and recommended Andrew leave home for a residential treatment program, and when finished, not return home. The evaluation was devastating to me. He wrote:

> *In the best-case scenario, it might be possible for Andrew to succeed in some sort of independent or supported living. In the worst-case scenario, he might need some built-in behavioral support. I regret we have no options for pursuing this kind of treatment in Connecticut. Fortunately for Andrew, he has some resources for health-care payment. I am pursuing these in coordination with his mother and his psychiatrist, Dr. McMase.*
>
> *Andrew's description of his condition was chaotic. He fluctuated between acknowledgement of his injury and the difficulty it presented, to gross denial of difficulty and outright claims that everything was going well despite evidence to the contrary.*

I couldn't read on. I was too upset with the content but realized that we needed to get Andrew into a residential program, sooner rather than later. In the interim, I continued to meet with Dr. Sarnelli, as I needed advice on how to practice tough love, using my mind more than my heart. Andrew had been through so much and was in such obvious pain. But for him to get on with life, in a real world, it had to be this way.

We found an in-patient behavioral program that looked excellent. I would again begin the insurance battle—documentation, phone calls, letters of necessity, etc.—since the facility was out of network. Andrew was still seeing his psychiatrist, Dr. McMase, whom he trusted and confided in. *Thank you, God, for that.*

One night I came home from work to find a note on the table. It said "Gone to Nantucket, be back in a week. Love, Andrew."

This was all the fuel I needed to add to the fire erupting inside me. I lay awake at night, worrying where he was and who was taking care of him or exploiting him. I was mentally confused and physically exhausted. I went to sleep reminding God that Andrew was in his hands, and he must watch over him.

Three days later he called. "Mom, I went to our cottage, and Dad was there. So I'm staying with him, and he'll be driving me home on Sunday."

A thousand-pound weight came off my shoulders. And then I laughed hysterically. James had probably planned a romantic rendezvous with his new girlfriend, when Andrew arrived on the doorstep. I was thrilled! *Thank you God!*

When he returned home, he appeared relaxed and relayed his adventure of hitchhiking to Cape Cod. Eight rides and five hours later, he spent his first night on Nantucket Island with strangers on a fifty-foot yacht. "They were just nice people trying to help me out," he said.

While he was gone, we had found a rehab program at the Tandem Institute in Texas. Funding had been approved, and a case manager was flying up to assess Andrew. I even had the chief of police involved in the plan. A week before, Andrew had forged a check and signed James's name. No one was going to press charges because everyone knew him and felt sorry for him. But this did help us. The police were going to pick him up for questioning about the bad check, and keep him until the Tandem case manager could assess him.

The plan went as scheduled. Andrew roamed around town and was taken into custody. However, he was smart and knew they couldn't hold him because his dad and the bank were not pressing charges. He pressured the police to let him go and demanded food from a specific deli. When I arrived, he was driving the police crazy.

"How's it going?" I asked the chief.

"I don't know how you do it. I'd be arrested if he lived with me."

"That's why we have to get him into this program."

Then Andrew walked in and said, "I saw your car here, Ma."

"Yes, I heard you were here."

"I know what you're trying to do, and it won't work. I'm not going to Texas. I've been in enough hospitals." Then he looked at the chief. "My mom's trying to control my life. She had me in Highgate for a year, and my dad said the only reason she came to visit me every week was she was having an affair with one of the doctors."

The chief jumped in. "Andrew, don't talk to your mom like that. Your mother's main concern has always been *you*, and don't forget that."

I shook my head. "Don't blame him, Chief—his dad's brainwashed him and is a sick man."

Another officer entered to inform Andrew that his lunch delivery was there.

"It's about time." Andrew got up, walked out, and turned one last time. "You better let me go pretty soon. I've got rights."

"Connie, he's right. I can't hold him much longer."

With luck on our side, the case manager from Tandem arrived. But ten minutes into the meeting, Andrew bolted. "Mom, I'm not going to Texas, and that's it." He picked up his backpack and hobbled out of the police station.

I hung my head and closed my eyes, hopeless. Something terrible was going to happen. I could feel it and had no way to stop it. I was aware that if his behavior continued, especially his use of alcohol,

Andrew could lose control and physically harm me. I felt I might be in danger. I would not enable bad behavior. I decided that if he touched me, I would call the police. But . . . could I really do it?

On Labor Day weekend, which would always remind me of the weekend he came out of the coma, as I was watching TV, I was distracted by someone stumbling on the road. It was Andrew. He was intoxicated. I was agitated and felt like a panther ready to attack. I had no more energy to put up with his drinking. Look what it had done to his father.

He tripped into the kitchen, his beautiful face distorted, his huge warm and tender eyes haunted and bloodshot.

"Andrew, you've been drinking. Look at yourself—you're drunk, just like your father. Can't you see what you're doing to yourself? I've had it. This is it! You can't stay here, not in this condition. Leave now!"

Andrew made light of my remarks, taunting me. "Sorry, Ma, but this is my home. I'm not leaving, and you can't make me. You're my conservator—you have to keep me, so there."

He deliberately hovered over me, trying to intimidate me. Enraged, I raised my arm to slap him across the face. At the same time he lifted his hand to strike me, but I blocked the blow as his hand hit my arm. I backed away and called 911. "How could you, Andrew? I can't believe you've resorted to this."

Into the phone I said, "This is Connie Kane on Green Road. I need the police right away. Andrew hit me, and I want him arrested."

I had played this scene over and over in my mind. I knew it would come to this and I'd need help from the law. Andrew had to hit rock bottom. But I was not prepared for it being the bottom for me as well. I was on the verge of collapse, heartbroken and full of guilt. It was the right thing to do, but all I could focus on was the police handcuffing him, his right hand in spasm. Helplessly I watched him, his partially paralyzed gait awkward, as they led him to the police cruiser.

What had I done? Where had I gone wrong? Would this ever end? Was there a God? I trusted in God and talked to him all day long as he was the mainstay in my life, giving me strength, but now I really needed his help to get through this mess.

I was broken and devoid of answers, in a suspended state of existence. I might as well have been removed from this earth. Had my life been in vain?

Chapter Fourteen

September 1992–June 1993

I WAS ALSO ARRESTED FOR "domestic violence," which was what the newspaper so articulately wrote for all the world to see. I called Bill Jones to represent me in court. He lived in town and knew my story. He assured me the case would be nullified, but this scandalous situation shattered me.

Meanwhile, Andrew was staying with James and his grandparents. James's sister Trudy was visiting from Florida and seemed to want to help, so I invited her to join me at a meeting with Dr. Sarnelli, and she accepted. I was optimistic that now perhaps Andrew would consider the Tandem program, and naively hoped that at long last Trudy sincerely wanted to help.

She showed up at the meeting in her usual designer style, exquisite gold jewelry, and an impressive Florida tan. It was obvious I was jealous and begrudged her life. I was drained emotionally, physically, and financially, and exasperated from constantly being kicked in the teeth. I resented the fact that James's family had done nothing to help. As I drowned, they watched and gloated. This was payback for my divorcing James. I felt like my last six years had been a total failure. I was blind with commitment for this twenty-year-old child who now probably hated me for doing what I thought was the right and safe thing.

True to form, Trudy did nothing for Andrew and with much indifference clarified that he could not stay, even temporarily, at his grandparents' home.

"My parents are too old to tolerate Andrew's problems. It's my job to help them."

I seethed as I watched her performance. She elaborated on how much care Bumpy and Dee needed. Yet she visited rarely—only long enough to box up and slyly remove treasures and antiques from the family house and items from our home that James had stored in the basement, things that should have gone to James's children, not Trudy. Todd had witnessed her in action. But now, I needed to address one more issue.

"Trudy, I need to ask you about Cane's wedding. Why weren't his only cousins invited? Has he grown so important that family means nothing to him?"

"We decided—you know how Andrew can be—that we just didn't want a scene. If we didn't invite one, we couldn't invite the rest. We thought that was the best solution."

Coldly, I looked at her. "You're ashamed of Andrew because he had an accident and a brain injury. I can't begin to tell you what this did to him, as well as to Todd and Laura. Andrew is still Cane's cousin, brain injury or not. There would have been a supervised plan in place."

Andrew was to be admired for his struggle, not hidden as if he didn't exist. I would have thought Cane would understand this, but I guess they didn't teach that in law school. It had become easier to pretend these cousins just didn't exist.

In September, I went to superior court for the first time, and it was an education. It was a zoo, everyone in jeans and T-shirts, arrested on family violence and abuse charges, and still fighting. Why was I shocked? I was there for the same reason.

Bill Jones told me to wait in a corner, where I observed and was observed. He handled the legalities, and I entered a small room with a judicial worker to go over the events, sign papers, then wait to be called to the courtroom. I was uncomfortable and sweating in my silk dress. As usual, I was overdressed. Would this Moose Jaw girl ever learn?

"Bill, have you seen Andrew? How does he look, and is James here? This tough love is the hardest thing I have ever done."

"They're both here. Andrew wants you taken off as conservator and to have his father put on."

"I have no objections. I need a break. But James is so irresponsible. Do you think he can handle this?"

"Maybe you should give him a chance. It might force him to be more involved—anything is better than nothing."

"You're right. It's an excellent idea. I can passively keep an eye on him. Tell them yes."

As we entered the courtroom, I was aghast to see Andrew sitting all alone. James had decided not to attend. I wiped away my tears, my eyes fixed on Andrew. What had we come to, after all those years of taking care of him? Andrew and I had been a team. And now . . . *God, I am furious with you. You are part of this team, and you're not holding up your part. I know this is only temporary, but I will need your guidance more than ever now. Please, hear my prayers.*

We approached the bench, and Andrew looked straight ahead, his hands shaking, right arm in spasm. I was barely able to stand. The court put a family violence protective order into effect, which meant

Andrew couldn't threaten, harass, assault, or hassle me, nor enter the family home unless accompanied by police.

In a matter of minutes it was over. I wanted to flee that ugly building. Actually, I would have liked to have left this earth, permanently. I arrived home just before Andrew, the police, and Dee. I was shocked that James had sent his mother, but I shouldn't have been, as she totally enabled him. She sat in the car, leaning on the horn, while Andrew packed his belongings.

Impatiently, she entered the house, and we immediately exchanged dagger glares, the police on her trail.

"Ma'am, you need to return to your car," they told her.

Dee thought she was above the law and ignored him. "You're a sick, unfit mother, living like a queen in the suburbs after divorcing my son, who gave you everything."

The police sensed impending hostility. "Ma'am, if you don't leave the house immediately, you'll be arrested."

She turned around and bellowed to Andrew, "Hurry up! We haven't got all day." And they left. I needed my therapist now, more than ever.

Over the next few weeks, I pushed myself spiritually—with nightly rosaries, and visits to church as well as Mass—and felt better emotionally and physically. I was power walking and sleeping better. Work had once again become a joy. Todd lived at home and constantly reaffirmed that I had done the right thing, even though I felt tremendous guilt.

Meanwhile, Bumpy was ill. His health had deteriorated, even though he seemed to have nine lives. One night he drove into a lake after a drinking binge and was submerged in water all night, until daybreak. When he arrived in the ER, his body temperature was so low we thought that was it. Five days later he was discharged. He was now in a convalescent home in Middlebury, and I visited him often. He was the only one in the family that I still loved.

"Con, James was up the other day, and he looked and smelled like a bum. But he's my son—what can I do? I told him he made a big mistake letting you go. He's got a girlfriend now, but he doesn't want anyone to have you."

He didn't have to worry about that! I think I had a sign on my back that read "Stay away, totally deranged."

My troubles worsened, due to a minor accident at work on the psych unit. I'd been helping bathe a patient in a tub who thought she was snorkeling, and let herself slide under the water. Immediately, I grabbed her and pulled her up, twisting my knee and feeling a snap with excruciating pain. I'd torn my meniscus and needed surgery right away.

I discussed this situation with God. *You knew I needed a rest. Thank you.*

A week later I was in the OR at St. John's Hospital. I said to Wayne, the anesthesiologist, an old dear friend of over twenty years, "It's about time you showed up. I won't let just anyone put me to sleep."

Wayne shook his head. "Bitch, bitch, bitch!"

I mumbled, "Just make me . . ."

In a few weeks I was back to work.

Todd and I were getting worried, since it was October, and we hadn't heard from Andrew. Todd checked a bar we heard Andrew frequented and sat down to order, but the bartender refused to serve him.

"Andrew, we don't want a scene again. You know you're not allowed in here."

Todd's body stiffened; he widened his eyes. "I'm not Andrew." He pulled out his license. "I didn't realize we looked that much alike. He's my brother. Have you seen him? I'm worried about him."

"He lives around the corner, is often here with his dad, who's a regular. He doesn't have any money. We told him he can't come back."

Todd left more upset than when he went in.

And then more trouble. I received a letter from Jack Lew, the probate court judge, saying that Andrew had retained a lawyer, Lyn Spring, who was seeking an order to have his conservatorship removed. She wanted this hearing to be expedited quickly. I reread the letter, shocked. Andrew's condition was getting worse, and this course of action would be dangerous. It was already unsafe with James as conservator.

I needed to meet with Attorney Spring. I entered an old office building, walked up a dirty, creaky staircase to her office, and was greeted by her partner. He was obese and unkempt, wearing a shirt with countless soiled spots and a wrinkled tie hanging loosely. This spoke volumes. Attorney Spring was a defensive woman who listened only to patronize me. She continued her personal agenda about why Andrew should have his own conservatorship, and it was obvious she had no knowledge of TBI. Was she taking advantage of him? Were her motives politically motivated? She had no idea what she was up against, as Judge Lew and my lawyer Bill were both on the same page. They knew the family and the situation and were witnessing Andrew's decline. Ms. Spring simply didn't know the facts.

On November 18, 1992, the hearing took place. Andrew arrived late, unkempt, unshaven, his hair long and dirty, and using a walking stick. My heart sank at the sight, and I was unable to hold back the tears. *My sweet baby, you are spiraling down.*

Bill argued the case. He'd known Andrew from birth and had seen him since the accident when he was well and when he wasn't. He asserted that, if anything, Andrew now needed more intervention, and that James and I should both assume conservatorship. However, James was a no-show, so we needed to meet again in two weeks.

Later that afternoon Judge Lew forwarded to me a letter he received from Attorney Spring. It read:

> Dear Judge Lew,
>
> It has come to my attention that you have been a friend of Mrs. Kane's for many years. To avoid the appearance of impropriety and to ensure impartiality, a judge without prior connections to the Kane family should preside over this matter, and I request you be removed.
>
> Because Mrs. Kane ordered Andrew from her home in the summer of 1992, and because of her history of violence and specifically the violence between Mrs. Kane and Andrew, Mrs. Kane could not remain Andrew's conservator even if he were incompetent. It is improper for Mrs. Kane to apply for conservatorship under these circumstances, and I am forced to wonder what her motives are for wishing to remain in control. However, Andrew is competent and seeks restoration at the earliest possible date. I request a hearing within 30 days.

I stopped reading the letter, furious with her ignorance and stupidity.

We met with a new judge at the next hearing. James and Andrew never looked at me.

Tension gripped the room. Andrew's attorney was going to have him evaluated by a new psychiatrist I had never heard of. I stared at Ms. Spring, thinking, *Jerk, you are out of your league.* Whatever Andrew had told her, and whatever she thought about me, she would be rudely awakened. I would not allow her to endanger Andrew's life any more than it already had been, and I would beat her at this stupid farce of a legal battle she was pursuing.

In the end, James was once again granted conservatorship. Andrew was still upset with me because of my involvement, but I knew in time this would resolve. As we all walked out of the courtroom, Ms. Spring's face was full of arrogance, but I caught her eye and smirked in triumph. I was still reeling from her nasty letter about my "history of family violence." How dare she sit in judgment of me when she had absolutely no idea of who I was or what my life entailed? Unfortunately, negative judgment would become a norm that I would have to deal with the rest of my life.

Thanksgiving was around the corner, and both my parents were coming to stay for a while. They were worried about Andrew. I invited him for dinner, but he refused and said he was going to be with James. He did agree to meet my parents for lunch downtown, where he lived. I picked them up afterward and offered Andrew a ride home, but he refused, stating he liked to walk. He looked better-groomed and no longer used a walking stick. When I brought them back home, they were both sick about Andrew and wondered what was to become of him. It bothered them even more that he had become so estranged from me and my family and seemed to only want James. And as much as they had loved James, they realized his drinking was going to be his demise, and sooner rather than later.

But my mother did notice the schefflera in the hallway. "I can't believe that plant. It must be almost six feet high."

"Yes, Ma, it just continues to grow and survive, even when we forget about it. It represents our family."

My father went without a drink the entire trip. I know this was because he loved Andrew and realized the severity of his situation. I'm not sure how I would have handled it if he hadn't realized how drinking would impact me.

And then another family friend called me. "I'm concerned about Andrew but am keeping an eye on him. He visits me regularly at my office, and I take him to coffee and lunch every now and then." I was relieved that friends felt free to call me. They knew I really cared, regardless of what Andrew or James might be saying about me. And even though the call worried me, it let me know I was not alone. I wasn't the only one who thought his situation looked like a ticking time bomb.

In December, my beloved father-in-law died. There was no question what my role should be, but it would take precise and delicate handling. I would support my children in the middle of a family that didn't want me. Todd talked to Andrew, and he agreed to come home for the day. Todd helped dress him in one of his good suits, and he looked so handsome. Laura was working in California, and James wouldn't send her the money to come home for the funeral, so I was not interfering. I called Dee to express my sympathy, and Todd, Andrew, and I attended the wake. That was the appropriate thing to do, and these were lessons I wanted my children to learn. It was not easy, as I felt everyone talked about how evil and psychopathic they thought I was, but I would stand tall, knowing in my heart I'd done the right and Christian thing. They were the dysfunctional ones.

Much to my surprise, I was asked to join the family at Mass the next day and ride with my children in one of the limousines. (Must have been the platter of food I sent over!) At least they felt our attendance was necessary, not like Cane's wedding, where we weren't wanted.

Even though I felt awkward filing into church with the family, I knew Bumpy would have wanted us to stand as a family, at least once more. During the ceremony, Andrew openly sobbed, often leaning on my shoulder. It had been a while since he'd shown any affection for me, and I savored the sentiment. After the funeral and burial, we were invited to the country club for brunch.

My first obligation was to speak to Dee. She surprised me by saying, "Thanks for coming. Bumpy would have been happy to see us all here together."

"I never considered not coming. We were family for twenty-five years, and I hope we can still share some quality family moments."

But the conversation quickly changed. Dee asked, "And what is Laura doing, and when is she returning to school?"

"She's traveling cross-country, will winter in Colorado and summer in Nantucket, and work at waitressing."

"For a bright girl, she's not too smart."

"Dee, she's been through a lot for a young girl. She needs time. She's a wonderful girl." I could see where this negative conversation was going. "Excuse me, I need to use the ladies' room."

On the way I saw Todd and said, "Please go to the bar and get me a stiff Bloody Mary. This family does me in."

"Mom, you're really handling yourself well."

"Thanks, it's not easy."

"I was just talking to Aunt Trudy. She said you looked good and wanted to know if you had your eyes done."

"Make that a double!"

Todd and I had taken the entire day off from work to spend time with Andrew. I was grateful for Todd's concern and sad that he'd found an apartment and would be moving. I would miss him, but he'd learned to fly, and that was what children were supposed to do.

I began socializing more—dinners out, day trips, and movies. I chose my friends cautiously: no negativity, smokers, or drinkers. Socializing agreed with me, as I became energized and happier than in years. My sense of humor resurfaced, and I joked in a mischievous and often naughty manner, but all in fun. I returned to work in the OR at Memorial Hospital and began singing and dancing while at work. I sought laughter, even if it meant busting on myself. Many times I left work feeling like I'd had so much fun I didn't deserve a paycheck, but the feeling was short-lived. I was not employed to improve my social skills, but perhaps, unbeknownst to me, I should have been.

It was now March—dreary and cold. I received a letter from the archdiocese, declaring that my marriage to James was null. I put the letter down, unprepared for my emotional reaction. When I divorced James, it had been my decision and choice. An annulment was worse.

Total strangers had looked at the marriage and felt there had been none. It hit me in the face that perhaps I'd made a terrible mistake with my marriage to James. I'd been committed, faithful, and monogamous, and had given the best twenty-five years of my life to the wrong man. This annulment would torment my psyche longer than the divorce.

At 3:11 one morning, the phone abruptly awoke me. Only bad news came at that hour. I answered, "Hello?"

A woman's voice spoke. "This is Memorial Hospital calling. Your husband's been in a car accident. He's conscious but going to the OR now."

Alarmed, I asked, "Is he in any danger?"

"No, he just wanted me to call you and the children."

I was relieved. "Tell Mr. Kane I'll let the children know, and we'll be up to see him. Mr. Kane is my ex-husband." I probably sounded coldhearted, but wanted her to know I was not running up to see him now. I would, however, do everything in my power to keep him healthy—he was my children's father. So where was his girlfriend?

James was drunk, had run a red light, and two kids crashed into him. I would have thought he'd have his license revoked or some criminal charges imposed upon him, but I don't think he was charged with anything. Maybe it was because he was so seriously injured. The doctors took out his spleen. He had lost a fair amount of blood but would recover. He was on a ventilator, since he was a smoker.

Todd, Andrew, and I went to visit him. The scene disturbed Todd. It was Andrew's accident all over again: the multitude of tubes attached to his body; the annoying clicking, winking, and blinking from the machines. James's doctor, with whom I had worked, entered the cubicle. I took him outside.

"I'm not sure if you're aware, but James is an alcoholic and will need to be detoxed or he'll go into DTs."

This was an enormous undertaking, as he needed massive doses of tranquilizers. I kept an eye on him constantly. A week later, he was unaware of my presence and getting worse. Andrew came daily, the emotional stress on him increasingly evident. But at least some good had come out of this, as we now spoke civilly to one another.

A female acquaintance, also an alcoholic, visited James. Amorously, she affectionately took his hands into hers, caressed him, proceeded to whisper sweet nothings, and he didn't flinch. Perhaps, subconsciously, the smell of alcohol had enticed him into a peaceful state, or a coma of safe refuge.

And then the real girlfriend showed up, shouting, "James doesn't want you here. What you've put him through is terrible!"

In the past I had liked her, but was appalled at her accusatory behavior. I told her, "We need to speak. Come with me." I directed her to a vacant cubicle and closed the door. "Look, you may be sleeping with James, but it doesn't give you a damn bit of authority."

"I've been trying to put him back together again."

"And what a wonderful job you've done. The night of the accident he was alone and drunk, trying to pick someone up. Just get one thing very clear. I am here as the mother of his children, to support them, and that's it. James is your trophy. I don't want him. If you're really concerned, you'd act more appropriately in front of him when he's in such a serious state. This is not in his best interests."

She walked out, shaking and agitated. The alcoholic acquaintance and girlfriend joined forces against me. They were so dysfunctional they couldn't see how damaging their behavior was. I knew what was right for James and what was wrong, and I was steadfast. Besides, they were on my turf!

The girlfriend continued to be a menace, called doctors, and tried to have me barred from visiting. She enlisted help from Trudy, who called and asked me not to intimidate the girlfriend or visit James. It was one huge control issue.

It blinded all of them to what really was at stake. James was listed in critical condition. Regardless of our issues, I wanted him better for his children, and nothing would stand in my way. It was three weeks post-op, and he was getting worse. They were unable to wean him from the respirator because his lungs were damaged from the accident and generally in bad shape from his years of smoking cigarettes. I realized I needed to bring Laura home from Colorado in case he died. She flew home, and Todd picked her up at the airport. He then picked up Andrew, and we all met for pizza and the renewal of family bonds.

Afterward, Laura and I went to the hospital. I tried to make light of the serious situation. "The nurse just informed me your dad was fed up with his breathing tube and pulled it out. They're going to keep it out and see how he does."

Laura grabbed my hand as we entered James's cubicle. The scene was intimidating. "Mom, you lied to me. He doesn't even look like Dad." She inched closer. His face was gray and swollen, and when he breathed, his chest rolled back and forth like a wave.

"Mom, all those tubes. When did his hair turn so gray?"

"His smoking and drinking caught up to him, but he's also being detoxed."

She stroked his hand. Regardless of how much pain he'd inflicted on her, he was still her father and she loved him. "Dad, it's Laura. Don't you recognize me and Mom? Can you see and hear us?"

As he slowly opened his eyes, they darted around the room. He was agitated, confused, and disoriented. His eyes widened as he attempted to focus on us. In a frail, scratchy, barely audible voice, similar to Marlon Brando in *the Godfather*, he responded, "Your mother's responsible for all this."

Laura and I stared at each other and rolled our eyes. *Here we go again.*

"Dad, Mom wasn't even there!"

"Doesn't matter. It's all her fault."

Jesting, I said, "Laura, I've developed special powers—be careful." I was and would forever be to blame for all his misfortune.

James went back to the OR. He'd broken a rib that kept his lungs from expanding fully, and now a membrane covered them and had to be removed. It was major surgery. I worked that day, and instead of taking a moment to say, "Hi, I hope you do well," I purposefully stayed away. I'm sure he was terrified—sober and stripped of his protective armor—and would be vulnerable and humane like the man I used to love. It would be just too painful for me, as I was still trying to heal.

From the OR, he was moved to a surgical floor because he'd developed ICU psychosis from being confined so long in the unit. This, along with what would have been a thirty-thousand-dollar detox program at a rehab center, put him on the road to recovery. And five weeks after the accident, he was discharged home. I was thrilled. No cigarettes or alcohol in his system—this was a new, positive start. He'd always said, "When the dust settles, we'll be back together again." Maybe now . . .

But little did I know that on the way home from the hospital to his parents he would ask his good friend, Sam, who picked him up, to stop so he could buy cigarettes and beer. He had no plans to quit drinking or smoking. I was sick from his decision.

Andrew was obviously struggling. The daily visits to see James had left him disheartened and disheveled, with no one looking out for him. He'd also made it very clear he did not want to return to my home and was content living in downtown Waterbury. Rock bottom was approaching, and I had no choice but to watch.

Then another emergency. Todd was home for Memorial Day weekend, visiting from Milford, a town forty minutes away, when Maria called. Andrew had called her to ask if she'd come and get him from his apartment, which she did.

She told me, "Andrew's in bad shape, scared, and talking about Vietnam and the Viet Cong coming after him." He wanted to come home.

Minutes later he was at the door—petrified, exhausted, paranoid, and hallucinating—totally out of touch with reality. He walked as if all his joints had loosened. Hopefully in his condition he did not witness the horror on my face as I greeted him.

Todd got him into the shower immediately and gave him clean clothes. Wearing gloves, I took the dirty ones and put them in a bag to throw away. I was surprised he'd roamed around Waterbury in that condition and the police hadn't picked him up.

He wanted to sleep, but before he nodded off I gently broached the subject of his going to a hospital. He agreed and was soon off to siesta land. The next day I went to work, but before I left I peeked into his room. He was sound asleep, so peaceful and beautiful, the demons at bay. I quietly closed the door and tiptoed out of the house. This had to be rock bottom. The only thing worse was death, and I refused to accept that. I was again ready to fight!

I rushed home from work, singing as I spoke. "Andrew, sweetie, I'm home." It was quiet. I went through the house—no Andrew. I walked across the street to Maria's—no Andrew. I was overwhelmed and desperate. In his room the dog waddled over. I said, "Maggie, where's Andrew?"

She perked up her ears and barked. I sat on his bed and cried, "Where are you? Where have you gone in this condition?" Again I looked up to the heavens. *God, it's your turn. He's on the streets, and anything can happen—keep him safe.*

Two days later the phone rang in the middle of the night. I jolted upright and said, "Hello?" There was no response. "Hello, hello, is anyone there? Andrew, is that you?" I was positive it was him and that he'd call back. He had no father keeping an eye on him, no friends, nowhere to turn, but at least I knew he was alive. I tossed and turned, watched the clock, and waited. He didn't call back. I got up and went to work.

Three days later at 2:10 a.m. the phone rang. Again I jolted awake. "Hello, hello, Andrew?" No one responded. "Andrew, talk to me. I love you."

"Mom, will you come and get me?" The phone went dead.

I jumped out of bed and bolted to the car. I wasn't sure where I was going, but I would search his neighborhood until I found him. I'd call the police to help. We had to find him alive before we found him dead.

Downtown Waterbury in the middle of a hot June night was not a safe place for a single white female to roam. I prayed, *God please stay with me and help me find him.*

My car rolled through the neighborhood as I looked for someone, anyone, I could ask about Andrew, but there was no one on the street. I continued to drive up and down until I saw movement coming from some bushes. It was pitch black, but someone was lurking, hiding, not wanting to be seen. My heart raced. *God, let this be a good person. I need to stay alive. I've still got a lot to do.*

And then a body appeared, barefoot, wearing only undershorts. It moved under the streetlight. It was Andrew. "Oh thank you, God!"

Gently I called to him. "Andrew, it's Mom. Please come over here. I just want to talk to you."

Initially he appeared happy to see me, but as he leaned into the car I was face-to-face with paranoia, and his expression changed instantly.

"Andrew, it's your mother. You called me. Let me take you home."

Fearfully and frantically he moved away from the car. "You're not my mother. I don't know who you are, but you're not my mother. Get away from me!"

I begged and cried but nothing worked. He quickly limped away into his apartment building. At that moment a police cruiser drove up the street and stopped.

"Ma'am, do you need help?"

"Yes, that young man who just walked into that building is my son. He has a TBI, and I think has gotten into drugs and alcohol and is totally psychotic. I'm a nurse. He needs to be in a hospital but doesn't recognize me. I don't know what apartment is his, but there must be a superintendent who can tell us. Please help me!"

Inside the apartment building we headed straight to the superintendent, a fulminating female who was not happy to be roused and fired off a brutal round of obscenities.

"And I ain't opening any door. He owes me money. Do you know what time it is? They don't pay me enough for this hassle. Get the hell out of here."

I admired the patience of the police officers as they persuaded her to open her door.

She pointed her finger at me. "You his mother?"

I graciously nodded, my voice shaking. "Yes, and thank you for your time."

"Some mother you are. He doesn't belong here. He's nuts, should be locked up, just a menace to society!"

To pacify this woman, I gritted my teeth, nodded, and agreed. "Please give us his key. He needs to go to a hospital. I'll pay what he owes you."

"Thirty-one dollars."

I handed her two twenties.

"I ain't got no change."

"It's okay. Please, the key."

She handed the key to the police.

After knocking and getting no response, we quietly opened the door. Todd had told me to never go into Andrew's apartment. So I focused on Andrew and not the aesthetics. The place was a rat hole. The police called an ambulance. Andrew had always been taught that the police were his friends, and I think deep down he was relieved and calmed by their presence.

"I don't need to be in a hospital."

"It's just an assessment." The police impressed me with their kindness and respect. Andrew was guided carefully to the ambulance, and it drove off to the ER at Memorial Hospital.

The night was still dark and very warm as I gazed to the heavens. I took a deep breath and walked to my car. Tomorrow would be a new day, and we would start the uphill climb again. Andrew would no longer roam the streets and be a target of the parasitic society that preyed on the weak, sick, and vulnerable.

Sleep-deprived, I fell into my car. *Thank you, God, for keeping him safe.*

Chapter Fifteen

June 1993–March 1994

WHILE DRIVING HOME, MY MIND raced. I was not giving up on Andrew the way everyone else had. We were still a team, and he was my priority. Yes, his life had changed, but so had mine. I was also a victim and found it increasingly difficult to socialize with my Middlebury friends. Tennis, lunch, shopping, and theater were no longer part of my life. I was the only one of my friends who was divorced and had to work. I was no longer in their league. We were worlds apart, and I didn't blame them for their affluent lifestyle. They had no idea what mine entailed, and I was the displaced person.

In minutes I was home. I called Memorial Hospital ER and spoke to the triage nurse. "Hi, it's Connie Kane. My son Andrew was just admitted there. I'm sure you're going to medicate him, and he'll hopefully sleep. I'll be in later this afternoon, but if you need me, I'm home. You have my phone number, right? I'm exhausted and going to bed now. If he wakes up, tell him his mother called and that I love him."

I crawled into bed at five thirty. Half a tranquilizer later I was asleep. I awoke at two p.m., a bit groggy, and went for a short walk before going to the hospital to see Andrew.

He was sound asleep, after having escalated and been put into four-point leather restraints. My stomach agonized at the visual. I hoped he was too sick to remember being tied down like an animal. When was this torture to end? I placed a call to James. Dee answered.

"It's Saturday. He's out and needs to socialize after what he's been through!"

I wanted to spit in her face. "Andrew's in the hospital, stable, but I need James's help."

"He's still convalescing from his accident and can't be part of this. You take care of it."

The phone clicked off.

"Bitch!"

Two days later, Andrew was calmer — still psychotic, but taken out of restraints. However, he soon became restless and within seconds jumped up on the bed and pulled the lights down from the ceiling. He was confused and frightened and couldn't understand or remember what the fuss was all about. Then he was "papered" (an involuntary commitment for his safety and the safety of others) to the state hospital at Fairview Heights, of which I'd heard nothing but horror stories.

The next day I would see for myself, and make them aware that Andrew has a TBI and not a psychiatric mental health issue. As diplomacy was my strong point — *ahem* — I would bring to their attention that this child of mine, regardless of his present condition, still remained priceless goods.

I parked at Fairview Heights Hospital, trying to find the building Andrew was in. I encountered other clients, their faces expressionless.

Many of them lived in their own worlds, engrossed in the private intimacy of the moment, unaware of the illness that imprisoned them. This was home and family. Society had no place or patience for them. Their disease—mental illness—was not kind to them. It isolated and abandoned them while at the same time insulating them from discrimination.

As I entered Andrew's building, I cringed. It was dark, dismal, and absent of color. Fear gripped me as I pushed a bell in front of a large all-encompassing door that appeared to have been put to the test frequently, perhaps by family, police, or clients, in a state of frustration, anger, or hysterics. In the distance I heard the sound of heavy shoes on a hard floor and enough rattling keys to fill an eight-inch ring.

The gatekeeper appeared. "Hello, I'm Eldon."

I smiled. "Hi, Eldon, I'm here to see Andrew Kane. I'm his mother. And what is your job here?"

"I'm a psychiatric technician."

"Thank you, Eldon."

I knew that meant "aide." We went through another set of locked doors to a recreation room, stark with bars on the window. Certainly not the window treatments I would choose.

"Sit down, Mrs. Kane. I'll bring him out."

I was wary of sitting anywhere. This was a hellhole, and I couldn't imagine Andrew being monitored appropriately, being treated with dignity, or—most importantly—getting better. The hole in my stomach was grinding deeper, but on the brighter side I knew this was temporary. Andrew was off the streets and by nature would get better because he was not a mental patient. An Indian doctor came to speak with me and explained that Andrew was heavily medicated and sleeping, and that the staff was keeping an eye on him.

I left him locked behind bars, for now. Outside I basked in the fresh air and sunshine. I would never take this for granted.

Two days later I returned. Andrew was wearing clothes I didn't recognize. He walked awkwardly, his limp was more pronounced, and his face was expressionless, almost robotic.

"Hi, Gigi, how are you? Are they treating you okay? I brought you some new clothes."

Very slurred, he answered, "Okay, I guess. They won't let me go outside. There's no air conditioning—it's so hot, Ma. I need to go back to bed."

"Don't they make you go to group therapy, exercise, occupational therapy? What meds are you on?"

He was becoming agitated. "I can't remember. Call the doctor. Ma, you better go."

He walked to the locked door, pushed a buzzer, and disappeared, never turning to say good-bye.

Tears rolled down my cheeks. My body was heavy, drowning in pain. *Please, God, help.* I sat in my car and sobbed, feeling hopeless, unsure of this outcome. Had he done more brain damage with the substance abuse?

James cleared out Andrew's apartment and dumped his belongings in my garage. I looked through the bags and was heartsick at what I saw: ragged clothing, worn shoes. I called James but Dee answered. "Andrew needs a pair of sneakers. He's in socks, and I'm afraid he's going to fall. James is in charge of his finances. Could he please get him some shoes?"

"James can't even buy clothes for himself—how do you expect him to buy shoes for Andrew?"

"Easy, he's a thirteen medium!"

"He can't do that!"

"You mean he won't."

If I wanted him to have shoes, I'd have to buy them. I left for the mall to shop for a strong, supportive yet stylish sneaker. He deserved at least that. I also picked up new duds that would make him feel better. And Dee would be happy that I was spending my money, since she hoped to put me into poverty. I could still hear her shrill voice, "You got the house. You got the kids!"

After week three of Andrew's hospitalization, we had still not heard from or seen James. By the end of two months, Andrew was begging to be released, and a meeting for his discharge was in place. What pained me most was the look on his face when James entered the room—as if God himself had arrived. He proudly announced, "That's my dad!"

I agreed to have Andrew come home to live with me, but I was going to Nantucket on vacation—which I desperately needed—with my sister Pat, who was flying in from Regina.

Andrew pleaded with James, "Dad, please let me come home with you, just for the week. You won't regret it. I promise."

"No, that's totally out of the question."

He loved James so much, yet the drunken jerk didn't even notice. I couldn't understand how James could so callously ignore him. But it was the betrayal on Andrew's face that tore me apart as he walked out of the meeting, crying and inconsolable. James didn't care that Andrew was locked up in this hellhole. I could only surmise that having him come stay would complicate his selfish lifestyle.

"Sweetie, I'll come and get you from the hospital as soon as I get back from vacation. I promise."

My sister and I rented a tiny one-room cottage in Nantucket with a minuscule kitchen, but it was perfect. I was refreshed from a wonderful week of sun and returned home to an eager Andrew ready to accept all the house rules Dr. Sarnelli and I had put together. The greeting was like it used to be. He hugged and kissed me and even threw in a few extra spontaneous playful kisses along the way.

"Ma, it feels great to leave that place. I've really learned my lesson—no more drinking or marijuana. Thanks for bringing me home."

"Okay, and we're starting today with Dr. Sarnelli and Dave Brown from the State Rehab Department. We're all going to work together to get you a job. We have an appointment this morning with Dr. Sarnelli. I also brought you the *Times* with the Style Section. I know how you love fashion."

"Gee, thanks, Ma." He kissed me again on the cheek.

Andrew started working at a local family-owned gourmet supermarket, bagging groceries and stocking shelves. They liked him. How could you not like this handsome, polite boy with a great sense of humor?

By mid-November, his employer called Dave Brown at State Rehab to report that Andrew smelled of alcohol.

Andrew said, "Yes, I'm guilty, but it was once and won't happen again. I want to keep this job."

Dr. Sarnelli was concerned and discussed outpatient alcohol programs. Andrew insisted he didn't have a problem. But I knew different when, at one point, he stayed out all night and came home at five thirty, bouncing off the walls, his face and body covered in dirt. I surmised he was drunk, had fallen, and spent the night in some ditch. No one would pick him up in that state. In fact, lately no one offered to give him rides, since most people were afraid of him and what he might do next. Friends rarely asked how he was doing, fearful of the truth. I suppose they thought I was disgraced or ashamed, but I wasn't. His behavior was dangerous, and I feared the rules of the street would prevail and he would be found dead. I loved this child and was certain somewhere out there was a program that would help stop this madness.

After Christmas I was going to leave psych at St. John's and go back full-time in the OR at Memorial Hospital. The only difference in changing positions was "going from the diagnosed to the undiagnosed." The doctors were quite offended when I made that comment. Of course I was joking . . .

Christmas was approaching, and I was taking all the kids back home to Moose Jaw. My mother planned and baked for months, the freezer filled to the brim. My father had been suffering from major depression since my brother's death and drowned his pain hourly in vodka. He drank first thing in the morning and was passed out by noon. It was a hell of a retirement for both of them, especially for my mother, who was sober and watched him slowly kill himself. She kept busy volunteering at an old-folks' home, at church, and in the choir. She had a beautiful untrained voice and sang lead solos. I was thankful for the strength she had passed on to me.

When we arrived in Regina, it was twenty degrees below zero. We were unable to leave the three-bedroom, one-and-a-half-bath home, even to momentarily jog, for fear of frostbite. The town was closed down because of the holiday week, and TV access was limited. My sister and her two children were also there, so we were nine people on top of one another, but it was comfy and warm, and we ate constantly.

I had bought duty-free liquor and thought I was going crazy when I searched high and low, unable to locate it. At this point I was ready to blow. "I know I bought liquor. Somebody took it."

My mother was surprised. "Connie, who would take it?"

I was shaking. "Someone did, and everyone is covering for them. I think Andrew's drinking—he's acting very sneaky."

My mother was aghast. "What do you mean?"

"Mom, I haven't told you half of what's going on in my life. It's too much, and you don't need to know, but at this point I can't take it anymore."

I sat my mother down and told her the truth. She loved Andrew, so I couldn't tell her everything. It would have destroyed her, and it nearly killed me to see her in tears. She never saw the turmoil Andrew caused with his shifty behavior. My dream for family normalcy was shattered, the daily tension strangling us. Was this how we were all going to end up, forever traumatized and destroyed?

The kids knew Andrew had taken the liquor but wouldn't rat him out, especially when I was so close to the edge. We desperately needed fresh air before this week turned into a horrible sentence.

At Christmas dinner my dad announced in a drunken slur, "This will be my last Christmas."

Instead of experiencing happy holidays and a merry Christmas, we won the prize for traveling nearly four thousand miles to host the most chaotic, stressful, dysfunctional family holiday ever.

We returned home, and Laura left for University of Colorado Boulder, where she was now studying for a degree in psychology. James had finally decided to help with her tuition. Andrew, Dr. Sarnelli, and I had an important meeting. If Andrew refused to admit that he needed help or look into a substance abuse treatment center, Dr. Sarnelli would no longer work with us. Also, if Andrew didn't make the phone call for help, he'd have to leave home.

Andrew procrastinated. I begged him, but after hours of discussion he refused any further treatment. It was during a mild, mid-March snowstorm that he left.

I was devastated. "Wait a minute—here's three hundred dollars." I hoped he'd check into the local B and B where he'd been given refuge in the past, think his situation over, come to his senses, and realize that he needed a rehab program.

"Thanks, Ma, I love you." He walked out of the house, wearing only a flannel shirt for warmth.

I had sentenced him to exile. What was I thinking? I knew I had done the right thing, but "right" was harder than hell and would not console me. I prayed through the weekend for God to keep him safe. I heard from no one, so had no idea if he was alive or dead on a street. I hoped he had called James or anyone, but I still was anguished with horrible thoughts. And then I heard he'd stopped to visit one of the neighbors. They were wonderful people, and I knew he was in good hands. Hopefully they would support my decision.

I was relieved, and a few days later went to work. I was conscientious and had learned to focus solely on my work during the hours I was on duty and leave my personal problems at home. My patients and peers deserved this. I was working in OR 9, when a call came over the intercom. "Your surgeon's detained. The case will be delayed an hour."

I had arranged the room for a breast implant procedure. On the counter was a box containing four silicon breast sizers. Mischievously, I put all of them inside my bra and . . . *voila*! Dolly Parton. Theatrically, I wandered out of the room to make rounds in the other OR rooms and offer help. Going from room to room caused laughter and major commotion, until an overhead page announced, "Connie Kane to administration, stat," which caused an even bigger uproar.

I quickly removed the implants and headed to the "principal's" office—my manager, whom I'd known for twenty years and who knew all my personal issues with Andrew.

"Okay, so I got a little carried away. Just kill me."

My manager looked at me strangely. "What are you talking about? The manager from the ER just left. Andrew's down there—go."

I flew out of the OR. In the ER, a nurse came over quickly. "I knew you'd want to be notified. The police brought him in at four a.m., since he was roaming the streets. They knew him and realized he needed a hospital and not jail."

Thank you, God. How many people with TBI without an advocate ended up in jail rather than a hospital setting? I would never let that happen to Andrew!

"He's in bad shape—delusional and hallucinating. We medicated him and he's asleep."

The nurse unlocked the door to a room stripped bare. Andrew was sound asleep, naked, with a sheet thrown over him.

"When he awakens, we'll shower him."

"Thanks, can I just sit for a few minutes?"

"Take your time."

I sat and stared at my twenty-two-year-old child, my baby, unshaven and disheveled. Painfully I summed up the reality of the situation. I had forced him out, and he was living on the streets. This, he would not survive. I left the room. "If anything changes, please call me."

"Don't worry. I will."

I went back to work. I was broken and unable to speak. I constantly left the room to wipe my tears and blow my nose. At three thirty I headed back to the ER and looked into Andrew's room, only to find it empty. I stumbled to the triage nurse. "Have you seen my son, Andrew Kane, in room three?"

She rummaged through papers and charts. "He was discharged at two thirty."

In a rage I asked, "How could he be discharged? He's sick and doesn't have a home. He can't be on the streets. Do you just discharge patients to get them out of here? Was it too much to find a proper placement for him? You were supposed to call me."

"Mrs. Kane, Crisis interviewed him. He wouldn't sign for voluntarily admittance, and we couldn't hold him. He said he's living at the shelter and would be there by eight p.m. We called the director, and she confirmed he's been staying there."

It was a week from hell. Andrew was continually brought to the ER by the police. He had learned to work the system. He would be medicated and sleep, and seem to hold it together, then return to live on the streets and stay at the shelter at night. He knew where to get help. Our parish priest generously gave him money, then called me only to reaffirm how very sick he was. I had no control over this destructive behavior and agonized constantly.

It was a few weeks later at two a.m. when the call came. Andrew had not made it back to the shelter before closing time and had been roaming the streets and ended up at a convenience store. He planned to spend the night there since it was freezing cold and he didn't have a winter jacket or socks on. The gal behind the counter knew the family and called me. I gave her James's number because he lived five minutes away, but I told her if there was a problem to call me back.

Five minutes later she called me. "I called that number, but a woman who said she was Andrew's grandmother told me her son was asleep and she wasn't going to bother him. She told me to call you and you would take care of it."

"That bitch. I'm sorry, I didn't mean you. I'm leaving now. Thanks for calling."

I was there in no time. One look and I knew Andrew was in a full-blown psychosis and needed to be in a hospital. I called the police, and they removed him to the ER at Memorial Hospital.

This time I went with them and spoke to the psychiatrist. And for the second time, Andrew was papered to the state facility, Fairview Heights. While waiting for his transfer, he attempted to assault a hospital guard. This was totally out of character for him, but his psychosis caused violent behavior.

The next day Laura—home from school for a week—and I went to Fairview Heights and met with Andrew's social worker. He felt Andrew was using cocaine as well as marijuana and alcohol. I tried to explain that with a brain injury there was a low tolerance to any form of drugs. "It would have been helpful if blood had been drawn in the ER for a toxicology screen, but in all the bedlam I'd forgotten to request it until it was too late." And then the social worker at Fairview Heights asked Laura, "Do you feel your Oedipus complex was fully completed in this dysfunctional family?"

At that moment I requested a change in social workers. There was no way this whacko was getting near Andrew. We visited Andrew for a few minutes, and I was alarmed by the deep psychosis we were facing again, as he whispered to me, "Jodie Foster is here. She comes to stay periodically and won't go anywhere else, and we are very close."

He was not able to part with that fixed delusion for weeks.

Meanwhile, back home my good friend and next-door neighbor, Dr. Sean, Laura's godfather, was in the hospital dying of cancer. He and James were close friends, but James had been estranged since the divorce. It upset Dr. Sean to witness Andrew's continual struggle without the help of a father. He died a few weeks later. I flew Laura home again for the funeral, and Todd was a pallbearer. Andrew was still in Fairview Heights and in no condition to attend. James was a no-show for the calling hours, and Todd and Laura were disgusted with him. At the last minute at church, he pushed his way to join Laura and me.

And as if nothing had happened, James spoke to Laura, "Hey, honey, it's good to see you. I didn't know you were home."

"Ma flew me in. She knew I needed to be here."

"Must have been expensive."

Money, money, money—that's all the Kanes ever thought about. Like family, we followed the procession and then sat together. My nostrils twitched at the smell of alcohol. Later, at a family brunch, Todd, Laura, and I stayed in the kitchen chatting, while James stayed in the living room. Deliberately we never crossed paths. To an astute observer, the chill in the air was obvious. No one dared mention that this was the first social setting we had shared since the divorce.

Laura and Todd left to visit some old friends, which made me happy that they were spending time together. I went home, exhausted. All this had taken a toll on me. I went to bed. It was so peaceful.

I was sound asleep when the phone blared, refusing to stop. I needed to reorient myself.

"Hello?" I was momentarily mute. "Who is this?"

"It's Dr. Tuney at Fairview Heights."

I listened for a few minutes, hyperventilating, then shouted, "What do you mean he's in braydacardia?"

Andrew was in an ambulance speeding to the ER at Danbury Hospital.

He was unresponsive, his pulse rate thirty-two—weak and deathly slow.

Chapter Sixteen

March 1994–October 1996

I SNARLED ON THE PHONE like a vicious animal at this Dr. Tuney, whom I had never met. "Spell your name for me, and what did you give him? Didn't you read his chart? He has a TBI and very sensitive to medication. I *told* you not to give him Haldol. I made several trips there, and gave you a detailed history so this wouldn't happen. Do you think he's some disabled welfare patient who doesn't know any better? He may be psychotic, but for damn sure I'm not, and let me warn you, I'll have your ass and sue that entire facility if anything happens to him! I'm on my way to the ER now."

"Mrs. Kane, I'm just the covering doctor."

"You're still responsible. Don't even start that crap with me; I'm a nurse." I hung up the phone, then called Todd and Laura to meet me in the ER at Danbury Hospital. All I knew was Andrew was unconscious with a deathly low heart rate, when supposedly he was being taken care of. He was safer on the streets! What if they'd killed him with a medication error?

Todd and Laura were in the ER when I arrived. I made my way to the reception desk.

"Excuse me, I'm Connie Kane. My son Andrew was brought here from Fairview Heights. I'd like to see him, please."

"Room six on your left, but the rules only allow one person at a time."

"Arrest me. Laura and Todd, let's go!"

Todd was hesitant. "Mom, they said only you can go in."

"Let them call security. We're all going. I need you, and we don't have time. Andrew might be dead."

We entered Andrew's room to find him asleep and hooked up to an IV and EKG machine. His pulse rate was forty. I checked his chest and he was breathing. *Thank you, God!*

Dr. Carey, the ER doctor on duty, entered the room, clomping on noisy clogs. He was an assertive young man in his mid-thirties. He asked Todd and Laura, who were still standing in the doorway, to come closer. "It's okay, come in. The rules drive me crazy too." He put us at ease. And then explained.

"There has been a medication error, so we are forcing fluids and keeping him monitored until he's stable. I'm sure he'll be fine, but the next eight hours will tell."

We took turns sitting with Andrew, and when he started to move and his vital signs returned to normal, I kissed Todd and Laura and told them to leave. Within a couple of hours Andrew opened his eyes. Dr. Carey entered the room.

"Andrew is safe and needs to rest There's no need for you to stay. Your sleep is more important. Go home, and I'll call you when I get off duty."

I headed straight home to bed, and at five-thirty a.m. the phone rang.

"Mrs. Kane, it's Dr. Carey. I have someone who wants to speak to you."

It was Andrew. "Ma, you've got to do something."

I was taken aback. "Why, what's the matter?"

"I'm starving and have to wait until six for breakfast. This is a hospital. We're sick people, and there should be food around. We have rights. They're sending me back to Fairview Heights, and I want to eat before I leave."

I burst out laughing. His complaining was music to my ears. "I'll be over before you're gone," I promised.

Later that morning, when Andrew returned to Fairview Heights, I met with the administrator there. The lioness from Moose Jaw had been pushed way too far, and Fairview Heights must have had a premonition that I had claws. The administrator was waiting and totally apologetic. He agreed that a mistake had occurred, but reassured me it would not happen again and that Andrew was very safe in their hands. If I had any concerns, I was to notify him immediately.

In the following days, my confidence was restored when a new social worker, Sally Goldman, was assigned to the case. I truly believed God sent us this Jewish angel, who recognized that Andrew belonged not at Fairview Heights but in a behavioral TBI program. She researched and found a place for him at The Hospital for Special Care in nearby New Britain. One slot had opened, and it was critical to move quickly, as these openings rarely became available. It was a one-to-one program that lasted up to two years. I was amazed at how quickly James, still the conservator, moved with the paperwork. Ten days later, Andrew met the criteria—Medicaid would pay for the funding, and he was accepted into the program. *Thank you, God.*

The neurobehavioral unit was a ten-bed unit secured within The Hospital for Special Care. According to the brochure, the program specialized in training acquired brain injury (ABI) individuals to organize their behaviors appropriately, and learn skills to maximize their independence and improve their overall quality of life. It provided a highly structured, safe, and supportive learning environment, with a discharge goal of reintegrating into the community with limited support services. This was the best of the best, and I was in heaven.

The eight admission criteria that patients were required to meet were:

1. a diagnosis of acquired brain injury
2. previously documented attempts at rehabilitation
3. having at least one year post-injury
4. medical stability
5. age of eighteen years or older
6. unstable behaviors requiring a secured unit
7. a demonstrable ability to learn
8. a conservatorship in place.

This was a perfect place for Andrew. What an opportunity we had—that Andrew would have. All this chaos would end, and he would get on with his life and finally accept his injury.

On discharge day from Fairview Heights, the clouds and sky appeared especially lively. Andrew was melancholy. He'd been there for two months, and his psychosis hadn't totally disappeared. Deep inside my secret vault, I feared he'd fried his brain. After all, how many brain cells had been killed with his drug use? No one really knew, and he had little recall. We were told this hangover could last for months. We'd only to look at his father to see what thirty years of alcoholism abuse had done to *his* brain. We hardly recognized James anymore.

In the car we discussed the new program. "We're very lucky to get you in. It's meant to be, and you'll only be thirty minutes from home. I'll be able to visit often."

"I guess so, Ma, but I'm going to miss Jodie. She gave me a blanket she crocheted."

"That was very kind. She must be a nice person. But, Andrew, you don't mean Jodie Foster. Please tell me it's not her."

He glared at me. "Yes, Ma, it is Jodie Foster."

This fixed delusion upset me. Let this pass, please.

The Hospital for Special Care was Andrew's ninth hospital admission since his accident eight years prior, and he'd spent a total of almost four years in a facility of some sort. It was apparent he would not be able to live independently and would need some sort of support, but I wasn't sure exactly what that was. I think I was in denial as to the extent of his injury. But I constantly remembered the words from Newington Children's Hospital when he was discharged following the accident: "I see no reason why Andrew can't go on to college and someday get married." Those words stayed foremost in my brain for a very long of time.

At The Hospital for Special Care we pressed the buzzer, and the smiling face of a young well-dressed woman greeted us. I had a momentary flashback to the Wellness Center when Obstinate Boy greeted me and slammed the door in my face! Mustn't think of those negative events.

June Gilbert was the social worker for the unit. She began the tour, and I strolled around in heaven. The nurses' station overlooked a spacious lounge with a huge TV. The walls flanked by sparkling glass allowed the outside in, even though it was a locked unit. Outside was a courtyard, housing a basketball court, blooming flowers, and tables for picnics. There was a laundry room, and the client rooms were large and spotless, resembling college dorms. The staff-to-patient ratio was high, with the focus to immediately address abnormal behavior. My eyes were bugging out of my head in delight.

They were very strict with regard to conservatorship, and permission was needed for anyone to visit, including me. I was fascinated with their knowledge, and knew at long last I would be able to sleep at night. And maybe finally would no longer need a tranquilizer for sleep.

Two weeks later, during a visit, Andrew greeted me with a smile, then took me to see his room. Looking directly at me he said, "Ma, this program isn't for me. They expect me to be perfect." He leaned closer and asked, "You're not wired, are you?"

"No, I'm not wired. Why would I be?" His paranoia was frightening, persisting too long.

"I just want to make sure they're not taping our visit."

"Why would they care about our visit?"

"They do, Ma, believe me. But Jodie Foster's coming to get me out."

"Andrew, I don't think so. When people get sick from drugs, they get confused. You'll feel better soon."

On the way out, I stopped to see the social worker, June. I said, "Hi, do you have a minute?"

"Sure, come in."

"This psychosis has been present for two and a half months. I'm very worried that he's had more permanent damage to his brain."

"Yes, we had quite a time with him earlier this week when Jackie Kennedy died. He wanted to contact them, said he was a family friend. He's very convincing and also said his cousin was Bob Crane from *Hogan's Heroes*. Is that true, or is it a delusion?"

"That's true. Bob Crane is a distant relative."

"Even so, his delusions present a bit of a dilemma for us."

"I know. He can be very theatrical. But this continual and lengthy psychosis is worrying me. I've planned a weekend away to visit with old friends, but I'm not comfortable leaving."

"Go—you need to get away. We've got a close eye on him every minute, and that's what he's finding difficult. Besides, his father is around in case something happens."

"June, you must know by now that James is not a reliable or responsible man."

She smiled professionally but did not utter a word.

It was two days before I was ready to go. I'd just finished an exhilarating power walk, and my endorphins were jumping, when the phone rang. It was June. "Mrs. Kane, I don't want to worry you, but Andrew has threatened suicide. The entire team agrees that he's trying to manipulate us because he isn't getting his way, but we need to treat it with all the caution that it deserves, so we're putting him back on one-to-one."

"I was just about to leave for that weekend away."

"If we felt this was a serious problem, we'd tell you. Go. He's in good hands. By the time you return, he'll probably be off suicide precautions."

I heeded her advice, and when I arrived at my friend's place, I opened up about Andrew and my concerns. "I'm used to hospitals and know whom I can trust. For eight years this has been my life. The Hospital for Special Care is the best with TBI. I've total confidence in the team—from the doctors, especially Dr. Stanwood, to the maintenance workers. Maybe I'll write a book or screenplay about my experience with TBI. Clout, glitz, and Hollywood would create awareness. I don't have connections or literary knowledge, but I do have passion, which is the main ingredient.

My friends were in shock. "Connie we had no idea, but apparently you can do anything."

"No, don't say that. I can't. I'm just not afraid to try. When you've already been to hell, and back, what's there to fear?"

When I returned home, a few days later Andrew was off of suicide precautions and finally free of psychosis and antipsychotic medications. He was in a good place.

Todd and Laura, however, were once again in turmoil with Aunt Trudy. Her daughter, Anita, was getting married, and they were invited to the wedding. They decided to forgive and forget after what had transpired two years ago with their cousin Cane's wedding and said they would attend, still desiring to bond with their father's family. When they responded, however, Trudy again showed her true colors and informed them there was no place at the hotel because she was saving rooms for her friends.

I was enraged that once again she had struck my children a malicious blow. She was simply inhumane. Todd was especially torn apart, but it was Laura who wrote a letter to Trudy. She told her how upset and disappointed they were with the way she treated them and how unwanted they felt. She went on to say how sickened she was that Trudy hadn't helped her brother, James, address the disease of alcoholism that was killing him. She ended with "I think you are so selfish that you don't care what happens to others as long as you get what you want. I feel sorry for you because I don't think you will ever know what true happiness is."

Todd and Laura did not attend the wedding.

In the spring I joined a gym and was working out regularly. I was less stressed, not having to worry about Andrew, and beginning to look fit. Every Thursday Andrew and I went out for dinner, and Sundays we went shopping. Occasionally, Todd took him out for dinner.

By September Andrew was able to come home for a weekend pass. Todd called and we planned a day trip to enjoy the foliage. He arrived early to spend time with Andrew. I rushed into the house after working out at the gym, happy and smiling. Todd was flustered and stared at me. He cringed and shook his head, "Oh no, my mother's in spandex!" Despite my wardrobe malfunction shock, we had a great day.

James rarely visited — he was too busy. At this point he could no longer hold a job, but he did have a steady girlfriend. He showed up for some of the meetings at The Hospital for Special Care, which surprised but pleased me, as Andrew's face illuminated when he entered the room. It was obvious he desperately loved his father and wanted to see him. Andrew called, wanting to visit him and his grandmother at their home, but James never returned his calls. Finally, Andrew got Dee on the phone and begged her to come for a visit. In turn, she hollered at him, "Stop calling your father. You just make him cry!"

I had taught my children to respect their elders, especially grandparents, and to try to show kindness in regard to their often different views, but at this moment I couldn't contain myself. Dee's vicious behavior was disgraceful in the way she treated Andrew in such a degrading manner. When he told me the story, I was livid. I couldn't understand her and wondered whether she was normal or if dementia caused this horrible behavior. I hoped that before she died she would someday treat my children with the same respect that they showed her.

A few weeks later, my mother came to visit. Todd was turning twenty-five, I fifty, and my mother seventy-five. Todd was treating us to a fancy dinner, so I "gussied up," donning a daring black dress. He entered and kissed us both.

"Granny, I'm the happiest man on earth. I've got a great job and a beautiful girlfriend I think I'm taking to the altar! What more could a man want?"

My mother was inquisitive. "And what makes her so special?"

"She's thin, tall, blonde, smart, sophisticated, and has a great sense of humor. You know, Mom — she's just like you!"

"That's probably the highest compliment you could ever pay me." I was so emotional that I excused myself to the ladies' room before my mascara ruined my face. As I returned, Todd was chatting with his grandmother.

Todd said, "Granny, you've got to do something. Did you see how low cut my mother's dress is?"

"Yes, and I think she looks wonderful."

Todd was shocked. "Granny!"

It was a wonderful celebration, despite my choice of dress.

I was feeling good and looking fit. Someone at my gym suggested I could model and gave me the name of a New York modeling agency. Surprisingly, I was invited to join their client list, and soon I was getting calls for little jobs. Cindy Crawford I was not, but vintage . . . ? Perhaps. I couldn't believe my ears when I received a call to do a clothing shoot. I didn't care what it was or how much it paid, but the excitement of going into New York was overwhelming. When you've survived a living hell, nothing will stand in the way of trying the impossible.

Just the idea of running into the city was a rush for me. It allowed me the freedom to leave behind all my problems and have some fun. I knew I was never going to make a lot of money, but modeling took me into another world, and that was a gift. So there I was, perched on a freezing rock in Central Park for hours wearing a hideous coat even a homeless person would reject. I also did some catalogue work and thought I was really in the money when I got paid three hundred dollars an hour.

But my chance for stardom came when I got a call to be an extra in the movie *The Mirror Has Two Faces* with Barbra Streisand and Jeff Bridges. They were shooting a scene in which Jeff Bridges was a professor speaking to an audience. They needed a hundred or so extras. I felt this was the moment that would make me famous. It was a few weeks before Christmas when I lugged a suitcase filled with several clothing changes to the shoot at Columbia University. It was eleven p.m. before we actors filed into an auditorium. I was seated at the end of a row, purposefully, I was sure, to make a statement.

Ms. Streisand moved up and down the aisle, meticulously directing the crew to change a vase on the podium a half an inch to the left, then two inches to the right. I'd never seen such long fingers. Did she have extra-long digits implanted?

We finished at three a.m., and there I was in the middle of Harlem with no way back to Grand Central Station. Desperate, I befriended the tallest street-wise crew member to help me find a cab. He told the driver, "Get her safe and sound to Grand Central."

I said, "Thank you. Merry Christmas. See you in the movies."

We sped through the totally foreign world of Harlem. The streets were carnival-like, jammed with what seemed like nerve-racking goings-on.

At Grand Central I jumped out of the cab and leapt over a homeless person, to flee inside to safety. However, the door was locked. I had three hours to kill before the station reopened. It was a festive season, but I was not about to roam the streets lugging a heavy suitcase.

I headed to the Grand Hyatt next to the station in search of a place to eat, drink, relax, or do whatever until I could get the seven a.m. train home, but everything was closed. I slinked to a sofa in the lobby and quietly sat down. Within ten minutes the manager came over.

"Excuse me, Miss—could I see your room key?"

Should I cry, or fess up? "I don't have a key. I just finished working... oh, not that kind of working, I mean..."

"I'm sorry, you'll have to leave. We have a policy regarding women sitting alone in our lobby, especially at this hour."

"It's not what you think. I'm not looking for business—no, not me."

"Please leave before I call security."

"Look, please, I'm a mother and a nurse and a good person. I just finished working to make additional money as a movie extra. I came from Connecticut alone. Grand Central is locked, and you don't want me on the streets. I have to get home to my children. I'll pay you to sit here. I won't fall asleep. I'll be appropriate, please." Tears sealed the deal.

"Okay, you can stay."

"Thank you so much, and look for me in the movies!" I was relieved and opened a magazine to read, but sensed a pair of eyes focused on me. A well-dressed, inebriated man stood in front of me.

"How much?"

"Oh my God. Please leave before I call the guard."

"Getting uppity in your old age."

I was ready to verbally assault this creep, but I remained appropriate and turned my head the other way. How dare he? Old age? I was a movie star!

I got home at ten in the morning. My check for seventy-five dollars reflected a day's work. But my glory would come when the movie was released and for five seconds the back of my head, along with a hundred others, would be on the screen.

A few days later, still on a high, I was sound asleep, when the phone rang at eleven p.m. It was Laura.

"Mom, I know it's late, but I had to call. I didn't know I was going to see you today!"

"See me today? Laura, are you all right?" *Oh my God, she's doing drugs again.*

"Mom, I'm fine, but you won't believe this. This morning I went to my psych class and entered the amphitheater to watch a video. As the lights dimmed, who was on the screen but my mother and brother! It was the video you and Andrew made when he was at Highgate."

"I hardly remember it—how was it?"

"Tough to watch, and nobody knew it was my brother and mother. The girl next to me whispered that if that had been her, she'd rather be dead. She didn't see my reaction and tears."

"Laura, I'm so sorry. It must have been hard for you. Where did it come from?"

"It's part of the curriculum in the Psychology Department and has been integrated into a three-part video about TBI, Alzheimer's Disease, and Korskoff's Syndrome. It's called *The World of Abnormal Psychology and Organic Mental Disorders*."

This was the beginning of sharing what we had experienced and hopefully helping others in similar situations—TBI, Andrew, alcohol, James.

"Mom, I never totally realized what you and Andrew went through, and I need to tell you that I'm proud and lucky to have you."

"Laura, this is the best phone call ever. I love you."

"I love you too."

I'd waited a long time to hear those words, as our relationship had been strained for many years. The next day I called Andrew at The Hospital for Special Care to relay the conversation, and without missing a beat he asked, "So where are my royalties?"

Andrew had been there eight months. They were hosting the annual Christmas party, and I ran into the social worker, June Gilbert. She informed me Andrew had made great strides. He admitted he was an alcoholic and was attending AA meetings, five times a week. Her words were a welcome Christmas present.

"There's a band called The Supremes playing downstairs—let's get going," Andrew shouted.

"Okay, but you'll have to let me hold your arm."

"Mom, you're so goofy!"

"I know, but I'm too old to change."

So many people at the party remarked how handsome Andrew was, and he just rolled his eyes, embarrassed. The party suited him. The auditorium rocked, toes tapped, wheelchairs danced. Handicaps and disabilities were forgotten for the moment. Andrew flew up on the stage to perform. I felt free, light, and exhilarated as I watched him, and tears rolled down my cheeks. These were happy tears, basking in the moment, and also pained tears because James didn't show up. As I observed the patients who seemed to have no family present, I wondered what had happened and if their families still loved them. I ached for what they had lost but rejoiced for all I had. Time was a precious commodity, and quality of life, family, and true friends were priceless. Andrew had paid a huge price for his family to learn this valuable lesson. On the way home I sang "The Wind beneath My Wings." That was our song, Andrew's and mine. *And thank you, God.*

The year 1996 was right around the corner. Andrew was twenty-five and in a safe place, and I now had time to expand my horizons. I started a German class, which I had spoken as a child and shamefully repressed, and a screenwriting class. How hard would it be to write a screenplay? I thought, even though I didn't have an English literature background and had never typed or used a computer. I loved passing from the sublime to the ridiculous, constantly committing absurdities, and was comfortable being the laughingstock. Yes indeed, I met the criteria to be successful. I commuted to Westport, Connecticut, for classes, but soon gave up German, since screenwriting was more of a commitment than I had realized.

More good news came. Todd and Christine, his girlfriend, had a wonderful announcement. At dinner he made a toast. "To the two most important women in my life."

My mouth dropped open. And before I could utter a word, he proposed to Christine and she accepted, then and there. With a frog in my throat, I said, "Welcome to our family. I'm happy Todd has chosen you."

"No, Mrs. Kane, thank you for giving me the most wonderful man in the world."

God had definitely put these two together for a special reason. They both had siblings with disabilities.

Meanwhile, Andrew was anxiously awaiting discharge from The Hospital for Special Care after fifteen months. I'd never seen him so happy and mature. He'd hooked up with a small TBI program in Chaplin, Connecticut, called Pride, and would be moving there over the July Fourth weekend. It was a supervised home, occupied by four clean-cut young men with TBIs similar to Andrew's. This new home was welcoming and neat and had staff present twenty-four hours a day to help clients with cooking, cleaning, and daily care. A van was accessible to drive clients wherever they wanted to go, including jobs, and to take one wheelchair client to college. Everything was finally perfect, and Andrew, too, was perfect. The next goal for him was to have his own apartment.

I was happy and content, busy cleaning house, when the doorbell rang. Looking like a rag, I went to the door to find two tall official-looking, clean-cut men, dressed in suits and khaki raincoats. I opened the door.

"Mrs. Kane, we're from the FBI. Could we talk to you for a moment?"

"Sure, but what's this about?"

"Your son Andrew was a patient at Highgate, correct?"

"Yes." I panicked—oh my God, his stay wasn't covered by insurance and they're going to put me in jail.

"Have you been in contact with anyone who worked there?"

"No, why?"

"We're investigating them for insurance fraud. It seems they were billing for services not rendered and have fled New Hampshire and we can't locate them."

"Really. Well, I'm not surprised." I relayed my year-long experience as they listened attentively.

When they left, I remembered but soon dismissed the time Andrew spent at Highgate. That was in the past, and today I had a social event to get ready for.

In my leisure time I had begun attending functions with the Canadian community in New York City. The president of the Canadian Society of New York proposed me as a member, and I was excited about attending a black-tie event—"A Night in Banff"—at Carnegie Hall. The emcee was Peter Jennings. I brought Maria along.

I felt at ease and at home with this group even though most of them were from Eastern Canada and I was from the Wild West. Canadians are unpretentious, warm, and respectful. Westerners take their time, speak slowly, never jaywalk, or run a yellow light. By moving to the Northeast I'd become Americanized—maybe too competitive and intense, and perhaps too opinionated. But now, ten years since the accident, I'd learned how to relax, reenergize, and listen more to my heart and be nonjudgmental. Later I would incorporate all this wisdom into a relaxation program for patients where I worked.

That night at Carnegie Hall, the lights dimmed. It was last call before the event commenced. I was chatting, when who did my wandering eyes see? No, not Santa Claus but Peter Jennings scurrying toward the bar. It was now or never, Connie!

Undaunted, I walked up to him until we were face-to-face. I extended my hand to shake his. "Hi, Mr. Jennings, I'm Connie Kane. We've been having dinner together every evening for years, and I think it's time we met."

He laughed and smiled. "Indeed we should, Connie."

By now he was swarmed. Maria and I left like two giggling schoolgirls and entered the auditorium for the main event. I told her, "He is so handsome, and even though he had a date with him, I could tell there was lust in that handshake."

Maria raised a suspicious eyebrow. "You really need to get out more."

The gala was a night to remember. It had been a very long time since I'd felt glamorous and sophisticated. At one thirty I returned home to a blinking light on my answering machine. I calmly kicked off my shoes and pressed the button.

"Hi, Ma, it's Andrew, your son. I just heard a song, I think by Celine Dion, and thought of you." He started to sing, "You were my strength when I was weak, you were my voice when I couldn't speak, you were my eyes when I couldn't see." I sat down, my knees weak. "Anyway, I just wanted to call and say thanks for being my eyes and voice when I was in the coma. Ma, I love you, bye."

A perfect ending to a perfect day.

That fall, Laura would start her junior year in Boulder at the University of Colorado, and Todd was planning his wedding. Andrew was ready to move into his own apartment under supervision from Pride. He had a job at McDonald's, which he enjoyed, but one of the girls he worked with kept calling him "retarded." I was more irate than he was. Uneducated people don't understand brain injury, and I felt this described about ninety-five percent of the population. I still hoped he would aspire to further his education and change that misperception.

He had a cute apartment, and we all contributed to furnishing it. James sent a sofa that smelled of cat urine, which we immediately tossed, along with the linens Dee sent that weren't good enough to be used as rags. Andrew was proud of this move and his family's support but never uttered a word against James and Dee. After all, James was still his dad, whom he adored and would never speak badly about. I could only imagine how it all made him feel.

I was enjoying writing my screenplay and found the process cathartic. I had only been in the class for six months and vaguely understood the three-act play structure, when I announced to my class that I was entering the Sundance Film Festival competition for screenwriters. My producer-instructor was shocked and said, "But, Connie, Sundance is probably the best in the world."

"Good, I like starting at the top." I wasn't sure what he meant, but I'd finished the first six pages, written a synopsis, and could submit them with an explanation of where I was in the project. My ten-year battle with Andrew had left me confident and wiser about how to deal with people. The ongoing life-or-death crisis had taught me to advocate and to start only where the power was. Starting at the bottom was time-consuming and compromising—not for me.

That summer was busy. James and I were hosting a rehearsal dinner for Todd's October wedding in Boston, and already there were problems with James paying his portion. If he backed out, Todd told me he would not invite him or his family to the wedding.

James and I agreed to share the bill to buy Andrew what he needed for the wedding. I shopped with Andrew to buy him a new suit, shirt, tie—the works. Later, when I told James what I had purchased, he argued that I'd spent too much money, and that Andrew certainly didn't need the cologne. He was becoming a cheapskate for everyone but himself.

To make matters worse, James wanted Trudy and her husband to be invited to the rehearsal dinner as well as the wedding. I was shocked they were coming. This was stressful for Todd. He tried to put the past behind him and be optimistic that Trudy and her family finally wanted to be family.

"Sweetie, on your wedding day, you will only be concentrating on your beautiful bride and your new life together. You won't even be aware that Trudy exists."

Meanwhile, in August, I arrived home energized from a power walk. The now six-foot-tall, ten-year-old schefflera plant needed to be watered. I addressed it, "Hey bud, another beautiful day." And then I skipped over to the blinking light on my answering machine. "This message is for Connie Kane, from Kathy at the Sundance Feature Film Program. We have reviewed your application for the January 1997 Sundance Screenwriters Lab and would like to invite you to submit your completed screenplay for the next round of consideration. Please send us your script by September sixth, and note your application number on the cover. If you have any questions . . ."

It was a thunderbolt! I was mute, numb, and then out of control. I jumped for joy, danced, and shrieked, "Yes, yes, oh my God! I can't believe this. I'm not a writer. I'm a mother, a nurse. Am I a writer? Maybe I am. And, oh my God, I think I just had an orgasm. At least I still know what that is!"

Totally exhilarated, I wandered to the backyard, lifted by an aura of accomplishment.

Thick brush from the bank now gently rested on the split-rail fence. It had grown over the railing, as if feeling it mandatory to cover the spot where it all happened ten years ago. The tree that held the swing was gone. I looked up to the heavens. The sun cradled me. The calm, puffy clouds frolicked in a blue sky. Around the trellis, swaying in the breeze, the red geraniums stood guard over the pink impatiens, flanked by their loyal vinca vine. I was one with nature and comforted by its presence. I felt so lucky. How much I'd grown! *Thank you, God.*

Each and every one of us has a story to tell, and my story had piqued the Sundance committee's interest. It did have value, and it would someday help someone else. However, I now had two weeks to complete the screenplay, when I wasn't quite sure what the three-act structure was all about. Although I did not make the next round of consideration, being asked validated who I was and what I was working on, and that would motivate me to continue writing.

October arrived, and I was overjoyed at the prospect of Todd's wedding. My Canadian family flew in, and, as usual, Mother picked up the tab for everyone to stay in Boston. On the big day it was beautiful and warm. Todd and Best Man Andrew waited in the alcove of the church. Everything went off without a hitch, except for Todd exclaiming, "Andrew, I'm gonna wet my pants if you don't hurry and fix my tie!"

Andrew's hands fumbled. "Okay, Bro, you're done."

Todd flew down the stairs to find a bathroom. Unbeknownst to him, Christine was now waiting at the altar. Andrew was on guard, checking the door for Todd's return. When Todd returned, Andrew chuckled and pointed to Christine standing impatiently.

"The show's begun and your fly's undone. I'm such a poet."

Lickety-split, Todd zipped up his fly and leaped to the altar. The guests snickered too. Andrew calmly followed and took his place beside Todd.

At the reception, when the wedding party was introduced, James and I walked in together. But when he grabbed my hand, it was overstepping and inappropriate. I graciously pulled away with a smile on my face. The seating arrangements were delicate. I sat with my family and friends, and James sat with his sister, Trudy, and his friends on the opposite side of the room. That seemed to work. But as I scanned the room, my eyes fell upon James, and a wave of nostalgia overcame me. I vividly remembered our wedding in Nantucket on a beautiful sunny day like today. And I smiled, remembering eating lobster with my family for the first time, which we naively tackled very hesitantly. At that time I thought I was the luckiest girl in the entire world.

Quickly nostalgia turned to reality as Andrew took the podium to make a toast. He was awesome and so beautiful. I needed to be careful of tears in this arena.

Watching Andrew, I realized how much all of us had grown in the last ten years. Today was a truly beautiful day and could never be taken away.

Finally, everyone was in a good place.

I would always continue to be a steadfast optimist, a resilient lioness, and would never give up on my children.

And the girl from Moose Jaw was once again happy.

Thank you, God!

Epilogue

Even though we can't ever erase the accident, and it was a horrific catastrophe for Andrew, it was because of his strength and courage that Todd, Laura, and I were enabled to forge ahead with a strength and determination that, without having experienced this, we perhaps would never have come to realize.

Laura constantly seeks to improve her skills as a yoga instructor and a psychotherapist with a private practice in Beacon Hill, Boston. She attributes her success to Andrew.

Todd is an exceptional father. His focus is family. He and his wife Christine are wonderful parents and role models. They continually support Andrew and have lovingly enlightened their family and friends about the common misperceptions of TBI. My three grandchildren, Colin, Lily, and Colton, will be better people because of their Uncle Andrew. They will make the world a kinder and better place.

I would never have been able to share this story and written this book, or had the courage to write a screenplay, without Andrew's example. And I wouldn't be the accomplished nurse I am today. Thank you, Andrew.

After all these many years of dealing with stress, I have learned a great deal, and I hope I am a better person. Because my heart has been beaten, broken, and in pain for so many years, it has softened, thus contributing a soft, gentle calmness to my character. In turn, I am able to use these tools to help the apprehensive patient prior to surgery, as I pass on my experience of learning how to relax.

I have started a program using my clinical skills, philosophy, and soft gentle voice that takes patients through relaxing breathing techniques, guided visual imagery, and Reiki—the Japanese technique for stress reduction that promotes healing. I use these techniques in the OR with anxious patients, and also coach patients with chronic back pain prior to having local back injections. The very best gift I receive is when patients have received the injection and I tell them it's over, and they tell me they never felt a thing. Often patients request that I please make a tape for them, and others just ask if I can go home with them. I'm still waiting to go home with that tall, dark, handsome male patient!

Nursing doesn't get much better than that!

I can't believe that relaxation has become *my* forte, as I never believed I would ever get to this point in my life. I love my job, even though most of my friends are now retired. But I still don't like getting up at five thirty a.m.

The schefflera plant is now twenty-six years old, still growing strong and still in my home. I have moved many times, but the plant is always foremost in the moving plan. It was an important gift from Andrew and a constant reminder to our family that we are resilient.

And though Andrew continued to need more hospitalizations and would often be very challenging, we never gave up on him. Through it all, he has been unaware of the poignant life lessons he taught us just by being himself—most importantly in visualizing life as a glass always half full, and the importance of laughing between the tears in order to survive.

Andrew lives in his own apartment with a 24/7 direct support staff at Goodwill Industries, in their Acquired Brain Injury Program, twenty minutes from me. Often he feels that is too close for comfort, as I still keep a strict eye on him and his program. And I do pity his case manager, who has to listen to me. But as of today I now have help from Lauren, MSW (Masters in Social Work), at Melissa's Project, a program of Guardian Ad Litem Services. She advocates for Andrew and works with our team to monitor and make sure everyone is collaborating, responsible, and doing their jobs. It is an example of interagency collaboration at its best and takes a huge load off of me, the conservator.

But I still feel it's my job to be always aware of his program, and I still know what is best for him.

After all, Andrew, I am your mother. And I will always love you, more.

Resources

It is my hope that in listing the following Connecticut agencies, it may help you in your search to support your loved one. Advocate to be heard, and you too will Rise Up . . .
Or, let me be your voice!
With much love,
Thank you and very truly yours,
C.C.

Today in 2014, we have a phenomenal team in place that focuses on Andrew and his daily well-being. Our team leader is Dr. Eugene B. Piasetsky, PhD, Neuropsychology and Brain Injury Rehabilitation Services, PC. He is located in Hamden, CT. His functions are:

- Designing clinical and behavioral strategies for team members to employ that take into account the clients psychological makeup, mood status and cognitive impairments arising from his brain injury.

- The strategies are offered and modified in collaboration with the team so as to optimize the team's effectiveness in working with the client so as to enable him to collaborate with the various services and to do what is necessary in order to function at his best within the community.

- Strategies further seek to provide pathways for the client to secure enjoyment and achieve personal goals.

- Provide direct clinical services to the client to foster his awareness and adjustment to his acquired difficulties and, where applicable, teach him to work around difficulties and/or reduce their impact in practical situations.

- Provide direct clinical services to assist the client in developing for himself an acceptable and positive framework within which to pursue personal goals.

- Provide guidance to the team in non-medical crisis management.

The following agencies are represented at our monthly team meetings.

1) **Greater Bridgeport Community Mental Health Center, Middle Street, Bridgeport CT.** Dr. Khan is one of the psychiatrists, along with case managers and nurses, associated with the team, who also monitor the clients.

    Outpatient Services (state operated)

    Ongoing community-based services are provided by a number of multi-disciplinary treatment teams. Core clinical services, offered by all of these teams, include: psychopharmacology, assessment, case management, individual, group and family psychotherapy and psycho- education.

Community Support Program (CSP): (Dr. Khan and his team) CSP is targeted to individuals who need the most intense level of community-based care. The program utilizes a team approach to provide intensive, rehabilitative community support, crisis intervention, individual and group skill-building, also known as recovery education. The majority of the interventions are community-based, delivered in the individual's home, neighborhood or community, which enables the team to become intimately familiar with the individual's surroundings, strengths and challenges, within the context of their environment. The desired outcome is to assist individuals toward an independent, enriched life based on their own choices and preferences.

2) **Department of Mental Health and Addiction Services (DMHAS) ABI Services:**

Main phone number 860-262-6725

Web site: http://www.ct.gov/dmhas

Community Integration Specialists (CIS):

The CIS is responsible for processing all referrals to the ABI Community Services Program within the designated services area; serving as a link for clients to in-patient services; arranging for clinical consultations; assisting in the development of treatment plans; serving as liaison to private/public services within the appropriate community; providing monitoring of services for DMHAS ABI clients; and providing support to consumers, family members and conservators. The CIS receives continuous training regarding brain injury services available within the particular geographic region. The CIS coordinates with other programs within DMHAS and with other departments within the state/local services constellation that can provide services, funds, etc., to the person with brain injury.

3) **Department of Social Services (DSS) ABI Waiver:**

1-855-626-6632

Acquired Brain Injury (ABI) Waiver

A Medicaid Waiver program that employs the principles of person-centered planning to provide a range of non-medical, home and community based services, to maintain adults who have an acquired brain injury (not a developmental or degenerative disorder), in the community. Without these services, the adult would otherwise require placement in one of four types of institutional settings. Adults must be age 18-64 to apply, must be able to participate in the development of a service plan in partnership with a Department social worker, or have a Conservator to do so, must meet all technical, procedural and financial requirements of the Medicaid program, or the Medicaid for Employed Disabled program. An adult deemed eligible for the ABI Waiver, is eligible for all Medicaid covered services. Application is made by contacting the Department's regional offices, and returning a completed ABI Waiver Request Form. LEVEL OF CARE REQUIREMENT: This means that, without waiver services, you would need to live in a nursing facility, a chronic disease hospital, or a long term Intermediate Care Facility.

What services are available under the ABI waiver? There are 19 services available under the ABI waiver. Some services may not be accessed in conjunction with other services.

- Case management: assistance to the individual in implementing and coordinating all sources of support and services to the waiver participant.

- Chore Services: services needed to maintain the participant's home in a sanitary and safe condition.

- Cognitive/Behavioral Programs: individualized programs to decrease severe maladaptive behaviors that would jeopardize the participant's ability to remain in the community.

- Community Living Support Services: supervised living in a community residential setting which provides up to 24 hour support services. Services may include medication management, self care, interpersonal skills, etc.

- Companion Services: non-medical care, supervision, and socialization services that have a therapeutic goal as noted in the participant's services plan.

- Environmental Accessibility Adaptations: physical adaptations to the participant's home to ensure the participant's health and safety, and to promote independence. Services may include ramp installation, bathroom modifications, doorway widening, etc.

- Family Training: training and counseling for individuals who live with or provide care to the waiver participant.

- Habilitation: services provided outside the participant's home, to assist the participant with obtaining or enhancing adaptive, socialization, and self-help skills to live successfully in the community.

- Pre-Vocational Services: services designed to prepare the participant for employment when the participant is not expected to be able to work, or participate in a transitional work program, within 1 year.

- Supported Employment Services: Paid employment with intensive supports provided in a variety of settings, for participants unlikely to secure competitive employment.

- Homemaker Services: General household activities including meal preparation, vacuuming, etc.

- Home Delivered Meals: Meals delivered to the participant when the person responsible is unable to do so.

- Independent Living Skills Training: Services designed and delivered on an independent or a group basis to improve the participant's ability to live independently in the community. Services may include training in self care, medication management, mobility, etc.

- Personal Care Assistance: Assistance with activities of daily living. These services may be provided by a family member of the participant if they meet the training requirements established by DSS.

- Personal Emergency Response Systems: Electronic Devices that enables individuals at a high risk for institutionalization to obtain help in an emergency.

- Respite Care: To provide short-term assistance to the participant if a caretaker is absent or in need of relief.

- Specialized Medical Equipment and Supplies: As specified in the participant's service plan that will enable the individual to perform activities of daily living.

- Substance Abuse Programs: Interventions to reduce or eliminate the use of alcohol or drugs by the participant.

- Transitional Living Services: Individualized, short-term, residential services providing up to 24 hour support provided only once in the participant's lifetime.

- Transportation: Mobility services offered after exhaustion of all other resources.

- Vehicle Modification Services: Alterations made to the vehicle that is the participant's primary mode of transportation to avoid institutionalization.

4) **Guardian Ad Litem Services:**

Naugatuck, CT 06770

Office Phone: (203) 723-4332 x115

Michael Mackniak, **Esq.**, MNMP, is the Executive Director of this service. It is a not for profit, 501 (c) 3 organization which improves the delivery of supportive services to individuals and community provider agencies in order to increase the effectiveness of services afforded to persons in need. The agency was founded as a collaboration between **Connecticut's Probate Court Administration and the Department of Mental Health and Addiction Services.**

Melissa's Project, a Division of Guardian Ad Litem Services coordinates, monitors, reports and plans with/for individuals in need of community services in order to enhance their level of social functioning and independence. The program is designed to assist persons who have a need for community services and community supports by offering multi-disciplined staff and personnel trained in the areas of law, psychology, social services and elder care.

We undertake the time consuming aspects of assisting individuals enrolled in our program to ensure that their needs are met and that they have access to quality healthcare and services that are available to them in the community. The type of care management we deliver is based upon our copyrighted "Guardian

Model" which utilizes a bio-psychosocial approach to treatment, specifically designed to the needs of each enrollee.

Melissa's Project provides comprehensive case coordination and intra-agency oversight services to enable individuals with mental illness to live independently. Established in 2002, Melissa's Project is run by a private non-profit organization with funding from State Legislature, DMHAS and the Office of the Probate Court Administrator. Individuals served by the project achieve better engagement with treatment and, as a direct result, experience significant reductions in revolving door hospitalizations, arrests and incarcerations.

www.ingramcontent.com/pod-product-compliance
Lightning Source LLC
Chambersburg PA
CBHW021355290426
44108CB00010B/256